The Floor in Congressional Life

LEGISLATIVE POLITICS & POLICY MAKING

Series Editors

Janet M. Box-Steffensmeier, Vernal Riffe Professor of Political Science,
The Ohio State University

David Canon, Professor of Political Science, University of Wisconsin, Madison

The Floor in Congressional Life
ANDREW J. TAYLOR

The Influence of Campaign Contributions in State Legislatures: The Effects of
Institutions and Politics
LYNDA W. POWELL

The Evolution of American Legislatures: Colonies, Territories, and States,
1619–2009
PEVERILL SQUIRE

Getting Primaried: The Changing Politics of Congressional Primary Challenges
ROBERT G. BOATRIGHT

Ambition, Competition, and Electoral Reform: The Politics of Congressional
Elections Across Time
JAMIE L. CARSON AND JASON M. ROBERTS

Partisan Gerrymandering and the Construction of American Democracy
ERIK J. ENGSTROM

The Floor in Congressional Life

ANDREW J. TAYLOR

The University of Michigan Press • Ann Arbor

First paperback edition 2013

Published in the United States of America by
The University of Michigan Press
Printed and bound by CPI Group (UK) Ltd, Croydon, CR0 4YY

2016   2015   2014   2013   5   4   3   2

A CIP catalog record for this book is available from the British Library.

Library of Congress Cataloging-in-Publication Data

Taylor, Andrew J., 1966–
        The floor in Congressional life / Andrew J. Taylor.
            p.   cm. — (Legislative politics & policy making)
        Includes bibliographical references and index.
        ISBN 978-0-472-11809-0 (cloth : alk. paper) —
        ISBN 978-0-472-02818-4 (e-book)
            1. United States. Congress—Rules and practice.
        2. Legislation—United States.   3. Parliamentary practice—United States.
        I. Title.
        KF4937.T39   2012
        328.73'05—dc23

                                                              2011037285

ISBN 978-0-472-03547-2 (pbk. : alk. paper)

Contents

Preface and Acknowledgments

In 1999, I received the American Political Science Association's William A. Steiger Congressional Fellowship. The award is named for a Republican House member from Wisconsin who served from 1966 until his death, at age 40, in December 1978. I was tremendously honored to receive the accolade, but one part weighed heavily on me. The Steiger is granted to the fellow in that particular year's class who is considered to be most concerned with promoting the interests of Congress as an institution. Did I really care about Congress? I believed I did, but I didn't really know why or how.

I had a bit of an epiphany on this subject during President Bill Clinton's final State of the Union address on January 27, 2000. Fortunate enough to be given a ticket by my boss of the time, Representative Christopher Shays of Connecticut, I sat in the visitors' gallery, absorbed by the evening's proceedings. I don't remember much of what Clinton said—perhaps largely because the speech was his longest State of the Union and by most accounts his most uninteresting. But I was also stargazing. There was Hillary (still a First Lady at the time) and Jesse Jackson. There were the members of the cabinet and top military brass although, somewhat unusually, no Supreme Court justices. And on the floor were more members of Congress than I'd ever seen in any one place at any one time.

The congregation of so many legislators was especially odd. Most Americans think of the House of Representatives and Senate as institutions whose entire memberships convene regularly to discuss and debate the issues of the day. These gatherings take place on the floors of both chambers. In the House, speakers walk to the front of the dais and talk, often from behind a lectern, to their colleagues, who sit on semicircular benches; to the public in the galleries above; and to the broader nation as it watches on television or reads the news of the debate on the Internet or in the next day's papers. In the upper house, Senators speak from behind assigned desks arrayed across the chamber floor, with the most junior members placed at the back. Both chambers are intimate, but visitors cannot help but be struck by the power and formality of the places. The House mace, at least when the members are not convened in the Committee of the Whole; the seriousness of the sergeant at arms; the industry of the debate reporters and record clerks; the portraits of Washington and Lafayette—all provide a weighty atmosphere. In the Senate, the desks seem to exude history. This all feels and looks like the heart of American democracy.

In reality, however, the bodies rarely meet in their entirety. In the past decade or so, the only time large numbers of members appear on the floor is during momentous debates and votes—the impeachment and trial of President Clinton, the authorization of the use of force against Iraq, and the health care reform bill of 2009–10, for example. Members do flock to the floor for addresses by the president and foreign heads of state or during other rare occasions—when the anthrax scare shut down the House office buildings in the fall of 2001, House members congregated on the floor because there really was nowhere else for them to go. But most of the time, when members are in Washington, they seem to be in their offices, working with staff or meeting with constituents or lobbyists; in committee hearing rooms; in the halls, rooms, or grounds of the Capitol complex, holding press conferences or attending caucus meetings; or perhaps somewhere else in the District, speaking to some think tank or another. The floor does not seem to be a place members feel they can efficiently and effectively use their limited time. When floor debate takes place on substantive legislation, very few members are in attendance. Those in the visitors' gallery frequently outnumber lawmakers.

On the night of Clinton's 2000 State of the Union, it occurred to me that the floor was worthy of greater study. As I walked out of the House chamber, bumping shoulders with members, and exited onto the snowy sidewalks of Capitol Hill, I continued to think about the floor. Two particular issues came to mind. The first was the floor's role in the legislative process; the second was the quality of legislative debate that takes place in the House and Senate chambers. I thought that on both counts, a marked deterioration seemed to have occurred over time. I wanted to know whether that sense was justified and, if so, what had caused the floor's demise. This book was born.

In the end, the book became an investigation of two interesting and important phenomena. As such, it has two independent parts that come together as a broad study of the floor in Congress. The first analysis is of the development and bicameral differences in the procedures and practices that govern the House and Senate floors. I explain why the House and Senate floors are so different and why the Senate floor is more powerful and individual Senators have greater floor rights than their House counterparts. Second, I explore intercameral differences and historical changes in the quality of floor proceedings. The findings and their implications are fused in a concluding chapter.

Throughout the book, my central motivation is to understand what makes a good legislature. A powerful floor on which members practice robust rights and engage in superlative proceedings is critical to the kind of legislative bodies we should want. I am also interested in determining how close the House and Senate are to these ideals and what pushes the congressional chambers toward those ideals or moves them farther away.

As always with such an endeavor, I have many people to thank. In the early days, the work was funded by a 2003 Dirksen Congressional Center grant and a 2003 North Carolina State University College of Humanities and Social Sciences summer stipend. Sarah Binder and Eric Schickler graciously provided data for various parts of the analysis.

Howard Reiter at UConn and my colleagues at N.C. State have been a constant source of guidance and encouragement. Because the American Political Science Association's Congressional Fellowship was so important to my career and instrumental to this project, everyone connected with it, especially Jeff Biggs, deserves my gratitude.

Numerous industrious and reliable students at N.C. State assisted with data: Bryce Ball, Steve Block, Lee Cobb, Josh Franklin, Sean Hildebrand, Chris Kotek, Brandon McRae, Brad Salmon, and Roxana Toma. Staff at D. H. Hill Library at N.C. State (especially Michele Hayslett) and Davis Library at UNC-Chapel Hill (especially Beth Rowe) were very helpful, too.

For reading and commenting on various parts of the manuscript, I thank Scott Adler, Matthew Green, Gerhard Loewenberg, Michael Mac-Kuen, Nathan Monroe, Jennifer Nicoll Victor, Wendy Schiller, and Jim Stimson. I greatly appreciate the comments of several anonymous reviewers as well as the advice and counsel of the editors of the University of Michigan Press's Legislative Politics & Policy Making series, Jan Box-Steffensmeier and David Canon. Where this book does not come up to snuff, it is because of me and not them.

Melody Herr, my editor at the University of Michigan Press, worked assiduously to get this book ready for publication. Melody's charm and good humor were invaluable on days when I would fret, her gentle prodding and calm encouragement vital when I would drag my heels.

Finally, I thank my family. Jennifer and I have had two children since this project started. This book is for them, my Matthew and Lindsay.

Introduction

The House and Senate Floors

The House and Senate floors seem to be at the center of congressional life. When Americans watch C-SPAN's programming, they are invariably viewing live or recorded coverage of happenings on one of the two bodies' floors. When the networks and cable news programs cover Congress, the public generally gets to see snippets of members speaking passionately from within the two chambers. If asked to think of the most dramatic and important things that have happened in Congress, informed citizens would likely point to floor action—southern senators filibustering civil rights legislation in the 1960s, the Clinton impeachment debate and Senate trial, discussions about whether to authorize military action in Vietnam or Iraq, perhaps the great debates about slavery in which senators such as John C. Calhoun (D-SC), Henry Clay (Whig-KY), and Daniel Webster (Whig-MA) demonstrated their superb oratory.

Even fictionalized portrayals of Congress showcase the floor. Hollywood's most famous congressional scene must be Jimmy Stewart's exhausting filibuster in the Senate in Frank Capra's *Mr. Smith Goes to Washington*. Once in a while, committees will attract notice. Just as television was discovering Congress, the Kefauver Committee's examination of organized crime mesmerized the nation, much in the same way that the Clarence Thomas Supreme Court nomination hearings transfixed viewers in the fall of 1991. House and Senate committee proceedings on Watergate captivated us as well. But the layperson's view is surely that the House and Senate floors form Congress's heart and that what happens on them shapes the attitudes and actions of legislators and the public alike.

Scholarly attention, conversely, is spread wider. Indeed, the floor plays at best a secondary role in the most influential theories of congressional organization and behavior. What happens there is considered to have a negligible effect on policy making and congressional life. The "majority party cartel" model of Cox and McCubbins (1993, 2005) posits that congressional procedures are shaped to serve the majority party and its policy interests. Presiding officers and standing committees are agents of the majority, especially in the House. Legislation is packaged to please the median member of the majority. Indeed, the majority party exercises such vigorous control of the agenda that the floor is reduced to rubber-stamping proposals. This is not quite the case in Aldrich and Rohde's "conditional party government" model because the importance of the majority party is temporally variable (Aldrich, Berger, and Rohde 2002; Aldrich and Rohde 2001; Rohde 1991). The majority's ability to control the agenda and policy outcomes is increased during times of interparty preference polarization and intraparty preference homogenization. Still, when these phenomena are high, the floor has little to no real influence on the substance and success of legislation.

The "gains-from-trade" or "distributive" model perhaps most articulately described by Weingast and Marshall (1988) places committees at the center of congressional action. Legislators who have high demands for particular policies obtain assignments on the committees that have jurisdiction over those policies. The floor operates as a sort of giant logroll in which members exchange deference to bills they personally consider unimportant for influence on those they have helped craft in committee and that are close to their interests. Even the "informational" model, which views committees as subservient of the chamber, does not envision a particularly important role for the floor (Gilligan and Krehbiel 1987, 1990; Krehbiel 1991). Here, committees, peopled by members who have policy preferences that reflect the full body, facilitate specialization that benefits the chamber's collective interest by overcoming informational deficiencies in a complex policy environment. Committees, in other words, are labor-dividing, time-saving, and information-gathering devices. They negate the need for a powerful floor. Krehbiel's (1991) explanation of informational theories conceptualizes the principal in the relationship as the floor only in the sense that the term is synonymous with *body* or *chamber.*

It is true a considerable amount of empirical work has looked at the floor. Much of the work on the significant behavioral and procedural changes in the House and Senate during the 1970s and 1980s focused on floor action (Bach and Smith 1988; Sinclair 1989; Smith 1989). Amending activity, which increased dramatically in this period, has been of particular interest (Bach 1986; Enelow 1981; Finocchiaro and Jenkins 2008; Fleisher and Bond 1983; Forgette and Saturno 1994; Jenkins and Munger 2003; Wilkerson 1999). Other scholars have looked at floor debates and speeches, the substance of floor proceedings (Bessette 1994; Harris 2005; Hill and Hurley 2002; Maltzman and Sigelman 1996; Morris 2001; Mucciaroni and Quirk 2006; Steiner et al. 2004).

Procedures and practices restricting floor behavior, such as the use of special rules in the House (Dion and Huber 1996; Krehbiel 1997; Marshall 2002) and unanimous consent agreements (UCAs) in the Senate (Ainsworth and Flathman 1995; Smith and Flathman 1989), have drawn widespread scholarly attention as well. So, too, in recent years has the obstructionist device of the Senate filibuster (Binder and Smith 2007; Koger 2010; Wawro and Schickler 2006). Probably hundreds of scholars have, at some time in their career, looked carefully at roll-call votes, providing treatments that range from analyses of recorded votes in their aggregate across time and chambers so as to discern basic patterns or construct general spatial models (Clinton, Jackman, and Rivers 2004; Krehbiel 1998; McCarty, Poole, and Rosenthal 2001; Poole and Rosenthal 1997) to those of a single or small number of related roll calls on specific issues such as trade (Biglaiser, Jackson, and Peake 2004; Conley 1999; Kahane 1996; Uslaner 1998).[1]

However, only one really comprehensive study of the floor has been undertaken. Steven S. Smith's *Call to Order: Floor Politics in the House and Senate* (1989) examines the sizable effects of amendments, conference committees, House special rules, and Senate UCAs on the new floor politics of the 1960s, 1970s, and 1980s. The book represents the most systematic analysis of the floor to date.

But Smith does not take a broad sweep of history. He concentrates exclusively on the second half of the 20th century. Moreover, the foundation he laid has not been built upon. Our understanding of the floor is still largely pieced together from studies that focus on other congressional institutions or fragments of floor action. In this book, I synthesize and add to this thinking and these findings in a panoramic study of the floor in congressional life.

The Essence of the Book

This book examines the floor broadly, as a discrete congressional institution to which all the parent body's members belong and with proceedings in which all members can participate.[2] It is the body in plenary. The floor has a critical but bounded role in the legislative process—the front end of which today is generally preempted by committee action, the back end often depicted by a final passage vote on a bill. It has, as a result, less formal authority than the body of which it is a part. The floor is not synonymous with the parent chamber, not least because House and Senate rules and practices have, over time, limited its power and allowed other institutions to influence the collective and authoritative decisions of each body.

I am particularly interested in two research questions about the floor. First, why are the House and Senate floors so distinct from one another? Put another way, why are bicameral differences in the procedures and practices that govern the floor so pronounced? This is an interesting question given that the House and Senate's organizational origins are essentially identical. The Constitution did not deem the bodies to be procedurally different. Today, however, the floor is considerably more important to the Senate's legislative process than to the House's. The formal gatekeeping and agenda-setting powers of House standing committees are comparatively great. It is very difficult for the floor to receive a bill if a committee refuses to report it, and committee-reported bills are often protected from floor amendment by restrictive special rules issued by the Rules Committee. Suspending chamber rules and moving ahead expeditiously can be done if a bill has the support of two-thirds of those voting and present, but this strategy, as a matter of practice, requires the explicit assent of the chair of the committee of jurisdiction and is only available at certain times, mainly for uncontroversial bills (Oleszek 2011, 135–40). In the Senate, by contrast, members can offer minor measures directly by motion or, because there is no rule that floor amendments be germane to the bill at hand, as additions to any piece of legislation. Senators can also invoke Rule XIV and place items on the calendar, effectively bypassing committee.[3]

Individual senators, moreover, have greater influence over floor proceedings than their House colleagues. In the lower chamber, the presiding officer—the Speaker or, when the body is convened in the Committee of the Whole, the chair—has the power to recognize those who can speak during floor debate. In the Senate, the member who holds the floor has the power of recognition. This power, along with the lack of a previous question motion—something that can be invoked by a simple majority in the House—provides the procedural basis for the chamber's famous filibuster.

This question is very important because although scholars have previously explored procedural change in Congress (Binder 1995, 1996, 1997;

Cox and McCubbins 2005; Dion 1997; Fink 2000; Schickler 2000, 2001), existing research focuses almost entirely on the House and on party politics and members' policy preferences as the drivers of organizational development. Binder (1997), for example, argues that large and ideologically coherent majority parties have pushed through the principal procedural changes that have undermined the floor. My work examines a broader set of plausible determinants of procedural evolution in a more explicitly bicameral analysis.

The answer to the first research question contributes to two important extant controversies and emerging approaches in congressional scholarship. My work informs the debate that surrounds the issue of procedural development in Congress. There is a significant literature on the topic (Binder 1995, 1996, 1997: Cox and McCubbins 2005; Dion 1997; Fink 2000; Schickler 2000, 2001), most of which asserts that procedures are largely endogenous to members' policy preferences, especially when these preferences are shaped by party. I reveal a greater role for other factors in the shaping of procedures, particularly membership size and workload.

The study chimes in on the critical debate about the importance of parties in Congress as well. The literature has kicked this issue around for quite some time. Its contributors are essentially divided between those who believe parties vigorously structure behavior and member preferences on policy and procedure (for example, Aldrich 1995; Cox and McCubbins 1993, 2005; Rohde 1991) and those who do not (for example, Krehbiel 1991, 1998). I show that parties matter, at least when it comes to organizational change, when they are distinct and when members conceive of procedural alterations in partisan terms. When the latter was not the case (that is, before the Civil War), congressional development was driven by forces largely unrelated to political party.

The second research question focuses on floor proceedings themselves. Again, my approach is explicitly bicameral and historical. Are popular stylized notions of floor debate accurate? There are two pieces of conventional wisdom about floor proceedings. The first is that Senate proceedings are superior to those in the House. Many people have held this view since James Madison uttered at the Constitutional Convention, "The use of the Senate is to consist in its proceedings with more coolness, with more system, and with more wisdom, than the popular branch" (Farrand 1966, 1:151). The second is that floor proceedings in both chambers have deteriorated over time. Americans today complain constantly about the partisan rancor they witness in Congress. Learned observers yearn for a return to the great orators of congressional history, such as the members of the Great Triumvirate, Calhoun, Clay, and Webster (B. Solomon 2000).

There exists no systematic historical analysis of the nature of floor debate in Congress, let alone a rigorous attempt to test these two propositions about floor proceedings. Previous work is limited to debate from particular eras (Bessette 1994; Mucciaroni and Quirk 2006; Wirls 2007) or during the usage of particular practices (Harris 2005; Maltzman and Sigelman 1996; Morris 2001; Rocca 2007).

My answers are bundled neatly together in this book, which takes its coherence as an extensive historical and bicameral analysis of the floor in Congress. This enterprise is hugely appropriate for normative reasons. Our understanding of representative democracy places emphasis on matters such as equality, participation, and transparency in a legislature. In a good legislative body, all members should be able adequately to represent their constituents. As far as is possible, no member should have more influence than any other. The represented should be able to hold legislators accountable for their actions. They need to witness their representatives' behavior. Legislative activity should educate the populace about political process and policy substance. In other words, the floor should be at the center of congressional life. The House and Senate floors are where all members get to speak. Each member, moreover, has one—and only one—vote. Contributions are formally recorded (in the *Congressional Record* since 1873) by order of the Constitution. Floor proceedings today are also covered live and "gavel to gavel" on television. The floor is the forum in which all constituents are represented, their representatives have equally weighted votes, and they can view clearly the quality of their representation.

There are fewer reasons for the American public to care about the power, organization, and behavior of congressional parties and committees. The influence and activities of standing committees and party conferences or caucuses are of most interest for their effects on the plenary. Committees' extensive procedural powers, for example are not problematic in and of themselves. Indeed, committee-centric theories such as gains from trade (Weingast and Marshall 1988) and information (Krehbiel 1991) show that committees can solve collective-action problems for the chambers and, by inference, help the floor be more efficient. But the public should have some concern because strong committees essentially shut many legislators out of the process of policy formation. The divvying up of policy jurisdictions among committees and the manner in which parties choose to assign members to them are also interesting and important. But these are not the kinds of activities that define legislative bodies and their fundamental contributions to representative democracy. Instead, Americans really should attend to such matters as the role of the floor in lawmaking, the extent of members' floor rights, and the quality of floor debate.

As a comprehensive evaluation of the floor in congressional life, therefore, the answers to these two distinct research questions together furnish a thorough exploration of three matters at the heart of congressional studies. The first is what makes a good legislature. I argue that the answer is a strong floor where members practice robust rights and engage in proceedings of superior quality—defined later as those that reflect the principles of accountability, education, representation, debate, and deliberation. The second is to grasp how well the House and Senate measure up to these aspirations and how the two chambers have developed across time and compare to one another today. The third is to understand the kinds of things that move the House and Senate closer to and farther away from the goals we ought to set for them.

Given that despite considerable differences, neither the House nor Senate fully meets these standards, the final chapter not only summarizes my findings but also proposes some reforms. The objective is to provide Americans who care about Congress with some direction as they think about how to improve it.

The Scope of the Book

This analysis of the floor has two distinct components. In the first, I ask and answer the question of why the floors of the House and Senate are so procedurally different. I shape my inquiry into the floor and the legislative process this way for two reasons. First, none of the work on the causes of procedural and organizational change in Congress—of which Binder (1995, 1996, 1997), Cox and McCubbins (2005), Dion (1997), Fink (2000), Schickler (2000, 2001), J. M. Roberts and Smith (2007) provide the most prominent—directly addresses the issue of House-Senate variation. This is interesting not least because, as noted earlier, bicameral procedural differences are numerous and in some cases deep.

Second, approaching floor procedures in this way provides an opportunity to explore the normative issues discussed previously. By examining the determinants of the basic bicameral differences in procedures that affect the floor, we can understand how to bring about the kind of legislative body we should want in our representative democracy.

I begin this particular investigation in chapter 1 by providing some theoretical foundations for the empirical analysis that follows. I first discuss two sets of characteristics that form dimensions along which the floors of legislative bodies can be placed. These dimensions allow for a clearer understanding of how the House and Senate floors differ and how each has changed over time. I call these the "floor power" and "floor rights" dimensions. The first is designed to order floors based on their influence in the parent body's legislative process. The second categorizes floors by the strength of the rights the parent body's members can exercise on them.

I next present three hypotheses about why the House and Senate floors are so different. The first is chamber size. It is largely exogenous of member preferences, motivations, and behavior and is essentially delineated by constitutional and entrenched statutory language. The second hypothesis is about workload. Workload is not anchored in the law and varies dramatically across chambers and time. It is an obvious candidate for explaining bicameral differences in floor power and rights. The final hypothesis, concerning party politics and policy preferences, borrows directly from and tests the conventional wisdom about the determinants of procedural change in Congress. Most of the extant literature describes congressional organization and rules largely as the product of members' policy interests and conflict between the two parties.

Throughout chapters 2 and 3, I test other hypotheses about procedural change affecting the House and Senate floors. These ideas form from fragments of theory about legislator turnover and changes in party control. The findings here are interesting in and of themselves, but the main focus is the three hypotheses, since only they can explain intercameral variation.

I use a longitudinal approach to analyze individual changes in House and Senate procedures and practices governing the floor. Procedures are dictated by formal rules and described by convention and precedent. They represent the fundamental ways in which a body works. Practices are not mandated but can be rightfully employed. Certain members decide about the use of practices at certain times. My approach allows for a direct and robust test of the hypotheses. The findings that emerge are somewhat complex, but they combine to tell what I think is a fairly simple, intuitively appealing, and novel story about why the House floor has less power in its parent body's legislative process than does the Senate's and why senators enjoy stronger floor rights than their colleagues on the other side of the Capitol.

Although the floor remains the focus, I take a different tack in the second part of the book, which encompasses chapters 4 and 5. Here I look at what happens on the floor. Specifically, I examine the two popular views of floor debate—that Senate proceedings are better (the "Senate-superior" hypothesis) and that it has generally deteriorated over time (the "worsen-over-time" hypothesis).

No previous scholar has systematically and empirically tested these arguments. In chapters 4 and 5, I create indicators of quality floor proceedings to conduct precisely these tests. It is tricky work, but I argue good floor proceedings must reflect five basic principles: accountability, education, representation, debate, and deliberation. Accountability refers to voters' capacity to judge their representatives through floor proceedings; education reflects the need for floor proceedings to inform the public about policy; and representation denotes the need for floor proceedings to reflect Americans' various interests. Debate and deliberation describe desirable forms of interaction between members on the floor. Debate involves the articulation and defense of a particular point of view. Deliberation describes a collective and thorough search for solutions to public problems.

These five principles are reflected in eight characteristics that are directly observable and from which I can form quantitative and qualitative measures: quantity, participation, equality, interaction, civility, reasoning, commonweal, and transparency. Floor proceedings that reflect the five central principles are essentially lengthy and transparent to the public. Individual members participate equally in discussions that display logical and sophisticated arguments. Members appeal to the collective good and conduct themselves civilly. Members also engage one another rather than merely present positions. I spend a considerable amount of time in chapter 4 fleshing out the principles and the characteristics that reflect them.

The Senate-superior and worsen-over-time hypotheses are tested using two different types of data. The first, "macrolevel" data, come from observations of the floor proceedings of entire Congresses. I examine the number of days and hours the House and Senate are in session during a Congress and, among other factors, evaluate media coverage of the floor across history. I also look at the number of occasions on which individual House and Senate members participated in floor proceedings in every fifth Congress from the 32nd (1851–53) to the 107th (2001–3). From this information, I glean systematic measures of the nature of participation.

Using the second type of data, "microlevel" data, I analyze floor proceedings on individual bills and resolutions. Each set of these data is defined by an issue to provide some comparability over time and across chambers. The issues are important in American history. This enables us to assume that the related proceedings are meaningful. The first issue is presidential impeachment and removal. Here I analyze and compare both chambers' proceedings in the Andrew Johnson and Bill Clinton episodes. The second is war declarations and selected authorizations of the presidential use of force, which provides 7 observations: the War of 1812, the Mexican-American War, the Spanish-American War, the declaration of war against Germany in 1917, the Tonkin Gulf Resolution, and congressional authorizations of the presidential use of force against Iraq in 1991 and 2002. The final issue is trade, which has always been controversial and salient in Congress. This category includes 31 observations, with verbatim records available for 25 of these cases.

For each debate, I note the number of columns in the *Congressional Globe* or *Congressional Record* filled by each member's remarks, the number of colloquies between members, and the number of times members who were asked to yield by colleagues did so. With the exception of the war data, I also examine the proportion of members who used a "commonweal" justification for their position. The findings, like those in the first part of the book, are complex and mixed. There is evidence to both confirm and reject the hypotheses.

Although floor proceedings in both chambers are not quite as bad as many believe them to be, they still could be better. Moreover, because the analysis in the first part of the book reveals that both chambers have generally moved in an undesirable direction as they have adopted and utilized various procedures and practices, I use the concluding chapter to make some predictions about the future of the floor in Congress and suggest some limited and realistic reforms to strengthen the House and Senate floors, invigorate member floor rights, and improve floor proceedings.

PART I

Floor Power and Rights

1 ◆ The Floor and the Legislative Process

Theoretical Underpinnings

The Constitution is essentially silent on the subject of congressional procedures and practices. It outlines procedures on the impeachment and trial of executive officials and judges and charges both chambers with selecting specified leaders. It also orders that a journal of proceedings be kept, allows for compulsory attendance and the expulsion of members, provides for a majority of each body to constitute a quorum, and enables one-fifth of a chamber's members to demand a recorded vote. But beyond these requirements, which are largely identical for both bodies, nothing is enumerated.[1]

Still, variations in the role of the floors in the legislative process and procedures governing their proceedings emerged quickly. By 1809, Representative Josiah Quincy (Fed-MA) had observed that the House "acts and reasons and votes, and performs all the operations of an animated being, and yet, judging from my own perceptions, I cannot refrain from concluding that all great political questions are settled somewhere else than on this floor" (*Congressional Quarterly* 1999, 42). The Senate, conversely, appeared to be more deliberative, and important business was conducted on the floor, even though, if anything, the upper chamber developed a standing committee system before the House did (Canon and Stewart 2001; Jenkins and Stewart 2002).

Today, the magnitude of individual differences is sometimes great, as, for example, in the rules governing floor amendments in the two houses. Other procedures and practices are identical across chambers, or differences are negligible and unimportant. For example, the House has five calendars, the Senate two. Juxtaposing the individual rules and conventions that govern the House and Senate floors is not particularly tricky. But contrasting procedures and practices in their aggregate—an exercise that permits a comprehensive comparison of the two bodies' floors and an investigation of why they are different—is considerably more difficult.

Placing the Floor in Time and Space

To address this challenge, I conceptualize the differences between the House and Senate floors as falling along two dimensions. The "floor power" dimension concerns the floor's ability to influence legislative product. At one end is a hypothetical pole represented by a body in which all collective authoritative decisions take place on the floor. Here, the floor essentially has a monopoly on legislative business. In such a body, the floor would not only have to approve of legislative product but would set its own agenda. It would determine the content of bills to be debated and voted on. There would be no gatekeeper—an institution that controls the flow of legislation to the floor and can block bills if it desires. At the other end is a hypothetical pole where the floor has no formal authority at all or where there is no floor and the body never meets or makes authoritative decisions in plenary.

The second dimension orders what happens on the floor. Here, the organizing principle is "floor rights," and bodies are arrayed based on how strong or weak individual members' floor rights are. At one hypothetical pole of this dimension, all members have equal and very robust rights that necessitate that proceedings must last as long as any individual member wants them to and all collective decisions are made unanimously. At the other pole, proceedings are controlled by a single dictator who acts with full discretion. As is the case with the floor power dimension, neither pole exists in the real world.

The two dimensions can be thought of as having "natural" and "restrictive" poles (fig. 1.1.).[2] A fully natural body meets only in plenary—that is, only on the floor—and has open-ended proceedings that are terminated by unanimity. Bills are passed only when members are in full agreement that they should. No member is privileged, and no individual or group has either gatekeeping or proposal powers. I use the term *natural* to describe such a body because others have hinted that this is a good way to portray such "institutionless" or, in McKelvey's (1986) words, "institution-free" legislatures. Krehbiel (1991, 248), for example, argues that "legislatures in

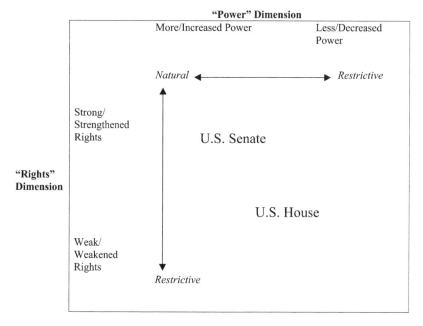

Fig. 1.1.   Thinking about the floor in time and space

their primitive states are egalitarian collective choice bodies." Cox (2005) describes this situation as a "legislative state of nature." In a seminal work on public-choice theory, Buchanan and Tullock (1962) state that the rule of unanimity is, in a normative sense, "ideal" and that institutions, even those as basic as simple majority rule, are "expedients" that have emerged as a way of diluting this more natural state of affairs.[3]

The entirely "restrictive" legislature has effectively no floor or a completely powerless floor controlled fully by a single dictatorial presiding officer. To say a body has become increasingly restrictive or is more restrictive than another conveys a sense that the body has been crafted to give the floor less power in the legislative process and/or weaken member floor rights.

Any placement of a body on these dimensions is far from precise. The normative implications discussed in the introduction are clear, however. Although productivity gains might be sacrificed—a point I discuss in the final chapter—we should want a body to be much closer to the natural pole than to the restrictive pole. It is also quite clear that, as figure 1.1 shows, the Senate is today generally a more natural body than the House. The Senate floor has more power than the House floor, and senators have stronger floor rights than do their colleagues in the lower chamber.

The approach is also therefore a useful way to gain an understanding of temporal changes and bicameral differences in congressional floor politics. For example, as the number of signatures needed for a discharge petition decreased—as it did from 218 to 145 in 1931—we can say the House became more natural because its floor increased its power. Utilizing such a longitudinal approach, we can determine what causes the House and Senate to change procedures and practices to move them in a natural or restrictive direction along each of the two dimensions. If the House exhibits more of a quality that moves the chambers demonstrably in a restrictive direction, that quality could well be contributing to House-Senate differences.

Procedural change in Congress appears to have been overwhelmingly restrictive (see chapter 2). Most important procedural changes and legislative practices have moved the House and Senate in the restrictive direction on both dimensions. Naturalization occurs but is relatively infrequent, often minimal in magnitude, and quite vulnerable to quick repeal. Given the general tendency for the bodies to move away from the natural pole, bicameral differences in floor power and rights essentially result from the House becoming more restrictive at a more rapid clip than is the case for the Senate.

Chapters 2 and 3 offer more detailed reasons for the general movement in the restrictive direction, but one highly plausible and general explanation is that restrictive procedures allow a body to fulfill its collective responsibility to produce policy and solve societal problems under most if not all conditions. More natural legislative bodies are prone to obstruction and what is often called legislative gridlock.

My framework allows me to compare procedures in different legislative bodies at a particular point in time. For example, table 1.1 reveals the rules that govern the termination of floor debate in 54 national and 99 American state legislative bodies. Greater procedural heterogeneity forces a more simplistic characterization of debate termination in the national body data, but regardless of the level of specificity, the table illustrates how legislative bodies can be ordered from more natural to most restrictive for this particular procedure. Debate termination clearly relates to the floor rights dimension, and the greater the proportion of members needed to bring proceedings on legislation to a halt and vote, the more robust the floor rights and therefore the more natural the chamber.

The findings reveal quite dramatically how much more natural, at least on this single procedure, the Senate is than the House. They also show that for debate termination, the House is not quite as restrictive as we might think. Numerous national and American state legislative bodies make it as easy or easier to cut off floor debate.

I am not the first scholar to think about congressional organization using these principles. Much work has been done on committees and parties and how they weaken the floor by controlling its agenda (Cox and Mc-Cubbins 2005, 2007; Maltzman 1997). Others have written extensively about how rules governing amendment activity can weaken or invigorate members' floor rights (Sinclair 1989; Smith 1989). Congressional scholars have also seen important connections between floor power and floor rights. For example, Smith (1989) shows how rank-and-file House members' frustrations with a tightly controlled floor agenda in the 1970s spilled over into a concerted effort to exploit and enhance floor rights.

Indeed, my theoretical framework is informed considerably by Smith's (1985, 1989) analyses of congressional floor politics. Smith characterizes legislative decision making using two dimensions: the number of units formally involved in the process and the number of individual participants who can affect the outcome. His approach is, however, broader than mine in that it is concerned directly with the influence of and the nature of decision making within institutions such as committees. I am concerned exclusively with the floor and am largely unconcerned with the power or role of participants within other units. For example, it does not matter particularly to me whether decision making within a committee is decentralized; I care whether committees are powerful. Moreover, the relationship between the number of units or participants on one hand and floor power or floor rights on the other is often unclear in Smith's work and may not be linear. The floor may or may not be an effective decision-making unit. There may be relatively large numbers of influential participants, such as committee and subcommittee chairs, when floor rights are minimal.

The similarities of and differences between Smith's framework and mine are displayed vividly by the congressional reforms of the 1960s and 1970s. Smith (1989, 5) argues that the Congress of the time moved toward what he calls a more "collegial" form of decision making in which there are few units and many participants and that features a "more floor-oriented process." In the vernacular I use, this was movement in the natural direction as the floor became more powerful and members exercised greater rights on it. Smith (1985, 208–11; 1989, 5–6) also notes that this period wit-

TABLE 1.1.   Debate Termination Procedures in 54 National and 99 American State Legislative Bodies

National Bodies

"Leadership Needed"		"Simple Majority Is Needed"		"Debate Is Open-Ended or a Super-Majority Is Needed"	
Argentina	both bodies	Australia	both bodies	Belgium	both bodies
Austria	both bodies	Canada	both bodies	Denmark	
Brazil	both bodies	Greece		Finland	
Chile	both bodies	Hungary		Iceland	
Czech Republic	both bodies	India	both bodies	Netherlands	both bodies
France	both bodies	Ireland	both bodies	Norway	
Germany	both bodies	Israel		Sweden	
Italy	both bodies	Japan	Councilors	United States	Senate
Japan	Representatives	Spain	both bodies		
Mexico	both bodies	United Kingdom	both bodies		
Poland	both bodies	United States	House		
Portugal		New Zealand			
Russia	both bodies				
Switzerland	both bodies				

Most Restrictive Procedure ⟶ **Most Natural Procedure**

American State Bodies

Simple Majority Present	Simple Majority Elected	3/5ths Pres.	3/5ths Elect.	2/3rds Pres.	2/3rds Elect.	3/4ths Pres.	3/4ths Elect.	No Rule
AR (H), AZ (HS), CA (HS), CT (HS), DE (H), FL (HS), GA (HS), HI (H), IA (S), IN (HS), KS (HS), LA (HS), MA(S), MD (HS), ME (H), MI (HS), MN (HS), MS (HS), MT (HS), NC (S), ND (HS), NH (HS), NJ (S), NM (S), NV (HS), NY (H), OH (H), OK (HS), OR (HS), PA (HS), RI (HS), SC (H), SD (HS), TX (HS), VA (S), WA (S), WI (HS), WV (HS), WY (S), United States (H)	CO (HS), IA (H), IL (HS), KY (HS), MO (HS), NE, NC (H), NY (S), OH (S)	AL (H), HI (S), SC (S)	United States (S)	AK (HS), AR (S), ID (HS), MA (H), NM (H), TN (HS), UT (H), VA (H), WA (H)	WY (H)	VT (H)	NJ (H)	AL (S), DE (S), ME (S), UT (S), VT (S)

Source: National legislative body data from Taylor 2006. State legislative body data collected by the author from rule books and conversations with state legislative clerks. Postal abbreviations used for U.S. states. In the United States the debate termination procedure is almost universally called the previous question motion.

Note: H = House or lower body; S = Senate or upper body.

nessed competition between the collegial model and his "decentralized" form of decision making, with many units and many individual participants. Whereas the collegial model was pushed by newer, more ideological members with broader policy interests, their senior and more pragmatic and parochial colleagues preferred decentralization, which enabled legislators to better shape outcomes within particular and narrow jurisdictions. Doing so meant protecting the prerogatives of committees and therefore a relatively weak floor and a body with more restrictive procedures and practices.

A Model of Procedural Change

Before we can address why the House and Senate floors are so different, we need to understand the mechanics of procedural change. Here I present a basic model of how congressional procedures move in a restrictive or natural direction.

The model is based on the idea that members are purposive agents of change. Members initiate revisions to procedures and practices even if the range of desirable and feasible choices available to them is constrained greatly by exogenous forces. Members propose and vote on amendments to the rules and alter, accelerate, and abandon practices. I assume that procedures and the use of practices are means by which members realize some greater goal. Other scholars of institutional change in Congress work from the idea that policy preferences dictate procedural choice (Binder 1995, 1996, 1997, 2006; Birkhead et al. 2010; Cox and McCubbins 2005; Dion 1997; Fink 2000; Schickler 2000, 2001), but member goals may also include reelection, advancement in the chamber, or a career beyond the body—that is, they may not always involve policy. All goals are furthered through legislation, however. Members therefore aspire, either individually or as part of a circumscribed group with shared goals, to increase their ability to influence legislation.

Members' specific procedural preferences are shaped by their current capacity to influence the legislative process—their centrality to decision making, we might say. Members wish to occupy positions of influence, formal or informal, or direct or indirect, so that they can help set the agenda and determine how the body disposes of legislation. From these perches, members can better realize their fundamental goals.

Those who are in positions of power—we might think of the Speaker and committee chairs in today's House of Representatives, for example—generally push to restrict procedures. A weaker floor where members exert fewer rights means that these individuals are better situated to determine legislative agendas and outcomes. Those who do not hold such positions will attempt to do one or both of two things. First, they will try to usurp the current leadership, perhaps via an election or some kind of parliamentary coup. Second, they will push to naturalize procedures. Movement in the natural direction will enhance these members' influence over the floor agenda and legislative outcomes.

Procedural change is a function of the capacity and will of these two groups of members—those who largely control the floor's agenda and proceedings and those who do not. Strong and determined members in formal leadership positions are likely to move procedures in a restrictive direction when faced by weak and unmotivated opposition. When those with little formal influence are galvanized, procedural change is more likely to move the other way. In chapter 2, I will use this basic model to test three plausible hypotheses about why the House is the more restrictive body. These three hypotheses leverage important and large differences between the House and Senate to see which of them can assist in an explanation of procedural disparity.

The Three Hypotheses

Chamber Size

The first hypothesis is built on the idea that the relative and changing size of a body are important determinants of institutional design. As R. Baker (2001, 72) puts it, "Senate rules differ from House rules largely because the Senate is a quarter the size of the House." More specifically, larger and growing bodies are likely to be more restrictive. As George Rothwell Brown (1922, 123) wrote in his influential study of congressional leadership, "The larger the size of the House, the greater the necessity for a strong and small body of resourceful leaders to act as its board of directors." Or as James Madison said of legislative assemblies in Federalist 58, "The greater the number composing them may be, the fewer will be the men who in fact direct their proceedings" (Hamilton, Madison, and Jay 1961, 360).

Some interesting theoretical and empirical work has examined the relationship between size and legislative procedures. This research has a variety of different theoretical foundations but essentially comes to the same conclusion: Large and growing bodies are more likely to have restrictive procedures, whereas small and shrinking bodies are more likely to have natural procedures. Much of this work is rooted in organizational theory and the general finding that increased size leads to hierarchy and centralization (Durkheim 1947; Michels 1949; Weber 1947). Polsby's (1968) seminal work on the "institutionalization" of the House of Representatives is perhaps the best example of organizational theory's application to legislatures. Polsby suggests that size has contributed to the "bounded" nature of the body, "universalistic and automated decision making," and complex internal procedures, which themselves allowed for the maturation of the committee system and the creation of powerful leaders.

Recent work on the Senate by Wawro and Schickler (2006) employs different thinking to come to the same general observation. They reveal that large increases in the size of the Senate do much to explain the establishment of cloture, the procedure used to limit debate and end filibusters in the chamber. The theory is taken from the work of Dixit (2004, 66), an economist, who argues that "a system based on voluntary information flows and self-enforcing equilibrium works for small or well-knit groups, whereas large groups need more formal institutions of information dissemination and enforcement." Such formal institutions are frequently more restrictive than the informal norms they replace. In this case, a codified cloture rule replaced the more natural "relation-based legislating" (Wawro and Schickler 2006).

Carrubba and Volden (2000) have offered a formal model that reveals that bodies with large memberships need to make their voting rules more exclusive—or weaken floor rights by permitting smaller coalitions to assent formally to collective decisions—because in such chambers, cooperation and coalition building become costly. In other words, members of large bodies are generally willing to support simple-majority rather than supermajority or unanimity rules so that the body can be productive. Analyses of bodies from abroad validate this thinking. In a theoretical piece on the European Union's Council of Ministers, Carrubba and Volden (2001) reveal that expanding bodies tend to weaken floor rights as well. In a large-N cross-sectional analysis, Taylor (2006) shows that larger bodies in democratic countries tend to restrict amendment rights and the ability of individual legislators to engage in floor obstruction.

In the congressional context, this theoretical and empirical work maintains that the House is more restrictive because it has always been much larger and grown more expansively than the Senate. The changing sizes of the bodies are shown in figure 1.2. The House grew much more rapidly

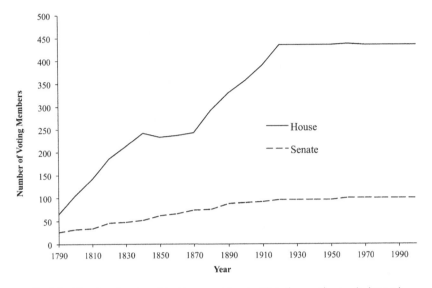

Fig. 1.2. The changing size of the House and Senate. (Data from author's calculations.)

than the Senate during the 19th century. House seats were distributed to states as they were admitted into the Union, and a variety of laws passed after the decennial censuses continually increased the size of the body until 1911, when Congress capped its membership at 435. In the 1st Congress (1789–91), the House was 2.5 times larger than the Senate; today, the ratio is 4.35 to 1.[4]

The work on chamber size and procedures generates the chamber-size hypothesis, which holds that (a) *larger bodies are more restrictive* and (b) *increases in size will lead to the adoption of more restrictive procedures and practices.*

The second part of the hypothesis is unidirectional. That decreases in size do not necessarily bring about a naturalization of procedures is consistent with my model of procedural change. Given the costs and difficulties of building coalitions and the challenges of managing larger bodies, the quantity of legislation produced under natural procedures declines as chambers get bigger. This development will be undesirable for many members, including those with little extant influence over decision making, because it will diminish their capacity to realize policy, electoral, and other goals. Unproductive bodies, for example, can accomplish little in the way of distributive policy or substantive legislative records that members seeking reelection can present to their constituents.

In other words, large and growing bodies are more likely to adopt restrictive procedures because a large swath of members, including many outside positions of influence, accepts such organizational arrangements. In small and shrinking bodies, however, no such agreement exists. Members who shape decision making believe that restrictive procedures are desirable, whereas their colleagues hold that naturalization should occur.

Note that the hypothesis is used to generate expectations about procedural change in both relatively large and growing bodies. Even in small bodies that are growing, the general membership's advocacy of natural procedures and resistance to restrictive ones will be altered. Members with little influence over the legislative process will perceive increased costs to more natural procedures as the body grows.

A study of the two chambers of Congress precludes a thorough test of the claim that large bodies are more restrictive than small ones, although an analysis of national bodies from across the world has shown such to be the case (Taylor 2006). I maintain that the relative sizes of the House and Senate help explain why the former is more restrictive than the latter. I will rigorously test the argument that the House's more rapid growth has led to its more restrictive procedures and practices.

Workload

The second hypothesis focuses on workload. The Framers created a largely symmetrical bicameral legislature in that the House and Senate have nearly equal powers and responsibilities. But across-chamber differences in workload quickly emerged. Lawmaking immediately became sequential, with the House generally working on bills first and the Senate then taking up those the lower chamber had approved (Binder 1997, 61–64; Swift 1996, 63–64; Wirls and Wirls 2004, 186–93). The House thus inevitably formulated, gathered information for, and discussed bills in depth. The Senate became more of a ratifying chamber, evaluating legislation rather than crafting it. The trend was reinforced by the constitutional obligation that the House initiate revenue bills, a rule that was quickly and informally extended to the practice of the lower chamber dealing first with all "money bills" (Kiewiet and McCubbins 1991, 12; Wirls and Wirls 2004, 187–89)—that is, spending as well as taxing. Figure 1.3 displays the number of private and public bills introduced in the House and Senate in the Congresses prior to the Civil War. Many more bills were introduced in the House, and the workloads of both chambers tended to increase.

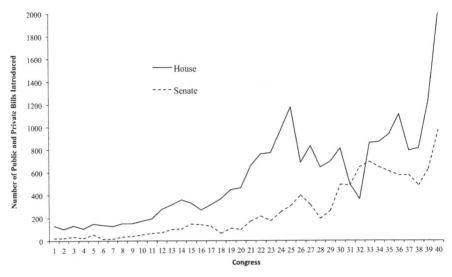

Fig. 1.3.   The number of bills introduced in the House and Senate, 1st (1789–91) to 40th (1867–69) Congresses. (Data for Congresses 1–17 from Sarah Binder. Data for Congresses 18–40 calculated from the Library of Congress "A Century of Lawmaking" Web site, http://memory.loc.gov/ammem/amlaw/lwhbsb.html.)

Although this particular lawmaking sequence is not as rigid today, the House still initiates a great deal more legislation than does the Senate. Taylor (2008) reports that of 950 important domestic policy bills in the 84th (1955–57) to 107th (2001–3) Congresses, about 64 percent were approved first by the House.[5]

Intercameral and longitudinal differences in workload have also been facilitated by the liberal bill introduction procedures both chambers developed. Unlike, for example, the United Kingdom's House of Commons, neither the U.S. House nor the Senate restricts either the members who can introduce bills or the time when they can be introduced. With many more members, the number of bills before the House at any one time is generally much larger than the number before the Senate. Furthermore, the number of bills has generally increased as constituent demands on members and the federal government's reach have grown. The number of bills peaked in the late 1970s, when upward of 18,000 bills were being introduced in the House each Congress; the figure has since settled down to around 5,000.[6]

Workload can be thought of and measured in different ways. As a concept, it means the extent of the burden placed on members by the legislative process. Much of this burden is the number of bills presented to them, but it is more than that. It includes the amount of legislative work they undertake more broadly—the effort expended on legislation in the form of bill drafting, committee work, floor time, and so forth. I generally use a measure that attempts to capture this idea fully.[7]

Chamber size has been largely ignored by empirical analyses of procedural design in Congress.[8] Workload has not. Binder's (1997, 204) influential study of longitudinal change in congressional procedures finds that a "conventional workload account makes only a marginal contribution to explaining House and Senate development." Fink (2000) comes to a similar conclusion in her study of early rules change proposals in the House. Both of these authors formulate and test a workload hypothesis that illuminates an intuitive relationship between workload and procedures and practices affecting the floor (Binder 1997, 45–47; Fink 2000). Binder and Fink essentially state that increasing workload diminishes the parliamentary rights of members of the minority party. This finding is consistent with my model of procedural change. Like large and growing memberships, large and growing workloads inhibit aggregate productivity, because sorting through proposals to identify those worthy of evaluation and approval is onerous, and scarce committee and floor time is wasted doing so. Members with little influence over decision making therefore recognize that natural procedures are costly when workload burdens are high, so such members are more likely to accept the need for increased restrictions. The usual conflict over procedural design will continue when workload is light or diminishing.

Table 1.2 shows procedural preferences and their hypothesized variance under conditions of chamber size and workload amount. The table reveals that consensus among members on procedures will occur only when bodies and workloads are large and/or growing. Under these conditions, members may agree to restrict procedures and to reject a naturalizing of them. Indeed, given that legislative bodies, including the U.S. House and Senate, tend to grow and have increasing workloads, the acceptance of restrictive procedures under increased memberships and business may well assist in explaining the general movement of chambers toward the restrictive pole of procedural types. The fundamental discord over procedures within a body is unlikely to bring about a reversion to the old way of doing things when memberships and work burdens shrink.

This leads to my workload hypothesis: (a) *bodies with heavier workloads are more restrictive,* and (b) *increases in workload will lead to the adoption of more restrictive procedures and practices.* The House has more restrictive procedures because its workload has been both large and growing. As is the case with Binder's (1997) measure of workload, which I use in chapter 3, the Senate's workload has often grown as dramatically as the House's. When it grows, there should be a greater propensity to adopt restrictive procedures. But the Senate's workload has invariably been lighter than the House's, a phenomenon that means the Senate is less likely to have restrictive procedures than the lower chamber.

Unlike the number of members, workload might be endogenous to legislators' policy preferences. Senate size is established by the Constitution, while House size is established largely by entrenched statute that is "protected" from frequent and substantive change by a deep-rooted legitimacy and the convoluted legislative process. Although workload is regulated by formal rules that are not easy to change, it is clearly also a product of member preferences. Workload is likely to be high, for example, if legislator ideal points are distant from status quo points. Under these conditions, members will generate numerous policy proposals for the body to consider.

Yet even if much workload is generated by members' positions on issues, we ought to observe a very different type of procedural change than that generally described by scholars of congressional development (Binder 1995, 1996, 1997; Birkhead et al. 2010; Cox and McCubbins 2005; Dion 1997; Fink 2000; Schickler 2000, 2001). A large majority of members could

TABLE 1.2. Chamber Size, Workload, and the Conditions under Which Members Should Accept or Reject Proposals to Alter Procedures

Nature of Proposed Procedural Change	Relationship of Group to Floor Agenda and Proceedings	Nature of Chamber Membership and/or Workload	
		Large and/or Growing	Small and/or Shrinking
Restrictive	Greatly Influence	Accept	Accept
	Has Little Influence	May Accept or Reject	Reject
Natural	Greatly Influence	Reject	Reject
	Has Little Influence	May Accept or Reject	Accept

have preferences induced by strong public demands for policy change, for example. In this case, ideal points are distant from the status quo and are likely to be arrayed to suggest little in the way of partisan polarization. The effect ought to generate workload and a climate amenable to the adoption of restrictive procedures.

Parties and Policy Preferences

The third hypothesis rests on somewhat different foundations. It assumes that partisanship and policy preferences drive procedural choice and outcomes. The basic argument is that all members want procedures that will generate policy outcomes as close as possible to their ideal points. Not all members will want the same procedural design at the same time because different members have different policy preferences. On any one bill, it is likely that some members would like to see procedures that expedite passage, while others would prefer the status quo and desire procedures that increase the chances that the bill will be defeated. There exists, as a consequence, a constant struggle over procedures and practices that shape the floor.

How should we expect this struggle to play out? In the basic model of procedural change, I argue that those who set the floor agenda and direct floor proceedings want restrictive rules. A principal reason is that these members' policy preferences are more likely to pass through the chamber when restrictive rules are in place. A weak floor on which members have few rights will find it difficult to block or alter proposed legislation. Members with little influence will push for naturalization so that they might offer proposals and so that legislation forwarded by those in power might be blocked or changed to the extent that it better reflects others' preferences.

The members who are most capable of influencing the legislative agenda and floor process essentially lead the majority party. It is particularly obvious that the legislative process in the contemporary House is directed by the Speaker, the Rules Committee, and standing committee chairs and their majorities, all of whom are largely accountable to the general membership of the majority party. Recent research on the Senate reveals that the majority party sets the floor agenda in that body as well, albeit to a lesser extent (Den Hartog and Monroe 2011; Gailmard and Jenkins 2007). Members of the minority party, on the other hand, are generally incapable of shaping the floor agenda and the conduct of floor proceedings.

If members of the two parties are assumed to have different positions on substantive issues, then the cleavages that separate policy and procedural preferences in a body line up along the same plane. Those who direct the legislative process disagree with those who do not on both policy and procedural grounds. Procedural change is determined by the power relationship between the two parties. The majority will succeed in restricting procedures—and then getting the policy outcomes it desires—when it is relatively powerful in its relationship with the minority. The minority will prevail, or at least block the majority, on procedural and subsequently policy matters at times when it is relatively powerful.

A rich and varied scholarship examines the role of party in procedural change. Binder's (1997) comprehensive longitudinal study of rules changes in the House and Senate shows that when the majority party strengthens—a concept measured using indicators of size and ideological cohesion—procedural alteration tends to dilute minority party rights. When the minority strengthens relative to the majority, it can bring about change in the opposite direction.[9] Fink (2000), conversely, demonstrates that rules that weakened minority party rights in the pre-1850 House came about when the majority party was divided and moved to protect itself. In his study of Congress and two foreign legislative bodies, Dion (1997, 245) argues that "small majorities are more cohesive, cohesive majorities lead to minority obstruction, minority obstruction leads to procedural changes on the part of the majority to limit obstruction." Schickler (2000) shows that the ideological position of the House's median member is critical to an understanding of the majority party's ability to stack the procedural deck. Majority party rights are invigorated when the chamber median is closer to the majority party's median. Minority party rights are expanded as the chamber median moves away from the majority party's median. Here, the chamber median is pivotal, and although she is always in the majority in a two-party body, she will support procedural change favored by the minority when she is close to that party's median. Binder (2006) has responded explicitly to Schickler's findings and reiterated her majority party strength argument.

All of this work has been influential for our understanding of longitudinal change in an individual body's procedures, especially the House. But can it be used to explain intercameral differences in congressional procedures and practices governing the floor? There are two plausible explanations to suggest that the answer to this question is yes. The first is that individual members' policy preferences should be arrayed differently in the House and Senate. Preference heterogeneity is likely to be great within states, which are generally larger than House districts and often include voters of diverse political persuasions and interests (R. Baker 2001, 106–18; Binder 2005, 156). In turn, senators' preferences are more likely to cluster around the chamber median when their ideal points are arrayed on a single dimension. The diversity of House members' districts, however, is likely to string their ideal points out along such a continuum.[10] Compared to their counterparts in the lower chamber, Senate parties should be less distinct and, given the interparty overlap in preferences, cohesive.[11] Intraparty preference homogeneity is, as Binder (1997) argues, a central element of party strength.[12]

Empirical evidence also shows that bodies with multimember districts, as is the case in the Senate, elect a less polarized membership than those with single-member districts such as the House. Using both longitudinal and cross-sectional techniques, Adams (1996), in a study of the Illinois legislature, and Richardson, Russell, and Cooper (2004), in a study of Arizona's legislature, show that whether examined as individuals or collectively in their parties, members elected to bodies in single-member districts are more ideologically extreme.

However, little empirical evidence supports theoretical claims that the preferences of individual House members and Senators are arrayed differently and that, as a result, Senate parties are less cohesive and polarized and the body's majority is weak. Several analyses of lengthy time series, for example, have discovered that partisan voting patterns are quite similar in both chambers (Aldrich, Berger, and Rohde 2002; Hurley and Wilson 1989), as have period-specific studies (Theriault 2004).[13]

Still, as noted previously, a second explanation exists for how member policy preferences and political parties can account for intercameral differences in procedures. It is taken directly from a body of recent work (Binder 1997, 2003; Binder and Smith 1997; J. M. Roberts and Smith 2007; Theriault 2008). This explanation argues that "path dependence" or the "stickiness" of "inherited rules" help explain procedural development. The path dependency argument essentially proposes that the Senate's entrenched and quite natural rules make it very difficult for strong majorities to restrict procedures. Furthermore, because the strength of parties is somewhat endogenous to procedural design, the Senate's rules inherently undermine the capacity of its majorities to alter procedures. In the House, however, it is difficult to naturalize procedures because members of the minority party cannot readily influence the floor agenda—particularly since the late 19th century (Cox and McCubbins 2005). In the lower chamber, procedures have proven easier for strong majorities to manipulate. In periods such as the 1890s and 1990s, this has enabled them to make the body's character markedly more restrictive. When the House changes like this, majorities strengthen further and the likelihood of additional movement in the restrictive direction is elevated as leaders use their enhanced procedural powers to corral rank-and-file members.

The intense focus on parties and policy preferences as the chief determinant of rules changes compels me to examine what Bensel (2000) calls an "instrumental party" model of procedural design. My main focus is an examination of whether power relations between majority and minority parties can explain intercameral differences and temporal changes in procedures and practices that affect the floor. I test my majority-party strength hypothesis: (a) *bodies with stronger majority parties are more restrictive, and those with weaker ones are more natural;* and (b) *increases in majority party strength will lead to the adoption of more restrictive procedures and practices, while decreases lead to the adoption of more natural procedures and practices.*

Unlike the previous hypotheses, the second part of this hypothesis is two-directional. Naturalization is explained by relatively weak majority—and therefore strong minority—parties. I do not test the first part of the hypothesis directly. I do not demonstrate that the House has, in the aggregate, more restrictive procedures today because it has generally had stronger majorities better positioned to weaken the floor and the rights members exercise on it. Instead, I examine whether the strengthening of majority parties generally brings about greater restriction and whether the relationship between majority party strength and changes in procedures and the use of practices is different in the House from what it is in the Senate.

Other Plausible Determinants of House-Senate Differences

Additional factors may explain bicameral variation in congressional procedures. Two that are central to the chambers' basic characters come immediately to mind. The first is term length. House members, of course, have two-year terms, while senators are elected for six years. With longer terms, senators have a greater incentive to invest time learning about many types of policy. Their body should have less need for the labor-dividing benefits that strong committees—and a weak floor—bring. A senator can better afford to engage with many issues, even those that, should they become law, will have negligible effect on her constituents. Senators have the advantage of an open, deliberative, and time-consuming process. They are more likely to want to protect the floor and their rights on it.

Related empirical work on senators' behavior over the course of a term bears out this finding. Many scholars have shown that individual senators align their activities most closely with constituency preferences in the last Congress of their term (Ahuja 1994; Bernstein 1991; Fenno 1982; Kuklinski 1978; Shapiro et al. 1990). Immediately after their election, senators do not feel tremendous urgency to attend to the matters on which their specific electorates judge them.

House members, conversely, have only two years to build a record to present to voters. They are likely to try directly and quickly to influence the most easily manipulable information on which constituents evaluate performance. Representatives are likely to concentrate on committee work because, to use Mayhew's (1974, 92) words, committees are "specialized small-group settings in which individual congressmen can make things happen and be perceived to make things happen." They are also likely to engage in casework, patronage, and distributive policy making, consuming time on business that is not subject to the broad deliberative process (Fiorina 1977; Herrera and Yawn 1999; Mayhew 1974). These activities do not require time-consuming coalition building and credit-diluting limelight sharing.

If rank-and-file House members have little interest in a powerful floor and their own rights on it, procedural change is likely to go in the restrictive direction. Put another way, a natural body consumes one of its members' most valued resources: time. When legislators have relatively little time, they are likely to acquiesce in or at least not oppose attempts to streamline the legislative process. Indeed, Carrubba and Volden's (2000) formal model shows that the more frequent a body's elections, the more likely members will accept weaker floor rights.

Constituency size might also explain bicameral procedural differences. Senators represent states and, with the exception of House members who come from at-large statewide districts, have bigger and generally more heterogeneous constituencies than their counterparts in the lower chamber. Together with their unique constitutional obligation to ratify treaties and confirm presidential appointments, this means that senators should have less interest in the kinds of narrow parochial issues with which House members concern themselves (Atlas, Hendershott, and Zupan 1997; Fiorina 1977; Mayhew 1974). Instead, they should focus more on national issues or, as normative treatments of representation have suggested, on the public good (Rehfeld 2005). Madison made this point in Federalist 10, when he argued that large and diverse representational units provide their elected officials with greater opportunities to pursue the nation's interest (Hamilton, Madison, and Jay 1961, 83).

Whereas shorter terms theoretically drive House members to delegate power to committees for time-saving and labor-dividing purposes, smaller and homogenous constituencies encourage representatives to strengthen committees to facilitate policy specialization. Representing such constituencies, House members can afford to neglect many issues and concentrate on a relatively few select others. Senators do not have this luxury, since their large and heterogeneous constituencies turn them into policy generalists and force them to attend to most legislative activity, including that which takes place on the floor.

Small constituencies also make distributive policy more appetizing because particularized benefits can be experienced only by a limited number of voters. The larger is the constituency, the smaller is the proportion of affected constituents. Indeed, as if to prove this point empirically, Lee and Oppenheimer (1999, 127–33) show that small-state senators gravitate toward committees that craft distributive policy, while large-state senators join committees that deal with national issues. The making of distributive policy places an emphasis on strong and autonomous committees and a deferential floor (Weingast and Marshall 1988).

Policy generalization, conversely, provides pressure to create procedures and practices that move a body in the natural direction. Electoral institutions that furnish incentives for members to generalize are likely to generate legislative rules promoting the power of the floor because the floor is the only institution that consists of all members—that is, those who collectively represent the nation—and that provides a forum in which many individual issues can be woven into a cohesive and singular public policy. If members are motivated to generalize, they are also likely to push for strong floor rights because they will be interested in legislative outcomes in numerous policy areas, not just a few.

Of course, constituency size might be related to chamber size. Chambers with larger constituencies are likely to be smaller. Both of these factors, moreover, push in the same direction: Bodies with larger constituencies and fewer members are hypothesized to be more natural. But these are different phenomena, both in a conceptual sense and in their effect on procedures and practices. In the case of Congress, for example, the Senate's large constituencies are not the direct product of chamber size but of the Framers' desire to recognize federal principles through congressional representation and their decision to create states as "staggered" multimember districts represented by two legislators selected at different times (Schiller 2000). When looked at through the lens of individual electoral pressures, large bodies create incentives to restrict procedures and practices because a powerful floor on which members have strong rights decreases productivity. Small constituencies move bodies in a restrictive direction because they encourage policy specialization, an activity best undertaken off the floor.

Term length does not vary across congressional history, of course. Constituency size does vary, but intercameral differences in constituency size have not changed very much. Moreover, several measurement difficulties are inherent to a longitudinal analysis using constituency size. States are of different sizes, and at least until the Apportionment Act of 1842, a significant proportion of House members were elected by the general-ticket method.[14] As a result, I cannot really test the propositions that term length and constituency size generate procedural change and differences in the House's and Senate's procedural characters.

Future scholars should potentially consider examining the effects of these two phenomena on legislative procedures and organization, however. Cross-sectional and comparative work such as Martorano's (2006) and Taylor's (2006) provide an opportunity to do precisely this sort of research.[15]

Path Dependency in the Development of Congressional Procedures

As noted previously, congressional scholars assume a kind of path dependency in the development of House and Senate procedures (Binder 1997, 2003; Binder and Smith 1997; J. M. Roberts and Smith 2007; Theriault 2008). These observers suggest that rules beget similar rules. The range of possible changes to procedures in any single Congress is narrowed considerably by extant arrangements. Bodies establish basic procedural characters that are difficult to alter and that survive over long periods of time.

Political scientists seem to agree on how path dependency has affected procedural development across congressional history. The Senate's decision to drop the previous question motion in 1806 and the House's decision to adopt an interpretation of the previous question that maintained the procedure ended debate on a bill in 1811 are critical (Binder 2003; J. M. Roberts and Smith 2007). Strong House majorities have used the previous question to overcome minority obstruction and have been well positioned to force rules changes that serve their policy interests—that is, to alter procedures generally in the restrictive direction. Robust Senate majorities, conversely, have consistently attempted to dilute minority rights but have frequently been unable to do so, largely because the procedural context, which allows minorities to filibuster, makes their efforts prohibitively difficult (Binder 1997, 167–201; J. M. Roberts and Smith 2007).

Another pivotal procedural moment, at least for the House, occurred in the late 19th century (Binder 2003; Cox and McCubbins 2005, 50–86). The body adopted Reed's Rules, preventing minority floor obstruction and allowed the majority-party-controlled Rules Committee to shape the conditions under which bills would be debated on the floor. The body moved stridently in the restrictive direction as a result. The development has yet to be reversed in even the slightest way.

According to this narrative then, the two chambers began to diverge very early on. As a response to procedural changes at the beginning of the 19th century, the House was to take the more restrictive trajectory, while the Senate followed a quite natural path. The events of the fifteen or so years before 1900 reinforced these developments.

Path dependency is important to my story as well. I argue that changes in House and Senate rules after the Civil War are relatively minor, largely because procedural journeys had been mapped out previously. I may not see the events of the 1880s and 1890s as quite as transformative for the House as do some observers, but I do recognize the fundamental role inherited rules play in congressional development.

Institutional stickiness or path dependency is very difficult to model, and I do not measure its impact on procedural change here. But if we assume it exists, any analysis of the development of congressional rules and practices should place greater emphasis on the earlier as well as the more important changes. My explanation of House-Senate differences does just this.

Conclusion

In my conceptualization of the procedures and practices governing the floors of the two congressional chambers, the Senate is clearly the more natural body. Its floor is more powerful than the House's, and its members enjoy more robust floor rights. In the following two chapters I will investigate why this is so. I will test my three hypotheses using data gathered from the expanse of congressional history. I begin with a quantitative analysis of congressional rules changes and alterations in the use of important practices.

2 ◆ Developing Procedural Character

A Quantitative Analytical History of House and Senate Floor Power and Rights

In this chapter, I begin my examination of the reasons why the House and Senate floors are so different by testing the three hypotheses on changes in House and Senate procedures and the use of House and Senate practices over time. If increases in size, workload, and majority party strength tend to push the bodies in a restrictive direction, evidence indicates that these matters contribute to aggregate bicameral differences in the power of the floors and the rights exercised on them. Since the House's membership and business have expanded more and its majorities have generally become more vigorous than those of the Senate, we can suggest with some confidence that the bodies' dissimilar procedural characters may largely be attributed to the various rates at which they have grown, taken on work, and seen their majority parties become more powerful. The hypotheses are tested on quantitative data about changes in House and Senate rules and practices over the course of congressional history. Although the findings are nuanced and varied, the preponderance of evidence is consistent with the hypotheses.

Explaining Changes in Formal Rules that Affect the House Floor

The Rules Changes

I start with an investigation of the House and changes to formal codified House rules shaping the floor from the 1st (1789–91) through 107th Congresses (2001–3). Codified rules are critical because they authorize the procedures that dictate practice and behavior. The rules I examine are explicitly mentioned in prominent histories of Congress. The sources were chosen because they provide thorough historical treatment of House procedure and are frequently used by congressional scholars.[1] They are listed in table 2.1 with the rules changes themselves.

TABLE 2.1. Changes to House Rules That Affect the Floor, 1789–2002

Year	Congress	Rules Change	Direction
1790	1st	Committees chosen by Speaker	Restrict (decrease floor power)
1794	3rd	Speaker appoints chair of Committee of the Whole	Restrict (decrease floor power)
1803	8th	Speaker right to name committee chairs and control of succession/committee majority reserves right to name chair	Restrict (decrease floor power)
1811	12th	Previous question rule adopted	Restrict (weaken floor rights)
1822	17th	2/3 vote needed to suspend the rules	Naturalize (strengthen floor rights)
1822	17th	Standing committees' right to report	Restrict (decrease floor power)
1841	27th	Majority vote can discharge Committee of the Whole	Restrict (weaken floor rights)
1841	27th	One hour rule	Restrict (weaken floor rights)
1847	30th	Five minute rule for amendments	Naturalize (strengthen floor rights) OR Restrict (weaken floor rights)
1880	46th	Package: Required debate on suspensions and previous question, allowed motion to recommit, etc.	Naturalize (strengthen floor rights)
1890	51st	Reed's Rules: End disappearing quorum and dilatory motions	Restrict (weaken floor rights)
1890	51st	Committee of the Whole quorum is 100	Restrict (weaken floor rights)
1892	52nd	Disappearing quorum rule reversed	Naturalize (strengthen floor rights)
1894	53rd	Disappearing quorum rule reinstated	Restrict (weaken floor rights)
1909	60th	Calendar Wednesday established	Naturalize (increase floor power)
1910	61st	Speaker cannot appoint committee members	Naturalize (increase floor power)
1910	61st	Speaker cannot be on Rules Committee	Naturalize (increase floor power)
1910	61st	Discharge petition created	Naturalize (increase floor power)

TABLE 2.1.—*Continued*

Year	Congress	Rules Change	Direction
1911	62nd	Committees and chairs selected by the House	Naturalize (increase floor power)
1924	68th	Discharge petition reduced to 150	Naturalize (increase floor power)
1925	69th	Discharge petition increased to 218	Restrict (decrease floor power)
1931	72nd	Discharge petition reduced to 145	Naturalize (increase floor power)
1935	74th	Discharge petition increased to 218	Restrict (decrease floor power)
1946	79th	Legislative Reorganization Act: decreases number of committees but gives them greater resources	Naturalize and Restrict (increase and decrease floor power)
1949	81st	21 day rule established	Naturalize (increase floor power)
1951	82nd	21 day rule repealed	Restrict (decrease floor power)
1961	87th	Rules Committee enlarged	Naturalize (increase floor power)
1965	89th	21 day rule reestablished	Naturalize (increase floor power)
1967	90th	21 day rule repealed	Restrict (decrease floor power)
1970	91st	Legislative Reorganization Act: weaken committees and chairs	Naturalize (increase floor power)
1973	93rd	Committees made more transparent and weakened (e.g., subcommittee bill of rights)	Naturalize (increase floor power)
1975	94th	Conference committees made more transparent	Naturalize (increase floor power)
1993	103rd	Discharge petitions transparent	Naturalize (increase floor power)
1995	104th	Republican rules: Weaken committees (e.g., term limits for chairs)	Naturalize (increase floor power)

Source: Alexander 1916; Binder 1997; Bolling 1968; Brown 1922; *Congressional Quarterly* 1982, 1999; Dion 1997; Follett 1896; Fuller 1909; Galloway 1976; Goodwin 1970; Hasbrouck 1927; Joint Committee on the Organization of Congress 1993; Josephy 1979; Luce 1922; Oleszek 2011; Peters 1997; Riddick 1949; Schickler 2000, 2001.

The rules changes have two critical characteristics. First, they affect the role of the floor in the legislative process and therefore constitute movement along the floor power dimension, or they shape floor proceedings and therefore constitute movement along the floor rights dimension. I am not particularly interested in the creation or abolition of standing committees, for example. With regard to rules governing standing committees, I am looking for obvious alterations in their collective power vis-à-vis the floor. In other words, does the change reveal real movement along the floor power dimension? For the most part, it was clear whether a rule change affected the floor and either discernibly naturalized or restricted procedures. In some cases, however, I had to make a judgment.

Second, and less subjectively, the rules changes are considered historically important. To qualify as important, a rules change had to be mentioned by at least half of my sources published after the change was made. There are 34 rules changes in the 107 Congresses—18 that naturalize procedures, 14 that restrict them, 1 that contains provisions that do both, and 1 that can be interpreted as moving the House in either direction.[2] Even a cursory look reveals the rules changes to be important and just about each one an essential part of any history of House procedures.[3]

The data highlight periods of stability and important clusters of change. Speaker Thomas Brackett Reed's (R-ME) rules of the 51st Congress (1889–91) that greatly restricted floor rights, the revolt against Speaker Joseph Cannon that increased floor power in the 61st Congress (1909–11), and packages that both naturalized and restricted procedures in the 17th (1821–23), 27th (1841–43), and 30th Congresses (1847–49) are probably the most prominent examples of clustered change.

Independent Variables

To test the chamber-size hypothesis on these data, I use a measure, *change in size*, that is the alteration in the number of members of the House from the Congress before the observation to the Congress of the observation as a percentage of the former.[4] As applied to longitudinal data, the chamber-size hypothesis holds that increases in chamber size will lead to the adoption of restrictive procedures.

I use a measure derived from Binder (1997, 218–19; 2006) to indicate workload.[5] Binder performs a factor analysis on the number of days in session, the number of public laws enacted, and the number of members of the House in each Congress.[6] It is not as full an accounting of legislative workload as we might like, but historical data on matters such as the number of committee meetings are not available. The principal differences between Binder's calculations and mine are that I use a continuous series—Binder breaks House workload into two, beginning the second part at the 54th Congress (1895–97)—and I update through the 107th Congress. I then transform this workload measure into a variable, *change in workload,* which is the change in the score from the previous Congress to the current Congress. It is reasonable to assume that in any one Congress, the body reacts to contemporaneous changes in the amount of workload rather than absolute workload levels. The effectiveness of existing rules is evaluated in the context of current burdens. As workload increases or decreases, these observations and the rules themselves will be altered accordingly.[7] I employ the measure to test the workload hypothesis: Increases in workload will lead to the adoption of restrictive procedures.

I employ two variables to test the majority party strength hypothesis. The first is a close variant of Binder's (1997, 220–24; 2006) indicator that measures majority party strength by multiplying the size of each party's representation in the House as a proportion of the entire chamber by its Rice cohesion score.[8] Binder then subtracts the minority's score from that of the majority. My *majority party strength* measure multiplies the size, as a proportion, of each party in a Congress with the standard deviation of its members' first dimension DW-NOMINATE scores subtracted from one.[9] Like Binder, I then subtract the minority score from the majority score.[10] Unlike the size and workload indicators, I do not use the change in the score from one Congress to the next. Majority party strength captures the capacity of a group of people, not a perception that is inevitably conceived in the context of recent conditions. It should be measured in absolute terms. À la Binder and the majority party strength hypothesis, I expect that Congresses where majority party strength is high will adopt restrictive procedures and that those with low majority party strength will adopt natural ones.

The second of these variables is Schickler's (2000) *change in ideological power balance*. This concept measures, in first dimension DW-NOMINATE, the absolute distance the median member of the majority is from the median member of the chamber subtracted from the absolute distance the median member of the minority is from the median member of the chamber. It then indicates the change in these numbers from the Congress before the one under observation to the Congress under observation.[11] It is designed to measure shifts in the floor median relative to the position of the two parties. Negative values denote the movement of the median toward the minority party; positive values denote the movement of the median toward the majority.

Although Schickler (2000) argues that his measure is not essentially partisan, it does, as Binder (2006) points out, make strong inferences about the relative power of the two parties. Greater ideological distance between the majority median and floor median indicates a more heterogeneous and/or smaller majority party. Like Binder, Schickler uses his variable in a model of rules changes designed to affect the relative power of the majority and minority parties. Still, as with the Binder-derived variable, we can extend this thinking and apply it to analysis of how rules affecting the floor will change. Consistent with Schickler, I hypothesize that movement of the floor median toward the majority will lead Congresses to adopt restrictive rules, with movement toward the minority leading to the naturalization of rules.[12]

Finally, I employ two variables that may theoretically be important to longitudinal models of changes in House rules, even if they cannot explain fundamental bicameral differences in the strength of the floor and floor rights. The first codes a Congress 1 if there has been a change in party control—that is, the former minority party is now the majority. Schickler (2000, 273–74) suggests that switches in party control may be accompanied by changes in rules because the two major parties have different preferences, and different legislative procedures can facilitate the creation of different policies. He uses the late-19th-century example of the Holman rule, which does not make my list but is included in two of the alternative data sets I analyze. This rule allowed expenditure-reducing amendments to appropriations bills and was an important procedural tool for Democrats in their relationship with Republican presidents (Kiewiet and McCubbins 1991; Stewart 1989).

Binder (1997) suggests a different connection between change in party control and alterations to the rules. She posits that a majority party, anticipating loss of control, may either tighten or relax procedures. Using my conceptualization of the dependent variable, we can make an additional theoretical link and discern a clear direction for the relationship. I hypothesize that party change will lead to a naturalization in procedures for two reasons. First, the new majority, having recently experienced minority status, will have a greater affinity for the floor and floor rights and a residual antithesis to procedures—like, for example, strong committees and presiding officers—that may have been used to undermine the party's power and block its legislative proposals in the previous Congress. Second, procedural change may well have been part of the old minority's public campaign to win control of the House. Binder (1997, 208) argues that "the public rarely focuses on procedural matters because it is usually difficult to make the connection between rules and policy outcomes." Former minority leader Bob Michel (R-IL) (1987) put it a little more bluntly when he noted that congressional procedures are "all 'inside baseball'" and "nothing is so boring to the layman as a litany of complaints over the more obscure provisions of House procedures." Still procedural change is sometimes a critical part of congressional campaigns. In 1890, Democrats vowed to reverse Speaker Thomas Brackett Reed's (R-ME) rules ending the disappearing quorum and preventing dilatory motions (Binder 1997, 129; W. A. Robinson 1930, 275; Schickler 2001, 44; Stealey 1906, 105). The 1908 Democratic party platform demanded, "The House of Representatives shall again become a deliberative body, controlled by a majority of the people's representatives, and not by the Speaker." Much closer to the present day, the House Republicans' 1994 "Contract with America" pledged opening-day procedural reforms designed, among other things, to undercut the power of committees. During the 2004 campaign, minority leader Nancy Pelosi (D-CA) proposed a "Minority Bill of Rights" that called for greater transparency for standing and conference committee proceedings, more open special rules to facilitate amending activity on the floor, and strict enforcement by the presiding officer of time limits for floor votes (Babington 2004). The Democrats' more successful 2006 campaign echoed many of these themes. After their victory in 2010, the Republicans' new House majority instituted a series of reforms discussed by their candidates on the stump, including a requirement that a bill be published on the Internet at least 72 hours before it goes to the floor. In each case, it is not surprising the minority party pledged during the campaign to naturalize House procedures. Legislative principles such as openness and deliberation appeal instinctively to the public.[13]

The last variable looks at turnover in a different way. It is the percentage of members in a Congress who were freshmen.[14] A large influx of new members represents a considerable exogenous shock to the House. As such, it may be viewed as an electoral repudiation of the status quo—whether that is a party, an ideology, a generation, or cadre of leaders—and as evidence of the need for new policies and, presumably, procedures. Moreover, given that senior and electorally safe members generally hold positions of influence over the floor agenda and proceedings (Cox and Mc-Cubbins 2007, 115–23), large incoming classes of lawmakers should attempt to naturalize procedures as they pursue their policy preferences. Large incoming classes may also undermine the legislative norms and traditions that legitimize powerful nonfloor institutions and inequality among members (Diermeier 1995). Such seemed to be the case in the mid-1970s (Schickler, McGhee, and Sides 2003; Smith 1989) and with the large freshman classes of 1992 and 1994 (Aldrich and Rohde 1997–98). Although Schickler (2001, 258) finds little empirical verification for a turnover explanation of formal rules changes in Congress, Battista (2003) has undertaken theoretical work to illustrate that membership change can have this type of effect.[15]

The party control variable is hypothesized to have no demonstrable effect on procedures in Congresses where it is coded 0. The absence of change will not necessarily lead to more restrictive procedures and practices. When there are few new freshmen, however, we should expect movement in the restrictive direction. Large numbers of freshmen bolster the coalition of members pressing for naturalization, but small freshman classes increase the relative power of the coalition pushing for restriction.

Results

Table 2.2 shows simple logit models of rules that restrict and naturalize House procedures. The dependent variable is coded 1 in the first model if the Congress experienced a rule that restricted procedures and coded 0 if this was not the case. In the second model, the dependent variable is coded 1 if the Congress approved a rule that naturalized procedures. The differences in the logit models are dramatic. In the model of rules changes that restrict procedures, change in size is the only variable with a coefficient that clearly reaches levels of statistical significance. Indeed, it is quite robust. Throughout this analysis, I examine the impact of moving the value of the variables one standard deviation—from half a standard deviation below their means to half a standard deviation above their means—while holding all other continuous variables in the model at their means and dummy variables at their modal values. When this is done to the change in size variable in this particular model, the probability of a Congress experiencing a rules change that restricts procedures increases from 6.8 percent (with 95 percent confidence bounds of 1.5 to 12.1) to 13.6 percent (confidence bounds of 5.3 to 21.9).

In the model of rules changes that naturalize House procedures, three variables reach levels of statistical significance. The freshman variable is robust but behaves counterintuitively, with rules naturalizing procedures more likely to be passed when there is less turnover. This is because rules naturalizing procedures were generally created in the 20th century, the era in which legislators made the House a career and turnover was low. I will present evidence that generally confirms the freshman hypothesis later.

The other two robust performances are as expected. When the ideological power balance variable decreases and the floor median moves toward the minority, the House is more likely to adopt rules that naturalize. Moreover, a change in party control is also likely to lead to rules that naturalize.

Table 2.3 applies the simple model to alternative dependent variables of rules changes. The first is Binder's (1997) list of rules alterations that create minority rights. The second dependent variable is Schickler's (2000). He uses a variety of sources to identify rules changes from the 40th (1867–69) to the 105th Congresses (1997–99) that advantage either the majority or minority party. He codes Congresses 1 if they adopted alterations to rules that advantaged the majority, −1 if revisions to rules assisted the minority. I consider the Congresses coded 1 to be those in which the House has moved in the restrictive direction, those with a −1 to have moved in the natural direction.

TABLE 2.2. A Model of Changes to the Rules That Affect the House Floor, 1789–2002

	Rules That Restrict		Rules That Naturalize	
	Coefficient (standard error)	Impact on y in Percentage Points of One Standard Deviation Increase	Coefficient (standard error)	Impact on y in Percentage Points of One Standard Deviation Increase
Change in size	8.73 (3.85)**	+6.8		
Change in workload	1.35 (1.10)	+4.0		
Majority party strength	−0.422 (2.80)	−0.2	−.469 (2.86)	−0.6
Change in ideological power balance	1.05 (2.20)	+1.7	−3.09 (1.73)**	−3.1
Freshmen	−0.007 (0.023)	−1.1	−0.042 (0.021)**	−7.0
Change in party control			1.11 (0.699)*	+15.7
Constant	−2.13 (.857)**		−0.502 (0.635)	
Log likelihood	−33.94		−42.81	
LR chi^2	11.27*		11.33*	
Nagelkerke R^2	0.191		0.169	
Percentage correctly predicted	90.65		84.11	

Source: Rules changes taken from table 2.1

Note: Method is logit. Coefficients are unstandardized. $N = 107$. Standard errors are in parentheses. Tests are one-tailed. "Impact on y" is the difference in the predicted probabilities in percentage points if $y = 1$ and x is manipulated from one-half standard deviation below its mean to one-half standard deviation above it (or from 0 to 1 for the change in party control dummy) while all other variables are kept at their means (and the change in party control dummy = 0). LR = likelihood ratio.

$^*p < .1$ $^{**}p < .05$

The third dependent variable is Cox and McCubbins's (2005, 78–81). They observe on matters related to procedure each resolution or amendment to a resolution that was subject to at least one roll-call vote and that was both in effect for at least six months and had detectable partisan consequences. I use those rules changes they highlight in bold because such alterations are important and seem to affect directly the role of the floor in the legislative process.[16] I determine whether a rule moves the House in a natural or restrictive direction. The Cox and McCubbins data run from the 46th (1879–81) to the 100th Congresses (1987–89).

Using these three data sets is somewhat problematic. Naturalization can be similar to but is not the same thing as rules changes that favor the minority party. Binder (1997) includes, for example, several instances of minority rights creation in committee proceedings—most notably, the

TABLE 2.3.　A Model of Changes to the Rules That Affect the House Floor Using Alternative Dependent Variables

| | Binder's Rules That Naturalize | Schickler Data | | Cox and McCubbins Data | |
| | | Naturalize | Restrict | Naturalize | Restrict |
	Coefficient (standard error)	Coefficient (standard error)	Coefficient (standard error)	Coefficient (standard error)	Coefficient (standard error)
Change in size			11.16 (9.62)		−5.71 (15.01)
Change in workload			0.131 (.838)		0.831 (.865)
Majority party strength	−7.45 (4.23)**	−5.53 (8.13)	3.12 (2.90)	5.26 (3.95)*	1.06 (3.03)
Change in ideological power balance	−5.57 (2.34)**	−12.07 (5.22)**	5.62 (2.45)**	−8.38 (3.25)**	2.58 (2.39)
Change in party control	−1.29 (1.01)	−0.675 (1.43)		1.53 (1.01)*	
Freshmen	−0.013 (.022)	−0.037 (.044)	−0.028 (.027)	−0.016 (.037)	0.029 (.031)
Constant	−0.594 (.741)	−1.39 (1.38)	−0.785 (.764)	−2.61 (1.16)**	−2.10 (.932)**
Log likelihood	−31.29	−14.78	−33.96	−21.24	−28.84
LR chi^2	20.53**	18.94**	13.87**	9.67**	4.73
Nagelkerke R^2	0.324	0.481	0.268	0.263	0.121
Percent correctly predicted	86.92	89.23	66.15	83.64	80.00
N	107	65 (40th–105th Congresses)		55 (46th–100th Congresses)	

Source: Dependent variables are from Binder 1997, Schickler 2000, and Cox and McCubbins 2005.

Note: Method is logit. Coefficients are unstandardized. Standard errors are in parentheses. Tests are one-tailed. LR = likelihood ratio.

*$p < .1$　　**$p < .05$

1970 Legislative Reorganization Act. These changes do not ostensibly affect the floor. Still, considerable theoretical overlap exists, and a hefty chunk of the rules changes flagged by these scholars make my list in the manner one would expect. Naturalizing floor rights and floor power clearly assists the minority party, as the coding schemes used by Binder and Schickler show. I think these measures make an adequate proxy for the kind of procedural change I am modeling here.

I examine the data sets for another reason. I wish to highlight that majority party strength and the related change in the ideological power balance variable can be important to explanations of changes to procedures that govern the House floor. As is readily seen, these variables are robust in the model of Binder's data.[17] The results reveal that when the median moves closer to the minority, rules bringing about naturalization tend to occur—increasing the value of the change in ideological power balance one standard deviation as I did earlier decreases the probability of a rules change naturalizing procedures from 5.3 percent (confidence bounds of −.4 to 10.9) to 2.2 percent (confidence bounds of −1.5 to 5.9). The result of a manipulation to the model when we shift the value of majority party strength in the usual way is to decrease the probability of such a rules change from 13.1 percent (confidence bounds of 2.9 to 23.2) to 5.4 percent (confidence bounds of 0 to 11.6).

The change in ideological power balance is also statistically significant and behaves as hypothesized in three of the four logit models of the Schickler and Cox and McCubbins data. For the Schickler data, in which procedures are naturalized, the probability of a Congress naturalizing procedures decreases from 9.3 percent (confidence bounds of −2.8 to 25.4) to 1.5 percent (confidence bounds of −3.7 to 4.6) when the value of the ideological power balance variable is raised in the usual way. For the Cox and McCubbins data on natural procedures, this predicted probability decreases from 18.1 percent (confidence bounds of 4.7 to 31.5) to 5.1 percent (confidence bounds of −2.0 to 12.2).[18]

Why does table 2.2 show considerable differences between the performance of the model of rules changes that restrict House procedures and that of rules changes that naturalize? I think the distribution of the rules changes over time can provide an answer. Table 2.1 shows that most rules changes that restrict procedures come in the early Congresses, whereas most of the changes that naturalize come in later years—essentially from the 60th Congress (1907–9) on. The determinants of revisions to formal rules as they affect the floor may vary over time. By way of a hypothetical example, the magnitude and perhaps the direction of a strong majority party effect on procedures may be different in 1830 than it is in 1980.

Table 2.4 reveals a logit model of the adoption of rules changes that restrict House procedures using the same independent variables. The first column contains results of a specification in which the first 39 Congresses (1789–1867) are used; the second column provides results of a specification in which the first 54 (1789–1897) Congresses are used; and the third column shows data from the 40th (1867–69) through 107th Congresses (2001–3). These are not arbitrary divisions of the data. The first is the period before the Civil War. A case can be made that the procedural distinctiveness of the bodies is clear as early as 1865. The second is the period prior to the establishment of Reed's Rules (the changes in House procedures that greatly reduced opportunities for minority floor obstruction)

TABLE 2.4. A Model of Changes to the Rules That Restrict the House Applied to Different Time Periods

	1st to 39th Congresses		1st to 54th Congresses		40th to 107th Congresses	
	Coefficient (standard error)	Impact on y in Percentage Points	Coefficient (standard error)	Impact on y in Percentage Points	Coefficient (standard error)	Impact on y in Percentage Points
Change in size	8.10 (4.30)**	+4.1	6.78 (4.04)**	+4.0	2.06 (12.58)	+1.0
Change in workload	9.55 (4.31)**	+9.2	8.66 (3.41)**	+11.0	0.486 (1.09)	+1.7
Majority party strength	4.95 (5.30)	+2.6	0.788 (3.81)	+0.5	–1.03 (4.35)	–1.1
Change in ideological power balance	3.10 (4.38)	+2.1	4.38 (3.97)	+3.8	0.313 (3.00)	+0.4
Freshmen	0.030 (.070)	+1.3	0.030 (.055)	+1.6	–0.005 (.035)	–0.6
Constant	–6.34 (4.10)*		–5.09 (3.04)**		–1.93 (1.00)**	
Log likelihood	–7.77		–13.07		–22.40	
LR chi^2	17.95**		19.15**		0.28	
Nagelkerke R^2	0.640		0.526		0.009	
Percent correctly predicted	97.44		94.44		89.71	
N	39		54		68	

Source: Rules changes taken from table 2.1.

Note: Method is logit. Coefficients are unstandardized. Standard errors are in parentheses. Tests are one-tailed. "Impact on y" is the difference in the predicted probabilities in percentage points if $y = 1$ and x is manipulated from one-half standard deviation below its mean to one-half standard deviation above it (or from 0 to 1 for the change in party control dummy) while all other variables are kept at their means (and the change in party control dummy = 0). LR = likelihood ratio.

*$p < .1$ **$p < .05$

and the Rules Committee's authority to issue special rules (the development that allowed the panel to set the conditions under which bills would be debated on the floor). Cox and McCubbins (2005, 50–86) suggest that the years around 1900 constitute a critical time for the House's procedural development. That era certainly seems to mark the end of the House's considerable acceleration in the restrictive direction. Parenthetically, we might also note that the body does not really grow after the turn of the 20th century and becomes fixed at 435 after the Reapportionment Act of 1929.

The results differ conspicuously, with size changes and now workload explaining a good deal of the restriction of procedures in the early years and all the variables performing poorly in the third specification. Indeed, with the other variables kept at their usual values, increasing the value of workload change from half of a standard deviation below its mean to half a standard deviation above its mean increases the probability of one of the first 39 Congresses experiencing a restriction of procedures from 1.4 percent (confidence bounds of –2.6 to 5.3) to 10.6 percent (confidence bounds of –4.4 to 25.6). The corresponding figures for change in size are 2.3 percent (confidence bounds of –3.2 to 7.8) to 6.4 percent (confidence bounds of –5.9 to 18.6). In the specification of the first 54 Congresses, these figures are 3.5 percent (confidence bounds of –2.2 to 9.3) to 7.5 percent (confidence bounds of –2.9 to 17.4) for size and 1.9 percent (confidence bounds of –2.2 to 6.1) to 12.8 (confidence bounds of 0.4 to 25.6) for workload.[19]

We can see that size and workload help explain restriction in the House, but only until about 1900—that is, during the time when most restrictive procedures were established. The argument that majority party strength is critical to an understanding of changes in important rules is best made when discussing the rules changes that occurred after that time or at least in the postbellum era. We have already recognized majority party strength to be important to the model of Binder's rules that naturalize and the ideological power balance variable to be quite robust in the models of the Schickler and Cox and McCubbins data. Most rules that naturalize come after the Civil War. Schickler's series begins with the 40th Congress (1867–69), while Cox and McCubbins's data begin with the 46th Congress (1879–81).

Formal Rules Governing Senate Floor Rights: A Brief History

Ideally, I would identify large individual changes to important formal procedures governing floor power and rights for the Senate as well. Doing so is, however, prohibitively difficult. The Senate does not change its rules nearly as much as the House does—Binder (1997), for example, cites 44 changes in House rules that govern minority party rights, but only 13 such changes in the Senate. There just is not enough variance for the researcher to get any analytical traction.[20]

The Senate does not change its formal rules much for three principal reasons. First, it is ostensibly a continuing body—that is, it does not need to approve formally a new or even existing set of standing rules at the beginning of every Congress.[21] With Senators split into three classes, not all of its members are elected at the same time, and the body need not reconstitute itself. Its rules are carried forward. Consequently, debates on Senate rules become a discussion of a proposal's merits rather than an exercise in organizing the body so that the work of a Congress can begin.

Second, the continuing body assumption means that any reform to the rules must be made within the framework of existing arrangements and is subject to a filibuster.[22] According to Binder and Smith (1997, 208), therefore, "Because inherited rules pose such a high threshold for change in the Senate, successful efforts to change the rules . . . should be expected on rare occasions." This is essentially the Senate half of the previously described path dependency argument.

The third reason is the body's reliance on precedent and tradition. The Senate rule book has always been significantly shorter than the House's, and the Senate looks to decisions from the chair to guide where codification leaves doubt. The Senate has also been held together by numerous widely agreed upon if unofficial rules of conduct, including what Sinclair (1989, 14–22) has called "apprenticeship." In the words of Matthews (1960, 93), "The new Senator is expected to keep his mouth shut, not to take the lead in floor fights, to listen and learn." Other important Senate norms include reciprocity, logrolling, and "institutional patriotism"—senators have frequently frowned on self-promotion and colleagues who care little for the body's collective interests.

Senate Rules and Unlimited Debate

As a result, I examine, in detail, the history of a single procedure critical to the understanding of floor rights in the Senate—that which grants unlimited debate. The data come from Wawro and Schickler (2006, 185–86). These authors catalog by year efforts to limit obstructionism on the Senate floor—either by resolution or by the establishment of precedent. They count both successful and unsuccessful attempts to alter the rules.[23] As they argue, attempts to reduce obstruction are important because, even if they fail, they restrain the use of the tactic as members who wish to block proceedings worry about antagonizing others (109–26). Only changes that would have consequences beyond the Congress in which they are introduced were counted.[24] The data stretch from the 1st Congress (1789–91) to the 79th Congress (1945–47) and contain 81 attempts to limit floor obstructionism, 19 of them successful. Much of the activity occurs between the 40th (1867–69) and 70th Congresses (1927–29). The most critical individual change is the 1917 adoption of Rule XXII, which permitted cloture and provided that floor debate on an item could be brought to a close with the assent of two-thirds of senators present and voting.

The Variables

I test the three hypotheses central to this analysis. Chamber size is explored employing a *change in size* variable that is calculated as the House's. The Senate's *change in workload* variable is also like the lower chamber's. It is the change from one Congress to the next in Binder's (1997) absolute score—an indicator constructed from a factor analysis of the number of days in session, the number of public laws enacted, and the number of members of the Senate in each Congress. Unlike the House version, however, Binder's Senate data are in a single continuous series and do not require manipulation.

I use two variables to test the hypothesis about parties and policy preferences. The first is *majority party strength* and is again calculated by multiplying the proportion of seats occupied by members of each party with its cohesion—a measure derived from the standard deviation of party members' first-dimension DW-NOMINATE scores subtracted from one. Minority party scores are then subtracted from those of the majority. The second is *change in ideological power balance*. It is derived from Schickler (2000) and is calculated in the same way as in the House analysis. Congresses with growing memberships and workloads, strong majority parties, and ideological balances of power that have shifted in favor of the majority ought to exhibit relatively large numbers of attempts, successful or not, to restrict floor obstruction.

As with the House analysis, I also incorporate the measure *freshmen*, or the proportion of the membership that is in its first Congress. I hypothesize that Congresses with relatively small numbers of freshmen will push to restrict floor rights.[25]

I add one more variable. *Filibuster* is the number of filibusters undertaken in the Senate in that Congress. The data are from Wawro and

Schickler (2006, 183–85).[26] Binder (1997, 167–201) argues that restrictions on Senate productivity—such as the number of filibusters—have brought about changes to Senate rules that suppress minority rights. Congresses in which there are relatively large numbers of filibusters, therefore, ought to witness greater numbers of attempts, successful and not, to limit floor obstruction.

In all analyses, the dependent variable is the number of *attempts tried* or *attempts successful* in a Congress. The latter was not modeled by Wawro and

TABLE 2.5. The Determinants of Attempted and Actual Changes to Rules Constraining Floor Obstruction in the Senate, 1789–1946

	Attempts Tried			Attempts Successful	
Change in size	2.71	4.45	3.45	0.087	2.34
	(4.49)	(4.37)	(2.75)	(4.56)	(6.51)
Change in workload	0.923	1.25	–0.121	0.275	1.65
	(0.658)*	(0.571)**	(0.363)	(0.630)	(1.06)*
Majority party strength	–0.668	–1.48	–1.97	2.19	3.98
	(1.57)	(1.39)	(1.13)*	(1.52)*	(2.20)**
Change in ideological power balance	0.014	0.248	0.253	–0.420	–0.911
	(1.46)	(0.806)	(1.21)	(1.17)	(1.68)
Freshmen	–0.060	–0.033	–0.049	–0.027	–0.048
	(0.025)**	(0.020)*	(0.017)**	(0.022)	(.035)*
Filibuster	0.067	0.018	0.011	–0.115	–0.306
	(0.224)	(0.127)	(0.132)	(0.222)	(0.352)
Constant	1.51	0.964	0.298	–1.08	–1.15
	(0.770)**	(0.659)	(0.304)	(0.777)	(1.17)
Log likelihood	–98.16	–97.58	–95.66	–48.94	–30.20
Nagelkerke R^2	0.133	0.147	0.163	0.072	0.206
Parameterization of dispersion	Mean	Constant			
α or δ	2.51	2.95	0.060		
	(0.853)	(1.19)	(0.158)		
LR of chi² dispersion test	50.16**	51.32**		68.66	
Percentage correctly predicted					84.81
Method	NBR	NBR	Zero–inflated NBR	Poisson	Logit

Source: Dependent variables from Wawro and Schickler 2006.

Note: Standard errors are in parentheses. $N = 79$. Tests are one-tailed. Chi² dispersion test is the likelihood ratio test of α or $\delta = 0$ for negative binomial regression (NBR) or the deviance statistic for the Poisson. A significant test is evidence of overdispersion and reveals the appropriateness of NBR. LR = likelihood ratio.

*$p < .1$ **$p < .05$

Schickler (2006). I utilize both a negative binomial regression and zero-inflated negative binomial regression for the attempts tried analysis because the dependent variable is not evenly dispersed. I employ Poisson regression for the attempts successful data.[27] Because there are only four Congresses in which more than one successful attempt took place, I also report a logit model of these particular data. Table 2.5 reveals the results.

Chamber Size

The findings show that on not one occasion does the change in size variable have a statistically significant coefficient of the predicted sign. The efforts, successful or not, to restrict obstruction and therefore weaken floor rights appear not to be brought about by a growing Senate. This is largely because there are very few attempts to change the rules prior to the Civil War, an era in which the Senate expanded dramatically. The finding is interesting in light of Wawro and Schickler's (2006, 181–95) analysis of the causes of Rule XXII and the establishment of cloture in 1917. They show a variable that is the size of the Senate—as opposed to my change in the size of the Senate—to be statistically significant in a count model of the by-year attempts to change the rules (193–95). In turn, they argue that the dramatic increase in the size of the Senate between 1886 (when it had 76 members) and 1912 (when it had 96) led to a significant increase in the number of filibusters and "an unraveling of relational legislating" (193). In other words, the cozy little Senate in which personal relationships could be used to manage conflict had been replaced by a much larger and impersonal body that needed a more restrictive and codified set of rules to ensure that it operated effectively.

Still, my findings do not necessarily refute a size argument. As a body grows, there may be a point beyond which it can no longer sustain a strong floor where members exercise robust rights. By my thinking, members outside formal positions of influence over the floor's agenda and proceedings have a considerably diminished interest in pushing for naturalization, and there is a much greater receptivity to efforts to weaken the floor and dilute floor rights. The body adopts more restrictive procedures as a consequence. Increases in size below—or indeed, perhaps both above and below—this threshold do little to make the body more restrictive.

If there was a critical size in the Senate, it was possibly in the region of 70 to 90 members. As Wawro and Schickler (2006, 185–95) suggest in their argument about the "close knittedness" of the Senate, efforts to limit floor obstruction took on a new seriousness after the 1880s. With the admission of North Dakota, South Dakota, Montana, Washington, Idaho, Wyoming, and Utah into the Union, the Senate grew from 76 to 88 members between the 50th (1887–9) and 51st (1889–91) Congresses.

Table 2.6 presents negative binomial regression models of the attempts tried data from the 50th Congress on. It is clear that after this point, senators moved to restrict floor obstruction as the body grew. Indeed, change in size performs more robustly than the other independent variables in these specifications of the basic model.

Comparative data on debate termination procedures and chamber size furnish some confirmatory evidence of this argument. The average size of American state legislative bodies that use a previous question more natural than the Senate's debate closure mechanism is 68.6. The average size of the bodies that use the House's version of the procedure and allow a simple majority of those present and voting to cut off debate is 77.7.

Wawro and Schickler (2006, 188–91) also argue that an influx of new members, many from states newly admitted into the Union, helped undermine relation-based legislating. Former House members contributed particularly to this effect because they were used to operating under constraining rules. The argument contradicts my hypothesis about membership changes. I suggest that increased turnover and therefore

TABLE 2.6. The Determinants of Attempted Changes to Rules Constraining Floor Obstruction in the Senate, 1887–1946

	Mean as Parameterization of Dispersion	Constant as Parameterization of Dispersion
Change in size	13.56 (10.08)*	12.09 (4.45)**
Change in workload	0.438 (0.626)	0.958 (0.651)*
Majority party strength	–2.84 (2.68)	–1.39 (2.46)
Change in ideological power balance	2.54 (1.81)*	1.84 (1.23)*
Freshmen	–0.057 (0.055)	0.002 (0.050)
Filibuster	–0.124 (0.214)	–0.061 (0.156)
Constant	1.69 (1.18)	0.237 (1.19)
Log likelihood	–43.41	–42.19
Nagelkerke R^2	0.202	0.270
α or δ	1.54 (0.829)	2.50 (1.44)
LR of chi^2 dispersion test	16.96**	19.40**

Source: Dependent variables from Wawro and Schickler 2006.

Note: Method is negative binomial regression. Standard errors are in parentheses. $N = 29$. Tests are one-tailed. Chi^2 dispersion test is the likelihood ratio test of α or $\delta = 0$. A significant test is evidence of overdispersion and reveals the appropriateness of NBR. LR = likelihood ratio.

*$p < .1$ **$p < .05$

numbers of freshmen ought to reduce attempts to undermine floor obstruction because stronger floor rights should appeal to junior members.
Table 2.5 vindicates my version of a new-member hypothesis. The freshman variable is quite robust and reveals that as the number of freshmen increases, there are fewer efforts to end floor obstruction. In substantive
terms, when the mean is used as the parameterization of dispersion, increasing the percentage of freshmen from half of a standard deviation below its mean to half above while keeping all other variables at their means
decreases the predicted count of attempts tried from 1.22 (confidence
bounds of .61 to 1.82) to .56 per Congress (confidence bounds of .21 to
.92). The freshman variable also has a negative coefficient at the $p < .1$ level
in the logit model of attempts successful. These findings are largely the result of the very few attempts to curtail obstruction that took place in the
antebellum Congress when turnover in the Senate was tremendous. Members of the Senate at this time generally served only one term, often less,
and the proportion of freshmen in many Congresses prior to the Civil War
frequently exceeded the standard third up for election.

Workload

Evidence confirms the workload hypothesis. It has a statistically significant
positive coefficient in several of the specifications. The finding is consistent with Wawro and Schickler's (2006, 191–95) results, although they use
an absolute measure of workload—taken from Binder (1997)—and not the
change in workload from one Congress to the next. I show that as workload increases, the Senate attempts to weaken floor rights and make legislative obstruction difficult. Binder and Smith (1997, 63–67) have already
suggested that increased workload contributed to the establishment of
Rule XXII. My findings provide some reinforcement to the argument that
workload restricts Senate procedures.

Majority Party Strength

The majority party strength variable has a coefficient with the predicted
sign in both of the model specifications for attempts successful shown in
table 2.5. In substantive terms, manipulating majority party strength in the
usual fashion increases the predicted number of successful attempts to restrict floor rights from .19 (with confidence bounds of .08 to .31) to .27 per
Congress (confidence bounds of .15 to .39) when the Poisson model is
used. The same manipulation in the logit model raises the predicted probability of a Congress having a successful attempt from 9.4 percent

(confidence bounds of 1.7 to 17.0) to 15.9 percent (confidence bounds of 6.0 to 25.8).

This reveals that party and policy preferences drive procedural choice in the Senate over a long period of time. For reasons discussed earlier, party is frequently thought of as less important in the upper chamber. In fact, the period when most of the successful attempts take place—that is, between roughly 1865 and 1917—saw a very partisan Senate. This partisanship was especially acute from the 55th (1897–99) to the 61st Congresses (1909–11), a time when the body grew dramatically and four of the nineteen successful attempts occurred. During this era, the majority party strength variable had a mean of .243. This compares to the mean of .192 for all other Congresses from the 1st (1789–91) to the 79th (1945–47). Furthermore, there is no doubt that the governing party was cohesive. The mean for the standard deviation of first dimension DW-NOMINATE scores of majority party members in the 40th (1867–9) through 65th Congresses (1919–21) is just .145. This number compares to .245 in the other Congresses in the data set and .132 for the House during the same period. When Rule XXII was established in 1917, the standard deviation of first-dimension DW-NOMINATE scores for all members of the majority is the second lowest, at .105, for any majority in any Congress from the 1st to 107th.[28] The majority is most cohesive, at .087, in the preceding 64th Congress (1917–19)—the Congress during which the filibuster against President Wilson's armed neutrality bill, the one that brought about Rule XXII, began.

Whether a cause or a consequence of this cohesiveness, the Senate parties of the time matured and strengthened as well. In the 1870s, the Democrats established committees to coordinate caucus business and select members for appointment to standing committees; in 1879, Senate officers became patronage positions of the majority party; in 1892, both parties formed permanent steering committees to create and administer party policy and strategy; and between 1913 and 1915, both parties formally established floor leaders and whips (Gamm and Smith 2002, 224–33).

The finding that partisanship and majority party power is important to an understanding of changes to rules governing floor obstruction is consistent with Koger's (2006) work. His examination of three attempts to reform Rule XXII and create a majority cloture procedure between 1918 and 1925 reveals that members of the majority party were significantly more likely to support the change than those in the minority and that within each party, legislators closest to the median member were most likely to support their party's position.

The second reason to be interested in the performance of the majority party strength variable in the attempts successful specifications is it is not replicated in the attempts tried specifications, a finding that leads Wawro and Schickler (2006) to reject a preference-based explanation of efforts to restrict floor obstruction in the Senate. Indeed, in one specification where attempts tried is the dependent variable, the majority party strength variable has a negative coefficient. My finding suggests that other antecedents, such as greater workload and particularly lower turnover, explain efforts to limit floor obstruction, but a strong majority party is necessary to write such attempts into the rules.

Binder (1997, 167–201) argues the opposite. She contends that strong Senate majorities frequently generated attempts to suppress minority rights but that the obstacles of supermajority procedures generally prevented such attempts from succeeding. Cross- or bipartisan pressures were often needed to create procedural change. The 1872 rules change that confined debate on amendments to appropriations legislation to five minutes, for example, was assured only after the minority Democrats were able to add a provision requiring that such amendments be germane, a revision for which they pushed because Republicans were using spending bills as a vehicle to expand the federal government's reach on many issues (Binder 1997, 184–85). More important, Rule XXII was brought about by widespread Democratic and Republican support of a bill to arm American merchant ships. "A little group" of eleven "willful men," as President Woodrow Wilson called them, was filibustering the legislation desired by a vast majority, and the only way to get it passed was to reform the rules. Fusing a widely supported policy with the need for procedural change brought about the breakthrough (Binder 1997, 189–91).

But my analysis suggests that procedural change can occur when the majority party is strong. Change might have involved formal minority party cooperation—93 percent of minority Republicans voted to bring about Rule XXII, for example—but this finding does not necessarily mean that majority party strength was irrelevant or even insufficient. The strength of the majority may force the minority to go along with procedural reform when it comes up for a vote. Altering formal rules may be more difficult in the Senate, but when there is change, it can frequently be attributed to large and cohesive majorities.

Other Variables

A quick comment on the performance of one other variable is in order. Unlike majority party strength, changes in the ideological balance of power in the Senate have no demonstrable effect on efforts to restrict practices over the entire data series. However, as table 2.6 shows, the variable behaves robustly and as predicted in the more modern data. Its performance is stronger than that of majority party strength but suggests a continued role for party and policy preferences in an explanation of when the Senate moves in a restrictive direction. Schickler (2000) sees the measure altering House procedures this way during the same period.

Unlimited Debate and the XVII Amendment

In 1913, the 17th Amendment was ratified, formalizing the direct election of senators. As a critical reform to Senate life, it is an obvious candidate as a cause of Rule XXII instituted four years later. A decline in the parties' command over their members—in Lapinski's (2004, 8) words, the amendment "put more control in the hands of Senators in securing their election"—purportedly led to a restriction in procedures and a weakening of floor rights. The thinking is that newly sensitized to popular opinion and with greater control over their own electoral prospects, senators were forced to respond to public discontent over obstructionist tactics.[29]

Dion (1997) argues that direct election explains why the Senate responded so rapidly to public outcry and moved to adopt the cloture procedure in 1917. Wawro and Schickler (2006, 195–208) reject this explanation. They show that popular control—whether through direct election, direct primary, voluntary party regulation, or preference votes—did not lead to the kind of increased turnover that would undermine relation-based legislating. Indeed, popularly controlled senators were as electorally vulnerable as those chosen by state legislators. Moreover, Wawro and Schickler's analysis of the filibuster of the 1908 Aldrich-Vreeland currency bill reveals that party and ideology, not popular control, explain the vote for or against a major Senate precedent on obstruction. This finding reinforces the argument that partisanship and policy preferences have driven restrictive procedures in the Senate.

To be sure, other evidence indicates that popular control had meaningful impact on Senate life. Crook and Hibbing (1997) believe that popular control brought about a more diverse membership. They also show that senators became more responsive to public opinion. Bernhard and Sala (2006) essentially reach the same conclusion, explaining that after 1913, senators moderated more as elections approached. Gailmard and Jenkins (2009) reveal that the 17th Amendment forced senators to reflect public ideology more; however, because they were no longer closely scrutinized by state legislators, same-state delegations became more diverse. Lapinski

(2004) argues that popular control increased the size of winning coalitions. Despite all of these findings, there is not much evidence to challenge the claim that Rule XXII's historical proximity to the 17th Amendment is largely coincidental. Part of this disconnect may result from the fact that many states had instituted popular control prior to 1913—L. Rogers (1926, 114) reports that by that time, 29 states already subjected senatorial candidates to direct primary and/or general election by the public. The rolling introduction of popular control might have mollified any effect the 17th Amendment had on procedural change.

The Continued Attack on Floor Obstruction

Important changes have occurred to Rule XXII since those listed in Wawro and Schickler's (2006) data set. Five come immediately to mind. The first, established in 1949, was a hodgepodge. It strengthened floor rights in that cloture could be invoked only by two-thirds of the chamber's members, not by two-thirds of those present and voting, but it allowed cloture on procedural matters with the exception to changes in formal rules (Koger 2010, 164–65). The scope of cloture was also enlarged to cover nominations and treaties (Binder 1997, 191–93). The second, engineered by majority leader Lyndon Johnson (D-TX) in 1959, lowered the cloture bar back to two-thirds present and voting and permitted cloture to be invoked on motions to proceed to rules changes. This change occurred in return for formal recognition of the Senate as a continuing body (Binder 1997, 193–95). The third change allowed cloture on most matters with the vote of three-fifths of the chamber (Binder 1997, 196–98). It was passed in 1975. The fourth and fifth changes, which undermined senators' ability to engage in postcloture filibusters, a practice perfected by Senator James Allen (D-AL), were passed in 1979 and 1986 (Koger 2010, 176–79). The 1979 change placed a 100-hour limit on postcloture debate. The 1986 alteration reduced this limit to 30 hours.

Binder (1997) claims that these changes have had mixed effects—that is, they have both suppressed and expanded the rights of minority party members.[30] But in the terms I use, it is clear, with the possible exception of 1949, that the changes have collectively restricted procedures by weakening floor rights. Moreover, in contrast with the analysis of pre–World War II changes, these procedural restrictions have not been the product of particularly strong majorities. The majority party strength scores are below the historical mean for all Congresses in which cloture reform takes place except the 94th (the 1975 change). In fact, significant majority party fracturing occurred on this issue. The first three attempts to weaken floor rights and obstruction were clearly the work of disgruntled liberal reformers of both parties who frequently witnessed the filibustering of bills designed to expand labor and especially civil rights (Binder 1997, 191–97). Their opponents were southern conservative Democrats who used obstruction to prevent efforts to move policy to the left. Binder (1997, 197–98) shows explicitly that the 1979 and 1986 changes were also adopted as the result of bipartisanship. With regard to restricting Senate floor rights in the past half century, members' procedural preferences seem to have been an extension of their policy preferences. But, unlike prior to World War II, these preferences have cut across, not between, parties.

The 1975 change provides a particularly good example. It was the culmination of a sustained effort to restrict floor obstruction undertaken by a coalition of liberals from both parties. At the beginning of every Congress from 1963 to 1975, Democrats such as Clinton Anderson (D-NM), Frank Church (D-ID), George McGovern (D-SD), and Walter Mondale (D-MN) teamed with Republicans including Clifford Case (R-NJ), Thruston Morton (R-KY), and James B. Pearson (R-KS) to try to lower the number of votes required to bring about cloture and put an end to conservative southerners' blocking of liberal goals. Even when, by the mid-1970s, civil rights had been largely taken off the agenda, the push to bring down the number of votes to invoke cloture remained bipartisan. Reform was ultimately realized when advocates for simple-majority cloture finally accepted that they could not achieve their goal and moved to pass a less restrictive procedure. Senate Resolution 4, the vehicle by which the Senate agreed to change Rule XXII and allow the invocation of cloture with three-fifths of members elected, was supported by only 40 of the Senate's 60 Democrats in March 1975, although 11 of the other 20 abstained. Sixteen Republicans voted for the measure, while 16 opposed it. The Democratic opponents were a diverse group that included liberals such as Church and Mike Gravel (D-AK), both of whom objected to a provision that reversed a decision made three weeks earlier that the Senate was not a continuing body, and renowned conservatives such as Allen.[31]

The practice of filibustering has been eroded by procedural changes other than formal alterations to Rule XXII. Most notable among these changes are the track system and statutory provisions that protect certain bills from the filibuster. The track system was instituted by Robert Byrd (D-WV) when he was majority whip in the 1970s (Smith 2010). It weakened floor rights because it allowed the majority leader—with unanimous consent or with the agreement of the minority leader—to have more than one bill pending on the floor as unfinished business. The Senate, in other words, could consider other bills while a filibuster was suspended and debate on the bill under consideration was put on hold. Floor obstruction, as a result, no longer ground the Senate to a halt, just a particular bill (Binder and Smith 1997, 15; Wawro and Schickler 2006, 261–62).

At the same time, Congress was feverishly folding debate limitation provisions into statute. Such restrictions had previously been built into law—most notably in the 1939 executive reorganization legislation (Binder and Smith 1997, 186–88)—but the 1960s and 1970s represented a dramatically more concerted and sustained use of them (Binder and Smith 1997, 188–94). On issues such as trade and the budget, laws were passed that prevented or undermined the use of the filibuster on future bills on the subjects. The Congressional Budget and Impoundment Control Act of 1974, for example, prevents budget resolutions and reconciliation bills—the omnibus pieces of legislation that often incorporate changes to tax law and entitlement spending—from being filibustered.

What might have caused the wave of procedural change restricting floor rights in the 1960s and 1970s? The answer is not easily discernible. It is again difficult to make a case for majority party strength. Around the 86th Congress (1959–61, and the last with Lyndon Johnson as majority leader), the majority party strengthened considerably. Indeed, in the five Congresses prior to 1960 (81st to 85th), the mean majority party strength score was only .016; in the Congresses of 1960–80 (86th to 96th), it was .177. But the latter figure is only slightly above the mean for the entire period between the 1st and 107th Congresses. And as already noted the Democratic majority was badly split on approaches to floor obstruction during the thirty years that followed World War II.

The Senate's workload did not grow particularly during this time, although members began to feel greater pressures from responsibilities other than legislating. Representational demands increased, and many began to travel to inform their policy decisions (Koger 2010, 167–68). Perhaps a better explanation, then, is provided by turnover, which decreased greatly at this time. Throughout the 1960s, most congressional elections saw significantly fewer than 10 new senators elected. Such numbers represent a considerable drop-off from the previous decade, when the mean was about 15.5. The entire period is also one of solid Democratic control, with little possibility of Republican takeover. In fact, the increase in the majority party strength score from the 1950s to the 1960–80 period can largely be attributed to the growth of the Democratic majority rather than to its coherence. This finding is consistent with my hypothesis about freshman classes. A plausible explanation, therefore, is that liberal reformers, witnessing their provocative agenda crash into a wall of obstruction on the Senate floor, wished to change Rule XXII and weaken floor rights. As increasingly senior members with greater prominence in American public life and formal influence over the Senate agenda, they cared less for the floor rights of individual members. They pushed vigorously for procedural change, confident in their own reelection and the durability of the Democratic Party's majority status.

House and Senate Practices That Affect the Floor

We can also test these hypotheses on discretionary behavior relevant to floor power and rights. Here I am looking at actions permissible under existing procedures. Such actions are not mandated by rules and precedents but can be employed under them. Certain members decide to use practices at certain times. These members need not constitute the majority required to change formal rules. Indeed, in the case of the House, one person, the Speaker, can decide how to use practices such as recognizing members on the floor. Little systematic information is available about the utilization of important practices in the past, and practices pivotal to the power of the floor and the rights exercised on it have been established or abolished by formal rules or come in and out of fashion to such an extent that studying long time series is frequently impossible. Still, some practices are important enough and have been employed long enough to permit examination.

Here, I analyze briefly the use of four practices, two in the House and two in the Senate. All are central to understanding either the floor's power in the legislative process or the strength of member floor rights. The results of this fairly quick analysis of a sample of practices, however, are more illustrative than definitive.

The Discharge Petition in the House

The first practice is the use of the House's discharge petition. As table 2.1 shows, the discharge petition was created in 1910. The rule first authorizing the practice was part of the House revolt against Speaker Joseph Cannon (R-IL) brought about by insurgent progressive Republicans and minority Democrats. The practice essentially undermines the power of standing committees because, if the petition is signed by the requisite number of members, a committee is dismissed of its responsibility for a bill and a motion to discharge is entered, to be called up by a willing member when the discharge calendar is in order. Today, the discharge is really the only way a simple majority of members can bypass obstructionist committees.[32] This practice therefore affects the power of the House floor in the body's legislative process.

Between 1910 and 1935, the rule was revised several times, with the most important alterations concerning the number of signatures required to discharge. The threshold bounced between 145 or 150 and a simple majority on a number of occasions, settling at 218 in 1935. The only significant change to occur since then is that as of 1993, signatures are made public as they are gathered. I therefore examine the practice of discharge petition usage from the 74th (1935–37) through 107th Congresses (2001–3).[33]

I analyze both the number of petitions that were filed and those that were successful—that is, where a petition brought about the discharge of a committee. As congressional scholars have argued, the act of filing a petition is not meaningless and can represent a concerted effort to have a bill debated on the floor (Burden 2003; Pearson and Schickler 2009). Petitions can be successful even if fewer than 218 signatures are gathered because they may result in the acquiescence of the standing committee of jurisdiction or the Rules Committee and the reporting of the bill, or something similar, to the floor. Relatively large numbers of filings and successful petitions reveal a practice reflective of a relatively strong floor and natural body. The discharge data I evaluate come from Beth (2001a).[34]

Figure 2.1 shows the number of discharge petitions filed and those that succeeded per Congress. The filing of discharge petitions drops off after about the 82nd Congress (1951–53), with usage revived, in patches, a little after the mid-1980s. The success of these petitions follows a similar pattern. To a certain extent, then, the practice of filing varies with expectations about petition success: Correlating the two produces a Pearson's r of .667.

I build explanatory models of the frequency of discharge petition filings and their success employing the variables I used in the models of the naturalization of House procedures—majority party strength, change in ideological power balance, change in party control, and number of freshmen. The model also includes a control variable, the number of *measures introduced* in a Congress divided by one thousand. This provides us with a basic

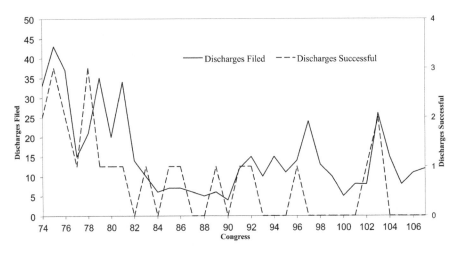

Fig. 2.1.   The number of discharge petitions filed and successful in the House, 1935–2002. (Data from Beth 2001a.)

grasp of the universe of items susceptible to discharge. For the filing data, I employ a negative binomial regression approach.[35] For the success data I use a Poisson model.

Table 2.7 reveals the results, showing that the filing and success of discharge petitions increases in Congresses when a disproportionate number of members are freshmen. This variable's coefficient is especially robust and suggests an expected strengthening of the floor as the body turns over. As the number of measures introduced goes down, the number of discharge petitions filed goes up. Although my model of procedural change does not posit that workload affects naturalization, this finding suggests practices that move the body in a natural direction are used less when the workload is high.

The majority party strength variable has a positive and statistically significant coefficient in the model of filings where the constant is used as the parameterization of dispersion. This finding runs counter to the majority party strength hypothesis and suggests that the number of discharge petitions filed increases as the majority strengthens. The finding is perhaps explained by the nature of discharge. Since the majority leadership does not control the practice of filing petitions, it may be one of the few ways that those who have little influence over the floor agenda—notably, members of the minority—can counter the pressure to push the House in a restrictive direction frequently exerted by a strong majority party.

Special Rules in the House

Another important practice is the issuance of special rules by the Rules Committee. Since 1883, the Rules Committee has been able to report rules that set out the conditions under which bills will be debated on the floor. A critical dimension of special rules is that they determine whether floor amendments can be offered. Those that prohibit or restrict amendments are generally called "restrictive" rules, while those that do not circumscribe

TABLE 2.7. The Determinants of the Use of the House Discharge Petition, 1935–2002

	Discharge Petitions Successful	Discharge Petitions Filed	
Majority party strength	1.20	0.881	1.47
	(1.89)	(0.747)	(0.685)**
Change in ideological	0.156	−0.134	−0.465
power balance	(1.91)	(0.697)	(0.614)
Change in party control	−0.647	−0.189	−0.086
	(0.671)	(0.221)	(0.198)
Freshmen	0.126	0.068	0.066
	(0.046)**	(0.015)**	(0.014)**
Measures introduced	−0.016	−0.025	−0.030
	(0.045)	(0.014)**	(0.014)**
Constant	−2.69	1.70	1.70
	(1.07)**	(0.306)**	(0.297)**
Parameterization of dispersion		Mean	Constant
α or δ		0.098	1.36
		(0.043)**	(0.567)**
LR of chi^2 dispersion test	23.50	16.84**	18.53**
Log likelihood	−30.66	−106.54	−105.70
Nagelkerke R^2	0.393	0.559	0.580
Method	Poisson	NBR	NBR

Source: Dependent variables from Beth 2001a.

Note: Standard errors are in parentheses. N = 34. Tests are one-tailed. Chi^2 dispersion test is the likelihood ratio test of α or δ = 0 for negative binomial regression (NBR) or the deviance statistic for the Poisson. A significant test is evidence of overdispersion and reveals the appropriateness of NBR. LR = likelihood ratio.

*$p < .1$ ** $p < .05$

amendments are "open" rules. This practice is thus important to understanding the strength of floor rights in the House at any particular point in time (Baron and Ferejohn 1989).

Congressional scholars disagree about what causes the Rules Committee to report restrictive rules. Many observers argue that the committee does so to ensure outcomes that are more extreme than the preference of the median member, generally protecting a bill that has been crafted to suit the majority party (Dion and Huber 1996; Marshall 2002; N. W. Monroe and Robinson 2008; Rohde 1991; Schickler 2001, 234–38). This view is based on the assumption that the Rules Committee is a tool of the majority and its leadership. Krehbiel (1997) proposes a majoritarian explanation consistent with informational and distributive models of congressional organization in which the committee produces a rule close to the preference of the chamber's median member.

Restrictive rules are largely a modern "discovery." Prior to the mid-1970s, the vast majority of bills could be altered on the floor, and special rules restricting amendments were rare (Oleszek 2011, 144–39).[36] In recent and thorough quantitative analyses, Owens and Wrighton (2008) and J. M. Roberts (2010) show that the issuance of restrictive special rules flourishes under a variety of conditions. Consistent with the switch in majority status hypothesis I have tested throughout the chapter, Owens and Wrighton reveal that changes in party control of the House lead to fewer restrictive rules—that is, the use of a practice that moves the body in the natural direction. Such a strategy certainly took place in the 1990s, when the change to a Republican majority in the 104th Congress (1995–97) had at least a short-term stanching effect on the employment of restrictive special rules. Having criticized the practice so vehemently in opposition, the new Republican leadership felt compelled to allow more open rules—and greater naturalization—with its party in the majority.[37] Fifty-four percent of nonappropriations measures had restrictive rules in 1995–96, compared to 70 percent in the previous Congress. By the 105th Congress (1997–99), however, the use of restrictive rules was again increasing, perhaps because the majority leadership had begun to understand the usefulness of such rules and not because the party it presided over had strengthened.[38] This finding also fits with Owens and Wrighton's story. They reveal an "emulation effect" in which a maturing majority copies its predecessor and over time calls for the Rules Committee to increase the number of restrictive rules issued.

More important for my analysis, Owens and Wrighton (2008) discover that a measure of partisan polarization does a great deal to explain the issuance of a large proportion of restrictive rules since the 1920s. J. M. Roberts (2010) concurs in his study of special rules from 1881 to 1937. When considerable ideological distance between and coherence within the parties has existed, as in the first dozen years of the 20th century and the period since about 1980, the Rules Committee has worked to protect committee-crafted bills from floor amendment.

Initial Recognition in the Senate

Just as increasing majority party strength seems to explain recent attempts to weaken the floor in the House, it looks to have had the same effect on practices in the upper body. Over the past couple of decades, a period of elevated majority party strength in the Senate, congressional scholars have observed a dilution of floor rights. Much of this weakening seems to stem from the assertiveness and partisanship of Senate majority leaders, most notably in their use of initial recognition. Senate precedents stipulate that if the majority leader wishes to be recognized first, the presiding officer must give the leader the floor.[39] Preemptive cloture furnishes a good example of how this advantage can be exploited. Here, the majority leader files a cloture motion when recognized and then takes up other measures until the motion has matured and is ready for a vote two days later (Evans and Oleszek 2001, 118). In the interim, no senator can offer or debate any amendments to the clotured item. Furthermore, if cloture is invoked, not only is debate limited, but any amendments offered must be germane to the bill at hand. The intent, therefore, is to fix debate length and restrict amending activity before bills are brought up. If the preemptive cloture attempt fails, the majority leader can just pull the bill from the floor.

The practice is increasingly common. As majority leader in the late 1990s and early 2000s, for example, Trent Lott (R-MS) frequently filed cloture motions, including 40 in 1999 alone (Evans and Oleszek 2001, 118–19).

Another way to restrict floor rights is to "fill the amendment tree." In this case, the majority leader uses initial recognition to offer first-degree and second-degree or perfecting amendments and thus prevents other senators from offering their own alternatives (Crespin and Monroe 2005; Evans and Oleszek 2001, 121–23; Schiller 2000; Smith 2010). Like preemptive cloture, this strategy has become increasingly popular, and Lott employed it frequently (Evans and Oleszek 2001, 122–23).[40]

Although systematic analyses of both practices are difficult, congressional scholars suggest that increased partisanship, party polarization, and, by inference, majority party strength are the reasons behind the discovery and increased use of preemptive cloture and filling the amendment tree. Sinclair (2000) argues that "more ideologically homogenous and better organized" Senate parties have meant that "Senate rules became permissive tools" in the 1990s. Evans and Oleszek (2001, 126) suggest that the robust utilization of the practices results from "a message-driven partisan environment."

Majority leaders can restrict amending activity and weaken floor rights in a third way. Amendments can be tabled by acceptance of a motion. Because the majority leader enjoys the privilege of initial recognition, he or she can immediately move to table an amendment (Crespin and Monroe 2005). The motion to table is an important practice because it is nondebatable and, if passed, effectively kills the amendment. Absent a filibuster, it allows for the expeditious defeat of amendments.

Regardless of who offers the motion to table, Crespin and Monroe (2005) and Den Hartog and Monroe (2011) argue explicitly that it is a partisan tool. The first pair of authors reveal the average proportion of all votes on which a majority party was on the losing side on motions to table was just 10 percent for the Congresses between the 95th (1977–79) and 104th (1995–97). The mean score, or roll rate, for the minority, by contrast, was 45 percent. The second pair shows the majority leadership to have used the practice largely to table motions introduced by members of the minority. These findings provide further evidence that the recent use of practices restricting Senate floor rights is caused by such phenomena as partisan polarization and homogenization, and strong majority parties.

Unanimous Consent Agreements in the Senate

The final practice, the unanimous consent agreement (UCA), is also designed to weaken floor rights in the Senate. UCAs are explicit arrangements to deal with a piece of legislation on the floor in a particular fashion. Although crafted by party leaders, they are ostensibly supported by all senators. The agreement is designed to restrict floor rights in some way so that legislative business may be expedited. Such restrictions traditionally include limits on debate length and the number and type of amendments that can be offered. Once accepted and promulgated, UCAs are as binding as any standing rule.

UCAs have been used to structure floor proceedings since the mid-1800s (Evans and Oleszek 2000, 86; J. M. Roberts and Smith 2007, 193–94).[41] By 1913, Senator Henry Cabot Lodge (R-MA) observed that the body's business is "largely transacted through unanimous consent agreements" (Oleszek 2011, 252). As a result, the practice provides a potential long time series for analysis. However, historical UCA data are scattered, and comparing UCAs with one another is highly problematic because many have several dimensions—agreements can deal with the entire floor process or just parts of it, may or may not mention amendments and debate lengths, and so forth (Evans and Oleszek 2000; Smith and Flathman 1989).

Still there are two critical periods in which the use of UCAs qualitatively and permanently changed. These provide us with a test, a little inelegant though it is, of the basic hypotheses about the change in a practice that affects the Senate floor. The first period is the 63rd Congress (1913–15). In 1914, the Senate reformed Rule XII to stipulate, among other things, that no unanimous consent request to take a final vote could be approved without a quorum and that a UCA could be revoked by unanimous consent (Evans and Oleszek 2000, 87–90; Gamm and Smith 2002; J. M. Roberts and Smith 2007; Wawro and Schickler 2006, 225–27). This change represented an increase in floor power and naturalization of procedures as the Senate responded to what many considered the leadership's abuse of UCAs. UCAs were formalized, and leaders was forced to expend more time and effort forging and enforcing them (Evans and Oleszek 2000, 90).

There are several candidates for causes of the 1914 rules change. Rule XII was adopted on a bipartisan 51–8 vote. The majority party strength score is quite low for the 63rd Congress—at .119 it is far below the mean for the 1st (1789–91) through 79th Congresses (1945–47), largely because the Democratic majority was quite slim (51 of the 96 senators were Democrats) and, despite cohesion on policy concerns, divided when it came to strategy. Indeed, the preceding year, progressive Democrats had removed the conservative Thomas S. Martin (D-VA) as majority leader, replacing him with John W. Kern (D-IN) (Gamm and Smith 2002, 230). Kern was not only more liberal than Martin but was also considerably more junior: He had served only two years in the Senate when he was picked to lead, while Martin had come to the body in 1895. Kern's appointment, therefore, indicated the importance of a new group of Senate Democrats.[42] This group was quite large—the 1909–15 period witnessed a great deal of turnover and the largest freshman classes since the mid-1870s—and its members were among the first senators to be selected popularly as the direct primary and binding preference votes, sometimes called the Oregon System, spread across the country. They were new to the majority as well, having ended eighteen years of Republican rule of the upper chamber in the 1912 elections.

The majority party strength, freshman, and party switch variables all seem to explain the 1914 rules change, and they perform as hypothesized. Procedures were changed as new, somewhat different (given the way its members had been selected), and disproportionately junior members of the majority flexed their muscles.[43] The effect, amplified by the majority's small size and these legislators' conflicts with more senior colleagues in the majority, was to strengthen the floor.

The second period of qualitative change in the use of UCAs came in the 1960s and 1970s. In this case, the change was evolutionary. It also required the support of a broad swath of the membership, not just a simple majority. As Lyndon Johnson's (D-TX) tenure as majority leader came to a close, there was a belief that the old approach to UCAs, which rested largely on time limits for debate and the principle of "uniform treatment of Senators and amendments" (Smith and Flathman 1989, 358), needed to be replaced because members were exploiting it to engage in obstructionist tactics. As a result, agreements became more complex, individualized, and piecemeal (J. M. Roberts and Smith 2007, 199; Smith 2010; Smith and Flathman 1989). UCAs began to specify, in considerable detail, particular amendments that would be in order and times when votes would be taken. Floor proceedings on measures were regularly governed by numerous UCAs, and a bill might go to the floor on one agreement as the Senate leadership negotiated others to close out debate and deal with amendments. By the end of Robert Byrd's (D-WV) tenure as majority leader in 1981, this new UCA regime was fully in place (Ainsworth and Flathman 1995; J. M. Roberts and Smith 2007, 199–200; Smith 1989, 105–8).

The new usage of UCAs was restrictive. As Ainsworth and Flathman (1995, 190) argue, "Moving from general provisions to individualized provisions affords the leader greater flexibility and enhances the ability to negotiate restrictive agreements." By enumerating amendments that could be offered, the new UCAs weakened the floor and members' rights on it.

Because the change in practice required the assent of large numbers of members, it is perhaps unsurprising that majority party strength does not drive this modification. As noted in the explanation for changes in procedures governing floor obstruction in the Senate of the 1960s and 1970s, the majority party was divided at this time. Instead, it is a period of low turnover. If the freshman variable largely explains the new UCA regime, it does so in the direction predicted. Moreover, the stability of membership could have facilitated logrolling on UCAs. With some confidence that colleagues could pay them back on future legislation where their preferences were strong, senators may have been more willing to restrict their floor rights and support UCAs on bills for which they cared less.

Workload does not play a role. We should expect the weakening of floor rights through a practice that requires the approval of large numbers of legislators when workload increases. If anything, congressional workloads were declining a little in the 1960s and 1970s.

Conclusion

This chapter reveals that changes in congressional procedures and practices have numerous and sometimes complex determinants. Changes in party control and, particularly, sizable freshman classes are repeatedly shown to result in naturalization. Restriction often occurs when a body's membership has not experienced great turnover.

In addition, with regard to the chapter's central task, considerable evidence confirms the chamber size, workload, and majority party strength hypotheses in analyses of procedural change and the use of practices in both the House and Senate. When they do have an effect, increasing size, workload, and majority party strength (however it is measured) push the bodies in a restrictive direction.

Third, majority party strength and changes in the ideological balance of power are important in the House, but largely only after the Civil War, if not 1900. Majority party strength and ideological power balance also help explain change in the Senate. This finding holds despite the path dependency argument and the suggestion that strong majorities are generally unable to change Senate procedures and practices because extant rules make it very difficult for them to do so.

Finally, chamber size and workload are important and robust determinants of movement in the restrictive direction. For the House, this finding especially holds during the 19th century. In the Senate, size remains important to procedural change as it moves into the 20th century. Like Wawro and Schickler (2006), I suggest not until around 1890 is the body large enough to permit growth to influence members' procedural preferences.

These findings consequently form the first part of an answer to the question about the bicameral divergence in procedures and practices governing the floors. The House became restrictive very quickly, when its size and workload were expanding more than the Senate's. By the late 19th century, the bodies' procedural paths were so distinct that while partisanship and policy preferences were to shape them into the future, any changes would not greatly alter their general directions. In the next chapter, I flesh out this answer in more detail by exploring the determinants of specific House-Senate differences, particularly in the antebellum period.

3 ◆ The Restrictive House and Natural Senate

The Story of Two Floors

The causes of changes to procedures and the use of practices affecting the floors of both chambers of Congress quite clearly vary over time. A large and influential literature argues persuasively that after the Civil War and particularly 1900, the strength of the majority party was a critical determinant of floor power and the strength of floor rights. When the majority party was robust and the minority weak, the House and Senate tended to move in a restrictive direction. They naturalized under the opposite conditions. In the 19th century, however, procedural change in both bodies seems to have been caused more by their increasing size and burgeoning workloads, especially in the House.

These developments form the beginning of an answer to the question that lies at the heart of part I of this book: Why are the House and Senate floors so different? In this chapter, I develop it further. I do so in two ways. First, I see whether the findings generated earlier are replicated in analyses of changes in four individual critical procedures. Second, I take these findings and combine them with those of chapter 2 to provide a detailed narrative about how the House and Senate floors became so different. I do this using a largely qualitative analysis of 19th-century congressional life.

The Roots of Specific Bicameral Differences

The analysis in chapter 2 suggests the general procedural character of the House was formed in the years before the Civil War by a rapidly growing membership and workload. In this section, I test the three hypotheses and this basic claim in an examination of changes in four individual procedures: those governing standing committees, those defining the powers of presiding officers, the germaneness rule regarding floor amendments, and the previous question. I choose these four procedures for two reasons. First, the House and Senate have adopted different versions of them, and in all cases, the House's versions are considerably more restrictive than the Senate's. Second, the form of these procedures that we recognize today emerged in the antebellum period. The focus on this era is not accidental. During this time, the fundamental procedural trajectories of the House and Senate diverged. The potential of procedures adopted at this time to weaken the House floor and reduce rights exercised on it were not fully exploited by the Speaker, committees, and members of the majority party prior to the Civil War, but much of the basic structure of the modern body was put in place. Together with two crucial late-19th-century innovations discussed later in this chapter—Reed's Rules and the establishment of the Rules Committee's prerogative to craft special rules—the four procedures essentially distinguish the contemporary House floor from its more natural Senate counterpart.

The data in table 2.1 indicate that the fork in the road indeed seems to have occurred before the Civil War. With the critical exceptions of Reed's Rules and special rules, table 2.1 suggests that most of the restriction of House procedures created by changes to formal rules happened before 1865. By then, the House had become distinct from the Senate, which remained the more natural legislative body. By 1900, the House floor's procedural evolution was essentially complete. The post-1900 rules changes, which generally naturalize, do not move the body back anywhere near its original state. Most of those later changes could justifiably be described as less important than the earlier restrictions. The creation of the discharge petition, Calendar Wednesday, and the post–World War II alterations that democratized and opened up committees but did not drastically undercut their essential powers are good examples. Other procedural alterations represented mere tinkering (for example, changes to the number of signatures needed to discharge) or were later reversed (the 21-day rule).

This section's argument is frequently unaccompanied by what might be considered direct and definitive evidence. House members do not provide confessions to the effect that growing membership or workload forced them to adopt restrictive procedures, and we have only paltry records of early congressional proceedings. As a result, we must rely on other indicators of the relationship between expanding memberships and business on one hand and procedural change on the other.

Committees and Their Procedural Rights

Committees emerged as a critical bicameral difference in the antebellum period. The standing committee system came of age in the Senate more quickly than it did in the House. The upper chamber established standing committees seemingly overnight—after the president's annual message in December 1816, Senator James Barbour (Rep-VA) submitted a resolution to create eleven standing committees that was approved without a formal vote (Swift 1996, 132). The transition from a system of exclusively select committees to one dominated by standing committees was more gradual on the other side of the Capitol (Gamm and Shepsle 1989).

This observation does little to betray the fact that standing committees are more influential in the House today. House committees enjoy greater formal powers than do Senate committees. These powers directly affect the influence possessed by the chambers' floors. The House provides its standing committees with strong gatekeeper powers, and special rules often are crafted to protect committee product from floor revision. In the Senate, members can frequently introduce bills on the floor as nongermane or substitute amendments to other bills or, in the case of uncontroversial legislation, by motion. Perfecting amendments are restricted only by unanimous consent agreements. Members of the modern House have fewer committee assignments than their Senate counterparts, enabling representatives to invest more time in individual committees. This also allows members to specialize in particular policy areas, a process facilitated by an arrangement that places them on committees that deal with issues of interest to them and their constituents (Hall and Grofman 1990; Londregan and Snyder 1994). House members consequently seem to care more about committee prerogatives.

This situation did not exist prior to the Civil War, but intercameral differences were already becoming apparent by that time. Table 2.1 reveals three important antebellum rules changes that increased the autonomy of House committees from the floor: the Speaker getting to appoint committees (1st Congress [1789–91]), the speaker obtaining a formal but qualified power to name committee chairs and control succession to that position (8th Congress [1803–5]), and standing committees receiving the right to report (17th Congress [1821–23]). The first two changes made committees largely the tool of the presiding officer. It is true that the 8th Congress rule also reserved the right of committee majorities to select their own chairs. But given that the Speaker appointed committee members, this development did not particularly increase the floor's ability to control committees; moreover, the provision was used just twice (Cooper 1970, 28).[1] Meaningful distance was put between the Speaker and committees only when reappointment to committees became an entrenched norm in the House in the mid- to late 1820s (Jenkins 1998).

Antebellum House committees thus offer a stark contrast to their Senate counterparts. In 1823, just after its rather rapid transition to standing committees from a select committee system, the upper chamber adopted a rule allowing its presiding officer, the president of the Senate and vice president of the United States, to choose committee members. After a torrid experience with this arrangement under the leadership of an assertive John C. Calhoun—Calhoun's predecessor, Daniel Tompkins, had routinely delegated the task to the president pro tempore—the full Senate overwhelmingly adopted a resolution seizing back the power in 1826 (Swift 1996, 134–35). Later that year, appointment procedures were changed further, with the entire Senate also appointing chairs. The president pro tempore was given the power to appoint in 1828, but the body was once again permitted to make selections in 1833. In 1846, the Senate allowed party caucuses to come up with lists of appointees; the full body's ratification of these suggestions was generally a formality (Gamm and Smith 2000, 112–17; Gamm and Smith 2002, 221–23; Haynes 1938, 1:273–76, 284–88). Soon thereafter, a seniority norm began to shape assignments as committees obtained a modicum of independence (Kravitz 1974).

Committees did not have quite the viselike grip on the agenda they have in the House today—members still had the power to discuss the referral of bills and move substantive resolutions on the floor—but they certainly had significant formal procedural rights to go along with their expanding autonomy. In 1822, House standing committees received authority to report bills, although they were doing it as a matter of course on certain measures, especially those crafted from parts of the president's address, as early as 1815 (Cooper 1988, 56–59). In 1837, bill introduction procedures were changed, and committees began routinely to receive bills before the floor did. During the twenty years immediately prior to the Civil War, the House adopted the custom of appointing members of the standing committee of jurisdiction to conference committees. Conference committees were also granted the privilege of reporting at any time (Rybicki 2003, 2007).

In the upper chamber, by contrast, members were able to introduce bills on the floor quite easily (Binder and Smith 1997, 46). More Senate public bills were introduced by members than by committees in the 1840s, while the reverse was true in the House (Cooper and Rybicki 2002, 186–88). Not until the 1850s were House members introducing as great a proportion of their chamber's public bills as Senators—between 50 and 60 percent per Congress. Haynes (1938 1:310) has argued that Senate committees have never really had a strong control of the prefloor process and special powers to report. Regardless, it is clear that antebellum House committees enjoyed greater procedural rights and independence from the floor than those in the Senate.

Both empirical evidence and cogent theoretical reasoning suggest that size and workload contributed significantly to these intercameral differences. A simple model using the entire 107 Congresses and incorporating just the change in size and change in workload variables predicts a restriction of House procedures in the 1st (1789–91) Congress at 75.0 percent and the 8th (1803–5) Congress at 63.4 percent—precisely when changes providing the Speaker with control of the composition of committees took place. If rules changes restricting House procedures were distributed randomly, each Congress would have a 12.1 percent chance of experiencing such a change.[2]

Furthermore, the period in which committees were made permanent instead of temporary—that is, the time when the more powerful standing committee system was established—coincides almost perfectly with an episode of significant and rapid growth in the size of both bodies. Between the 13th Congress (1813–15)—the one immediately prior to Barbour's resolution that essentially created the upper body's standing committee system—and the 17th Congress (1821–23), the Senate grew by one-third. This suggests that increases in the Senate's membership pushed the body to adopt restrictive procedures even when it was quite small, an idea on which I cast doubt in chapter 2. Still, from the 12th Congress (1811–13) to the 18th Congress (1823–25)—roughly the period in which the House committee system is overhauled in a similar way (Jenkins and Stewart 2002)—the lower body grew by 60 members, or 42 percent. With the exception of the 14th Congress (1815–17), this was also a period during which both bodies' workloads increased perceptibly.

The argument for chamber size as an antecedent to a stronger House committee system is bolstered further by the rapid emergence of the lower chamber as the initiator of legislative business. By the 5th Congress (1797–99), senators were introducing more bills per member than were their House colleagues (Swift 1996, 168–70). In addition, the Senate worked exclusively on the executive business of appointments and treaties (Wirls and Wirls 2004, 189–93). But in the early Congresses—up to the 14th (1815–17) according to Binder's (1997, 63) calculations, perhaps the 17th (1821–23) by Swift's calculations (1996, 168–70)—the vast majority of bills that consumed the legislature's attention were first introduced in the House and passed along to the Senate if approved (Binder 1997, 62–64; Binder and Smith 1997, 40–42; Kerr 1895, 92–96: Lancaster 1928; Swift 1996, 64). Although bill origination rates evened out after about the 14th Congress, a tradition of concurrent lawmaking had not fully formed until after House committees had received some critical procedural rights.

This point is important because it suggests that the formal powers House committees enjoy and that their Senate counterparts do not are somewhat attributable to a sequential system of lawmaking in which the larger lower chamber gathered information and formulated and refined legislation before passing it across the Capitol for the upper body's confirmation. The House needed stronger committees more than the Senate did.

On the surface, such an arrangement seems largely to have been accidental. The House took the lead particularly on fiscal policy, a major issue that incorporated a considerable amount of legislative business. Article I, Section 7 of the Constitution obliged the House to originate bills raising revenue, a directive that was interpreted quite broadly as a mandate to generate "supply bills"—what we now call appropriations—as well. The understanding stemmed directly from the use of the terms *money bills* (which included both taxing and spending) and *revenue bills* as synonyms by the Founders and their English contemporaries (Haynes 1938, 1:455; Wirls and Wirls 2004, 187–89). The bundling of tax and appropriations measures was formalized when the House set up a select committee to deal specifically with government expenditures and revenues in the 1st Congress (1789–91). In 1802, this panel was replaced by a standing committee, Ways and Means (Kiewiet and McCubbins 1991, 12). The early Ways and Means Committee had responsibility for spending bills, although this power was taken away from it as the House created standing committees specifically to oversee expenditures in the departments of the federal government in the 13th (1813–15) and 14th (1815–17) Congresses.

But theoretical and empirical work suggests that the sequence of law-making in American legislatures is a direct result of the relative sizes of the two chambers. Using a game-theoretic model tested on state legislatures, J. R. Rogers (1998, 2005) has argued that the lower information acquisition costs enjoyed by bigger bodies makes it easier for them to take a first-mover position in bicameral settings. This is especially the case when preferences are homogenous, since the two chambers will coordinate to allow the larger to acquire information and originate and the smaller to ratify. J. R. Rogers (2001) has also shown that designed sequencing is rational in a system of symmetrical bicameralism—that is, where both chambers have roughly equal powers, as in the U.S. Congress (Lijphart 1999, 206–7).[3]

Given that Jefferson's Republican supporters dominated both chambers of Congress between 1800 and the mid-1820s and that preferences were therefore quite homogenous, J. R. Rogers's (1998, 2005) theory does a good job predicting the House's first-mover status at this time. If bicameral coordination were occurring, the larger House would have worked hard to reduce the information acquiring costs it was expending on behalf of Congress as a whole. According to some influential scholars, the best way for a chamber efficiently to garner information is to divide labor among small groups of members in committees that receive formal autonomy and procedural rights (Gilligan and Krehbiel 1987, 1990; Krehbiel 1991). In Krehbiel's (1991, 74) words, an "organizational design that fosters informative committees" is an obvious and frequently used way to leverage information in legislatures. Data on the average life spans of congressional select committees prior to 1830 corroborate the idea that greater effort to collect information and write legislation was expended in the larger lower chamber. In just about every Congress, select committees lived longer in the House—in some instances, especially before the 14th Congress (1815–17), they lasted twice as long as those in the Senate (Canon and Stewart 2001).

Congressional scholars who subscribe to the informational model of organization argue that committees decrease information acquisition costs because they allow members to specialize in policy areas. However, the evidence suggests that House committee members in the early Congresses did not specialize as we think of the term today. Turnover on committees was high. House standing committees, with the exception of the period between the 15th (1817–19) and 25th (1837–39) Congresses, frequently contained upward of 50 percent new members. Before the Civil War, turnover in the House was a little higher than it was in the Senate, even after controlling for electoral change (Canon and Stewart 2001, 175–77).

Yet it is likely that modern approaches to the development of policy specialization were unnecessary in the early 19th century. Members were often appointed to committees because they had a preexisting familiarity with the issues of jurisdiction (Cooper 1988, 31–32; Luce 1922, 111). The policy milieu was also considerably simpler than it is today. Because of the small size and low sophistication of the electorate, as well as difficulties traveling to and from Washington, members had considerably fewer representational demands on their time. They could focus on legislative business. This relative lack of specialization does not undercut Jenkins and Stewart's (2002, 235) contention that the emergence of an established standing committee system in the House "contains many elements that are perfectly consistent with Krehbiel's (1991) informational view."

Majority party strength does not do a particularly good job of explaining the emergence of the House's more powerful committee system. If the restrictive procedures discussed here were pushed through by strong majority parties, we would expect them to benefit by the changes. But granting the speaker appointment power hardly brought about majority party stacking of committees. Moreover, as figures 3.1 and 3.2 show, the Speaker's ability to appoint members and name chairs was not demonstrably used to further the majority's interests on important standing committees in the House. The figures show the first-dimension DW-NOMINATE scores of the speaker, majority party median, and chamber median as well as the median member and chairs of the Commerce and Manufactures and Ways and Means Committees from the 4th Congress (1795–97) to the 1820s.[4] I choose these two committees because they provide the best examples of critical standing committees with responsibilities for general legislation in this early period (Jenkins and Stewart 2002, 198–206). Figure 3.1 reveals that speaker control was clearly not used to push Commerce and Manufactures in the direction of the majority party. Both the committee median and chair scores are generally closer to the chamber median than to the majority party median, especially after the 6th Congress (1799–1801). Indeed, both the chair and committee median are sometimes on the opposite side of the chamber median from the majority median.

The Ways and Means data shown in figure 3.2 are a little less clear, but they cannot be used to make a strong case that rules changes were used to push the committee toward the majority party's position. Moreover, for both committees, the committee median and chair tend to move closer to the speaker's position when Henry Clay leads the House. Clay was speaker from the 12th (1811–13) to 18th (1823–25) Congresses, with the exception of about a year between 1814 and 1815, when he was in Europe, and part

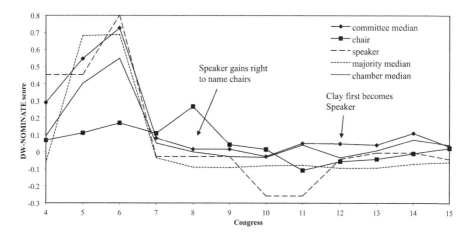

Fig. 3.1. The DW-NOMINATE scores of the Commerce and Manufactures Committee in comparative perspective, 4th (1795–97) to 15th (1817–19) Congresses. (Data from author's calculations.)

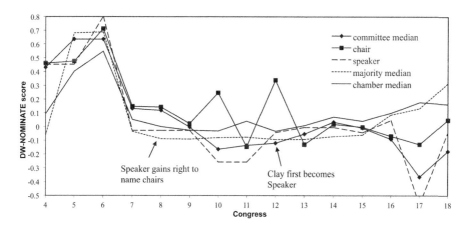

Fig. 3.2. The DW-NOMINATE scores of the Ways and Means Committee in comparative perspective, 4th (1795–97) to 18th (1823–25) Congresses. (Data from author's calculations.)

of the second session of the 16th Congress and all of the 17th Congress, from late 1820 through December 1822, when he was not a member of the House. The data are consistent with a common argument presented in the literature about Clay's forceful leadership and his personal "committee stacking" (Stewart 2007; Strahan 2002, 2007, 44–78; Strahan et al. 2000). Therefore, if the powers to appoint committee members and chairs had any tangible effect, it was to make them more responsive to the Speaker and the chamber median, not the majority.[5]

The Power of the Presiding Officer

As table 2.1 and the preceding discussion reveal, the House's presiding officer soon garnered important procedural powers. By the 11th Congress (1809–11), that the Speaker chose the chair of the Committee of the Whole and members and chairs of standing and select committees had become a settled fact of House life. The Speaker also immediately received almost unfettered discretion in regulating floor debate. The origins of this particular power can be found in Rule XIV, Section 2 of the 1st Congress (1789–91), which stated, "When two or more members happen to rise at once, the Speaker shall name who is first to speak." As Alexander (1916, 57) has written, "This did not mean a haphazard recognition, for early in the history of the House unwritten laws governing recognition began to accumulate." Constraints emerged, especially with regard to recognizing members of the reporting committee and alternating between members who favored and those who opposed the bill (Hinds 1907, sec. 1438, 923). But the Speaker received broad discretionary powers when it came to recognition.

The Senate's presiding officer—formally its president—has also enjoyed the power of recognition since the 1st Congress.[6] Unlike the Speaker, however, this person—and, indeed, any other senator—cannot interrupt the member who has the floor, a regulation first established by precedent in 1826 when Vice President John Calhoun ruled that he could not stop John Randolph's (Jackson-VA) tirade against President John Quincy Adams and Secretary of State Henry Clay. Today, this procedure can be found in Rule XIX. This regulation, along with the absence of a previous question, allows for Senate filibusters.

Although many accounts describe early Senate floor proceedings as not unusually protracted and ungovernable (Binder and Smith 1997, 39–50; Haynes 1938, 1:394–405), the body had laid the foundations for its tradition of unlimited debate and strong floor rights well before the Civil War.

By the 1840s, the dilatory tactics of Senate minorities were such an irritant that some senators began to propose reforms to make the chamber more like the House. In 1841, Henry Clay (Whig-KY) suggested that the Senate readopt the previous question and establish the hour rule (Binder and Smith 1997, 74–75; Wawro and Schickler 2006, 73–75), created earlier in the year it was the first procedure formally to limit the length of debates in the House. In 1850, Stephen Douglas (D-IL) introduced another resolution to resurrect the previous question (Haynes 1938, 1:395). The next year, the Senate narrowly defeated a resolution to make the motion to proceed nondebatable. Only after Representative Preston Brooks's (D-SC) brutal caning of Senator Charles Sumner (R-MA) in 1856 did the Senate establish a rule allowing the presiding officer to intervene during debate and impose order (Gamm and Smith 2000, 119–20). Today the provision that "if any member in speaking, or otherwise, transgress the rules of the Senate, the Presiding Officer shall, or any member may, call to order" can also be found in Rule XIX.

The relative weakness of the Senate's presiding officer is no doubt greatly attributable to the Constitution's designation of the U.S. vice president as president of the body (Gamm and Smith 2000). Frequent interbranch antagonisms in the first third of the 19th century—including those over committee assignments discussed earlier—aggravated the sense that the Senate should have one of its own to direct its proceedings, and the body set about undercutting its president's authority.

The Constitution already provided for a president pro tempore to fill in for the Senate's president when the latter was away on executive business. This person was to be a sitting senator. But the position was and remains little more than honorific. Before 1890, for example, the Senate did not recognize the president pro tempore when the vice president was physically in the chamber. As a result, most antebellum presidents pro tem served for stretches of less than fifty days (Gamm and Smith 2000, 115). In theory, this principle also meant that a new president pro tem needed to be elected every time the vice president left the Senate chamber, although in practice president pro tems were frequently in waiting, assuming the post on such occasions (Gamm and Smith 2000, 107). Before the 1880s, it was unclear whether the president pro tem could appoint a temporary presiding officer when he was away, further undermining the office (Gamm and Smith 2000, 109–11).

Evidence favors a size and workload explanation for the emergence of a relatively powerful presiding officer in the House. The formal rules changes that enhanced speaker power listed in table 2.1—the power to appoint committees (1st Congress [1789–91]), the chair of the Committee of the Whole (3rd Congress [1793–95]), and chairs of standing and select committees (8th Congress [1803–5])—coincide with the growth of the House and its workload. As noted in the previous section, a logit model consisting of just the change in size and workload variables predicts strongly the probability of restriction in the 1st and 8th Congresses. It predicts an 87.8 percent probability of restriction in the 3rd Congress.

The Germaneness of Amendments

The third critical procedural difference is that, in the words of current House rules, "No motion or proposition on a subject different from that under consideration shall be admitted under color of amendment" (Rule XVI, Clause 7). Floor amendments, in other words, must be germane. The Senate's rules place strict germaneness requirements on amendments to appropriations and reconciliation bills, budget resolutions, and those offered after the invocation of cloture, but unlike the House, the Senate has never had a general germaneness rule (Oleszek 2011, 65–66). When not constrained by germaneness, senators can, in theory at least, introduce a bill as an amendment to another bill on a vastly different subject.

The House's germaneness rule is integral to the strong proposal and gatekeeping powers standing committees have in the chamber. The strict tests—of which there are six—greatly protect legislative product reported out of committee and prevent members from introducing much potential legislation directly on the floor (Oleszek 2011, 195–97). The rule clearly weakens the House floor and the rights exercised on it.

The House requirement goes back to the original standing rules created at the beginning of the 1st Congress in March 1789. At the time the rule read, "No new motion or proposition shall be admitted under color of amendment as a substitute for a question or proposition under debate." According to *Hinds' Precedents of the House of Representatives* (Hines 1907, sec. 5825, 422), this language was widely interpreted as at least barring nongermane substitutes. The current language, which extends the rule to amendments in any form, was adopted in the widespread rules changes of March 1822.[7]

Any attempt to discern why the House has the rule and the Senate does not ought to focus on the lower chamber. Typical 18th-century parliamentary procedure allowed amendments of any type, including those, in Jefferson's contemporaneous words, "made so as totally to alter the nature of the proposition" (*Jefferson's Manual* 2005, 109th Cong., 243). Neither the British House of Commons nor, as far as we can tell, American colonial and state legislatures had germaneness restrictions. Unfortunately, however, we know very little, if anything, about why the House established the rule in 1789 and extended it in 1822. Neither the *House Journal* nor the *Annals of Congress* describes any debate surrounding the provision. Also obfuscating analysis of the 1822 action is the fact that it was part of a large package of rules changes.

Still, one legislative body did have a germaneness rule prior to the U.S. House. In May 1781, the Continental Congress revised its rules to include a provision almost identical to what the House adopted in 1789.[8] Again there exists no information in either the *Journals of the Continental Congress* or the writings of the principals that can help us understand the genesis of the rule. Luckily, the Continental Congress's action provides clues about why the House and not the Senate has the procedure. As Aldrich and Grant (1993) have argued, many of the issues that were important in the Continental Congress—most substantive but some procedural—carried over into the proceedings of the 1st Congress.

We can, for example, examine political conditions leading up to the creation of the rule in the Continental Congress. Here the evidence does not suggest that anything like majority party strength was an antecedent. In 1781, "delegate preferences were widely dispersed" (Jillson and Wilson 1994, 240). Not until 1783 did regional groups of delegates coalesce and "a powerful group of middle state and Chesapeake delegates, clustered around Hamilton and Madison, [seem] poised to seize control of the institution" (240). Instead we can present a stronger case for a burgeoning workload. Jillson and Wilson (1994, 96) show that the number of ad hoc committees in the Continental Congress—an indicator of and contributor to the demands on delegates—grew rapidly and linearly from 178 in 1779 to 345 in 1781. Moreover, the number of roll-call votes totaled only 45 in 1777 but averaged 180 per year between 1778 and 1780 (there were 156 in 1780) (Lord 1943). In no year after 1781 did the vote total reach 180.

With absenteeism reaching epidemic proportions—attendance declined from around 52 members in 1774 to about 33 in 1781—expectations in 1781 were that individual delegate workloads would only grow. This worry was exacerbated by the adoption of supermajority voting requirements in the Articles of Confederation in March 1781. The Articles necessitated the assent of the delegations of seven states for the passage of ordinary legislation, but nine delegations on important issues such as treaties and military and financial matters. In a body with a tradition of "an open agenda, limited agenda-setting powers in the chair and committees, and issue-by-issue consideration of legislative matters" (Jillson and Wilson 1994, 149–50), extra workloads were especially problematic. The Continental Congress directly addressed the issue early in 1781 by placing executive departments under singularly responsible secretaries (Jillson and Wilson 1994, 112–14). We might assume that the adoption of the germaneness requirement in the rules changes of May 1781 had a similar labor-saving goal.

Second, we can compare the Continental Congress with contemporaneous American legislatures in a cross-sectional analysis. Such a test persuades us again to reject the proposition that cleavages on policy preferences explain the germaneness requirement. Main (1967) argues that state senates were largely divided along a relatively simple and single cleavage during the revolutionary period. Small farmers, debtors, and revolutionaries frequently opposed a more aristocratic and loyalist faction. Conversely, not least because of the great regional differences between the states, the voting patterns of delegates to the Continental Congress are best explained by at least one additional dimension (Jillson and Wilson 1994, 167–94). Policy differences in the Continental Congress were, therefore, less likely to resemble the bifurcated arrangement inherent in a body split into two opposing factions with clear policy preferences.

Instead, differences in workload can help. Although true comparisons are unavailable, it seems safe to assume that the Continental Congress groaned more loudly under the demands placed on it. State legislatures' workloads also increased during the revolution, largely because of the emergence of new issues. The number of committees in state bodies grew (Harlow 1917, 64–78). But state legislatures in colonial America produced few laws (Olson 1992). The Continental Congress's increasing workload was felt particularly acutely because it also interacted with the body's inefficient procedures. As John Matthews, a South Carolina delegate, wrote in 1778, "I have frequently heard heavy complaints in our [South Carolina] Assembly, of the tedious progress of business, but I will venture to say, you do more business in one day, than we do, in three" (Burnett 1926, 421).

Given that the House emerged quickly and resolutely as the initiator of legislation, its first members may have realized that they would have a larger workload than members of the more reactive Senate. In that light, adopting a germaneness rule made sense.[9]

Still, a workload explanation of the House's unique germaneness requirement is highly notional. Indeed, although the period immediately after 1822 is one of a substantial acceleration in legislative business, the absolute and changing measures of workload I have used are relatively low for the 17th Congress (1821–23).

Regardless of the origins of the germaneness requirement, it is clear that the House's decisions surrounding the procedure in 1789 and 1822 were crucial. Speaker Andrew Stevenson's (D-VA) December 1827 ruling that an amendment on the jurisdiction of the Committee on Manufactures was not germane is the earliest reference to the requirement in *Hinds' Precedents* (Hinds 1907, sec. 5853, 437). By the mid-1830s, frequent rulings had declared amendments out of order because they were unrelated in some way to the bill under debate (Hinds 1907, sec. 5883). In the Senate, the first instance of a ruling permitting an amendment over the objection that it was not germane occurred in 1853 (*Congressional Globe*, 32nd Congress, 1st sess., 820). As a result, the germaneness provision—along with fixed jurisdiction, the beginnings of reporting rights, and the emergence of today's bill introduction procedures (Cooper and Rybicki 2002; Cooper and Young 1989)—formed an integral part of the large differences in the powers of House and Senate standing committees that were visible by the 1860s. The history of germaneness reveals that a distinguishing procedural characteristic of the House and Senate floors can have inauspicious beginnings.

The Previous Question

A critical difference between floor proceedings in the two congressional chambers is that a majority can terminate debate in the House by approving a previous question motion. In December 1811, at the commencement of the 12th Congress, the lower chamber formally enumerated the previous question as we know it today. The prior February, at the end of the 11th Congress, the House had effectively adopted the rule when it overturned Speaker Joseph Varnum's (R-MA) interpretation that the invocation of the previous question did not terminate proceedings during a debate on the expansion of a trade embargo with Britain. The Senate had dropped the provision from its rule book five years earlier.[10]

A discussion of procedural differences across congressional chambers must pay close attention to the adoption of the previous question in the House. Binder (1997, 43–67) offers the principal analysis of the rule's creation. She argues that the previous question was adopted in 1811 because a strong majority party presided over a body divided greatly by partisanship on the issue of war with Britain and in which the minority had begun to employ obstructionist tactics. Indeed, according to Koger (2010, 60–62), six filibusters took place between 1807 and 1811, and four of them had direct bearing on the conflict with the British.

Binder's position is based on three observations. First, the Senate dropped its previous question motion in 1806, at a time when the chamber's majority was relatively weak.[11] The 12th Congress (1811–13), conversely, is part of an era of Republican domination of the House in which a large and cohesive majority mastered the Federalist opposition. The period from the 9th (1805–7) to 12th Congresses saw sustained and heightened majority party strength. Second, recorded votes to sustain the Speaker's ruling on the previous question motion when applied to substantive matters in the 10th (1807–9) and 11th (1809–11) Congresses—there is no record of the vote on the creation of the rule itself—reveal a severe partisan cleavage (Binder 1997, 58–61). Third, Binder (1997, 57) finds a dramatic increase in dilatory and impeding motions just after 1810. In contrast, the minority was not using such tactics in the 10th Congress, when the House overturned a decision by Varnum that the previous question ended debate and brought the matter at hand to an immediate vote. Varnum used this vote as the precedent for his 1811 ruling. The minority also was not behaving this way in the 8th Congress, when the House reversed a similar ruling from the chair that approval of the previous question terminated proceedings.[12]

Indeed, Binder's explanation is particularly persuasive in light of the debate on the adoption of the previous question rule that took place on December 23, 1811 (*Annals of Congress*, 12th Cong., 1st sess., 569–81). A connection, shaped tremendously by partisan politics, seems to exist between policy and procedural preference that is absent in most other legislative matters of the day. The debate is repeatedly characterized, in the words of Josiah Quincy (Fed-MA), as "a mere contest for power between the majority and the minority" (*Annals of Congress*, 12th Cong., 1st sess., 572).

But some evidence indicates that a burgeoning workload might have played a role as well. Binder (1997, 51–53) dismisses workload as a contributing factor because increases in legislative business come after the previous question is established, the result of this critical tool of obstruction being taken away from the minority. Yet as figure 3.3 reveals, sizable increases in workload—as measured by my change in workload variable and compared to most other Congresses of the era—generally occurred be-

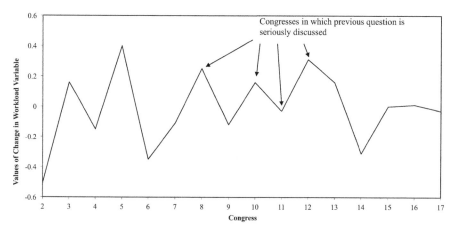

Fig. 3.3. Increases in the House workload from the previous Congress, 2nd (1791–93) to 17th (1821–23) Congresses. (Data: author's calculations from Binder 1997.)

tween the 7th and 8th, 9th and 10th, 10th and 11th, and 11th and 12th Congresses, with the second half of each of these pairs featuring serious discussion about revising the previous question rule and giving it its modern meaning. The establishment of the modern previous question came at the beginning of the 12th Congress, but members were surely capable of anticipating the legislative business they had on their plate. The previous question procedure was debated seriously at times when the House felt increasingly burdened by work.

A workload argument is assisted by the fact that in absolute terms, the volume of work in the 12th Congress was the highest since the 1st and the third-highest of all the Congresses prior to the 22nd (1831–33). And a logit model of the first 39 Congresses that contains just the change in workload variable predicts a 42.7 percent chance of the enactment of a rule restricting procedures in the 12th Congress, while the average for all these Congresses is 15.4 percent.[13]

Binder also gives short shrift to an organized, cohesive, and ebullient group of new members. By early standards, the freshmen who entered the 12th Congress were only moderate in size, but they are known for their strident views on issues and desire for policy change. Of the 65 newcomers, 52 were Republicans. Moreover, many were ardent war hawks, generally young men from the South and West determined to see the ongoing hostilities with Britain boil over into armed conflict. As an obvious sign of their influence and grasp of procedural issues, the group's ostensible leader, Henry Clay, was elected Speaker. In turn, Clay ensured that those who supported the cohort's policy positions chaired critical committees—Peter B. Porter (Rep-NY) headed Foreign Relations, David R. Williams (Rep-SC) led Military Affairs, and Ezekiel Bacon (Rep-MA) became chair of Ways and Means.[14] Although some historians have suggested that the influence of this class on more senior Republicans should not be overestimated (Risjord 1965, 123–26), its members possessed a perspicuous agenda and an acute understanding of how the House could be controlled. Indeed, Clay was in the chair when Hugh Nelson, a Republican freshman from Virginia, proposed the amendment to House rules codifying the new version of the previous question. To be sure, the freshman argument is undercut somewhat by the contention that it was the overturning of Varnum's ruling in February 1811, at the end of the 11th Congress, that effectively established the modern previous question. But as a senator, Clay had cheered hawkish Republican House members on from the sidelines as they moved to create the new procedure (Benton 1856, 2:257). He and his junior colleagues were fully aware of the importance of enumerating the procedure at the beginning of the next one.

Binder's argument makes implicit note of the freshman class of the 12th Congress by suggesting that it merely added to the strength of the Republican majority. But it can be argued that the war hawks represented, as perhaps did the classes of 1974 and 1994, the independent importance of electoral shocks to procedural change. Even if we could know what the public really wanted from the 1810 and 1811 elections, it is unlikely, of course, that procedural change was at the top of the list.[15] Such a clear vindication of the war agenda—expressed by westerners' belief that the British were assisting Indian opposition and easterners' view that the British were threatening American maritime and trading interests—seems to have necessitated procedural alterations, however.

Unlike 1974 and 1994, an energetic and resourceful freshman class helped bring about a restriction of House rules. This development runs counter to the hypothesis presented earlier that a large number of new members—contorted a bit here to mean an energetic freshman class—will naturalize procedures. Why the unpredicted outcome? Perhaps, as Clay's immediate ascension to the speakership vividly illustrated, seniority was unnecessary at the time for membership in important House institutions and influence over the floor agenda and proceedings. As Polsby (1968, 149) argues in his seminal article on institutionalization, during Clay's era, "leadership in the House was relatively open to lateral entry." The war hawks, unlike modern freshman classes, realized that natural procedures were as much, if not more, their enemy as their friend.

It is more difficult, however, to assert that the House's growth contributes to the adoption of the previous question. In 1811, only Illinois, Indiana, Louisiana, and Mississippi were likely to be admitted to the Union soon, and they had such small populations that their entry would do little to swell the chamber's ranks. Still, the once-in-a-decade expansion of the House was scheduled to take place after the 1810 census in the 13th Congress (1813–15)—and the House grew a substantial 27 percent, from 141 to 182, at that time. This development provides at least a modicum of evidence that the body's growth may have impinged on the decision to adopt the modern version of the previous question. Indeed, Binder (1997, 64) states that size may have played a role in the Senate's jettisoning of the previous question since "a much smaller Senate membership also reduced demand for managing the flow of Senate business."

In the end however, any analysis of this critical change in House rules must largely accept Binder's interpretation of events, with the qualification that a nascent workload, cohesive and energetic freshman class, and perhaps increasing size made some contribution. The previous question was adopted because a strong majority was unable to pass the legislation it desired. The creation of this procedure is, therefore, somewhat unusual. Whereas I have argued that procedural change in the House prior to the Civil War largely resulted from a growing workload and size, the previous question seems best explained by party politics and policy preferences. Why?

Three reasons stand out. First, the substantive issue that generated the procedural change was peculiarly salient. There had, of course, been many important issues during the first quarter century of the republic's existence, but impending war with Britain seems to have pushed partisan sensibilities to a height not seen since at least 1800, if ever. The tensions with the mother country covered a vast array of issues—trade and prosperity, security and relations with the Indians, national pride, deep regional divides, and America's role in the world—that continually brought political discourse around to the issue. "Never did the American Congress assemble under circumstances of greater interest and responsibility," wrote the *Boston Chronicle* as the 12th Congress convened (Hickey 1989, 29). The war also quite neatly divided the Republicans and Federalists. As a result, congressional parties cared deeply enough about policy outcomes to pay careful attention to procedures.

Second, the previous question was consistent with the Republican majority's thinking about legislative procedures. The previous question adopted in 1811 was a majoritarian procedure created to prevent minorities from delaying floor proceedings. Other contemporaneous attempts to restrict House rules generally undermined the floor and therefore diluted the influence of floor majorities. At least in the early days, Jeffersonian thought deplored rules designed to stifle the will of a House majority (Cooper 1970). The previous question did not offend such sensibilities.

Third, perhaps because of the political stakes, the large and cohesive Republicans faced an unusually obdurate minority willing to use previously latent parliamentary powers to block the majority's agenda. Binder (1997, 56–58) reveals dramatic spikes in the usage of obstructionist floor motions in the 11th and 12th Congresses. These tactics provided the majority with the incentive to adopt the previous question.

To suggest that the adoption of the previous question was the product of policy preferences and a strong majority party is not a small concession. Binder (1997) and J. M. Roberts and Smith (2007) argue that the 1811 decision set the House on a certain and distinct procedural path. It gave it, to use Binder and Smith's (1995) words, its "acquired procedural tendency." It is an exaggeration to state that the decision placed the House on an irreversible trajectory. But the existence of a previous question that could be invoked by a majority would make it more difficult to move procedures in the natural direction. It is also clearly an important reason why the House and Senate floors differed so greatly by the time of the Civil War.

Size, Workload, and Majority Party Strength in the Antebellum Congress: Two Vignettes and Some Additional Thoughts

To strengthen my argument, I undertake two tasks in this brief section. The first is to focus on two periods in which membership and workload growth in the House and Senate bring about the kind of procedural change we should expect: 1789–1811 and the 1840s. In the first period, I contrast House and Senate size; in the second, I look at how Congress's burgeoning workloads brought about efforts to restrict procedures in both chambers.

The twenty or so years that straddled 1800 witnessed remarkable growth in the size of the House. In the 1790, 1800, and 1810 censuses, Americans discovered that the country's population had grown dramatically and that to hew close to the Constitution's admonition in Article I, Section 2, that "the Number of Representatives shall not exceed one for every thirty Thousand," the House had to keep up. Thirty-six members were added to the 3rd Congress (1793–95), another 35 to the 8th Congress (1803–5), and 39 to the 13th Congress (1813–15). The House had 65 members in the 1st Congress and 182 by the 13th. In percentage terms, this represents by far the most rapid growth for any quarter-century span in American history.

At this time, only five new states were admitted to the Union—Vermont, Kentucky, Tennessee, Ohio, and Louisiana. The Senate, therefore, grew much more slowly. Moreover, the prospects for Senate expansion, particularly in the 1790s and first half of the first decade of the 18th century, were not particularly great. The Louisiana Purchase of 1803 and the establishment of the Indiana and Mississippi Territories around the same time more than doubled the geographic size of the country. But very low population densities in the territories meant that existing states, worried about these areas gaining Senate representation and altering power relations in the body, could make a strong case against admission into the Union (Lawson and Seidman 2005, 32). Squabbles with Spain and the presence of British and French traders and their Indian allies along the western frontier added to the slim prospects for statehood. So did Federalist opposition to Republican efforts at augmentation. In this regard, the Louisiana Purchase was particularly controversial. Federalists fretted greatly about the diminution of their values and economic interests in a country expanding under Jeffersonian principles (Onuf 2005; Theriault 2006). Several Federalists attempted to prove that the land obtained belonged to Spain rather than to France and thereby derail the acquisition (Fleming 2003, 145–51). In the House, a resolution denying the president's request to buy the territory was defeated by just two votes.

The Senate saw a lot of turnover at this time. The original states generally had about seven or eight senators who served at some point in the 1789–1811 period. Even by the 12th Congress (1811–13), mean service was less than one full term (Wirls and Wirls 2004, 173). Most senators departed for other public offices (Wirls and Wirls 2004, 171–73). But unlike their counterparts in the House, these men were invariably members of the country's small and interconnected political elite. They were protected tremendously from public scrutiny. Senators were selected by state legislators, their independence was deemed of national interest, and until 1794 at least, their deliberations took place in secret (Swift 1996, 56–61). Newspaper coverage of the Senate was minimal (Swift 1996, 60–61). Little institutional consciousness existed, and senators faced few external pressures to bring about procedural change. Moreover, as noted earlier, the workload of this time was light, and daily sessions were frequently short, with little of substance accomplished (Swift 1996, 79–80).

The House, conversely, saw a need to address membership growth. With a greater workload as well, it laid the foundations in this period for a dramatic increase in the power of the Speaker. The *Annals of Congress* and *House Journal* are essentially silent on the debates that surrounded the adoption of the rules that gave the speaker the power to appoint committees and their chairs. But these original sources are littered with examples of members discussing the strains a growing membership and workload were placing on the House over the first twenty years. During debates over the apportionment bills in the 2nd (1791–93), 7th (1801–3), and 12th (1811–13) Congresses, for example, members frequently remarked on the problems of an expanding House. Although much talk concerned the appropriateness of divisors used to calculate the number of new seats, most legislators were acutely aware of the implications of membership growth for House operations. In the 7th Congress, Representative Thomas Morris (Fed-NY) worried that a large House would, without necessary procedural safeguards, become like France's "mob convention" (*Annals of Congress*, 7th Cong., 1st sess., 340). Such supporters of expansion as Senator Samuel White (Fed-DE) believed that the growing House could be managed by procedural innovation and would not be "too large and unwieldy for the convenient and ordinary purposes of business." After all, Virginia's House of Delegates and the British House of Commons had devised efficient rules for dealing with large memberships (*Annals of Congress*, 7th Cong., 1st sess., 46–47).

A reading of the scholarship of the era also provides a sense that House members believed that organizational centralization or restrictive procedures were necessary. The Senate sat around waiting for the House to act, feeling no real need to examine procedures. The early House was the incubator of legislation and, as James Madison (Rep-VA) noted, was unfortunately characterized by "delays and perplexities" caused by its few formal rules and "the want of precedents" (*Congressional Quarterly* 1999, 40). Others, like Representative Fisher Ames (Fed-MA), blamed the need for legislating to be conducted in the cumbersome Committee of the Whole (*Congressional Quarterly* 1999, 40).

During the 1840s, both bodies' workloads grew considerably. The number of bills introduced in the Senate, for example, escalated from about 300 per Congress at the beginning of the decade to about 600 by its end. In both bodies, the number of days on which roll-call votes took place increased markedly (Koger 2010, 81–84). Congress was also forced to address a great number of pressing policy problems. The 1840s featured debates on legislation concerning trade, banking and finance, westward expansion, and slavery and sectionalism. These issues, particularly slavery, deeply split Congress.

As a result, opponents resorted to obstructionist tactics. Koger (2010, 43–45) shows that the number of dilatory motions introduced in the Senate and especially in the House increased palpably during the 26th Congress (1839–41). There were many incidents of obstructionism in both bodies, particularly on measures related to slavery and new territories (64–67). The Democratic blocking of the important bank bill of 1841 is considered one of the first significant filibusters in Senate history (Binder and Smith 1997, 91). Members, in turn, felt pressed for time and presumably looked to restrictive procedural innovations for relief. The House's Gag Rule, established in 1841, is one example. On the Senate side, the decade witnessed a consequential ruling from the presiding officer that a motion to table was not debatable (Wawro and Schickler 2006, 66–68). In 1841, moreover, Henry Clay (Whig-KY) called for the Senate to readopt its previous question procedure. This was just the first of the decade's many serious attempts to extract favorable rulings from the chair or to alter formal rules in ways that would mitigate nascent obstructionism in the Senate.

The section's second task is to provide a bit more confidence with which to reject the majority party strength hypothesis when it is applied to the data of the antebellum era. Given that the House moves much more rapidly in a restrictive direction, we should expect its majority parties generally to be stronger than their Senate counterparts at this time. Such is not really the case, however. The antebellum mean majority party strength score is .216 for the House and .211 for the Senate. House majority parties are generally a little more cohesive than their Senate counterparts—the standard deviation of House majority member first-dimension DW-NOMINATE scores for the first 39 Congresses is .205; it is .254 for the Senate—but Senate majorities generally occupied a larger proportion of the body's seats (64.4 percent compared to 60.7 percent in the House). The intercameral differences in these figures for the 68 post–Civil War Congresses in the study are almost identical to those for the antebellum period except for the fact that the size of House majorities has been essentially the same as those in the Senate.

Binder's Work and Antebellum Procedural Change

Binder (1997, 86–107) has argued that the relative strengths of the majority and minority parties brought about procedural change prior to the Civil
War. She does not really talk about membership size and discusses workload largely in passing. She has inferred a much stronger link between
party and procedure in this period. Specifically, she discusses four packages
of antebellum rules changes in this light. I dealt with one of these, the previous question, earlier.

Two of the remaining changes appear to have at best only indirect partisan antecedents, however. During the debate over the two-thirds suspension procedure in 1822, for example, Binder (1997, 90) states that "there
was no neat partisan division" over proposals to change the rules.[16] Jenkins
and Stewart (2002, 219) confirm this finding and suggest that no meaningful partisan cleavage at all existed in the 17th Congress. Binder (1997,
104–7) also suggests that the contradictory impact of the five-minute rule
in 1847 mitigated partisan disagreement over that reform. It both naturalized procedures in that it effectively guaranteed a debate on amendments
and restricted them in that five minutes was less than existing rules allowed.

Binder (1997, 43–67) more forcefully argues that the 1841 rules package resulted from partisan division and the majority party using its strength
to weaken minority rights or restrict procedures. Much of the case for the
1841 rules changes that allowed a majority to discharge a bill from the
Committee of the Whole and that limited members' floor speeches to an
hour is made through an analysis of roll-call votes on the proposals and related substantive policy issues.

The 1841 package is an interesting case. It was caught up in a battle
over the Gag Rule, which prohibited the consideration of antislavery petitions in the House (Binder 1997, 99–104; Jenkins and Stewart 2003;
Meinke 2007). The rule was established in 1836, and over the next eight
years it became a proxy for policy disputes over slavery. There were numerous attempts to end it. These efforts generally pitted Whigs, who
wanted to end the rule, against Democrats, who wanted it to continue, but
also mirrored a regional cleavage into which slavery had wedged (Jenkins
and Stewart 2003; Meinke 2007). In June 1841, the House first voted to
adopt temporarily the rules of the previous 26th Congress (1839–41),
without the Gag Rule. The legislative vehicle was a floor amendment offered by John Quincy Adams (Whig-MA). Thirty-seven percent of Whigs

voted against Adams's amendment, while 35 percent of Democrats supported it. When a special committee proposed making these rules permanent just a week later, however, the House rejected the report, effectively continuing the former rules complete with the gag provision. Two days after that, the antigag forces, led by Adams, reached a compromise with their rivals that delayed resolution of the issue until a later date. In July, the special committee came up with a new set of rules for the 27th Congress that included the two provisions of interest to us here (Binder 1997, 99–104; Jenkins and Stewart 2003). This package passed later that month.

The votes on the discharge and one-hour rule changes were standalone votes, separated from the gag issue by the compromise that postponed the controversy over antislavery petitions (Binder 1997, 101–2). Binder consequently suggests that the agreement effectively took slavery off the table and allowed members to concentrate on procedural matters.

But the initial iterations of the discharge and one-hour rules were surely framed as an attempt to postpone the Gag Rule for a while and move quickly on to other legislative business, particularly finalizing the rules. The procedural changes themselves remained secondary to many in the majority. In June 1841, Caleb Cushing (Whig-MA) pleaded that his party "come to the rescue of their country, and organize the House, under whatever rules; because, if we do not, we shall become, as we are now becoming, the laughing-stock, the scorn, the contempt, of the people of the United States" (Binder 1997, 102). The Whigs were frantically trying to get past the necessary task of setting the rules so they could make law. The Gag Rule was part of this job, not a nuisance to be dealt with before they could take their time organizing the House. Whig members seemed to care little about the contents of the rules package after the Gag Rule was set aside. The discharge and one-hour rules should, therefore, be evaluated as part of a larger deal to get the rules approved and not as strategic and unilateral attempts by a robust majority party to change extant procedures in a favorable direction. Indeed, the vote was not especially partisan—19 percent of Whigs opposed the package, and 26 percent of Democrats supported it. As I suggested earlier, a strong argument can be made that the changes in 1841 were brought about by a burgeoning membership and workload, itself intensified by members' increased willingness to engage in floor obstruction.

The Gag Rule, moreover, continued to cast a long shadow over the business of the 27th Congress. According to the index of the *Congressional Record*, sixteen references to abolition petitions arose after the issue was supposedly resolved. Adams tried to rescind the Gag Rule in the Congress's third session, in December 1842. Even after the slavery petition issue was "over," votes to approve subsequent rules changes broke down along the line that divided pro- and antislavery members. This line cut across the parties nearly as much as it did between them. As such, the issue did not galvanize the majority party and weaken its opposition.

Party and Members' Policy and Procedural Preferences

Congressional procedures were moved in a restrictive direction by a growing membership and workload in the 19th century and largely by a strengthening majority party in the 20th century. Most of the important procedural differences between the restrictive House and natural Senate occurred in the 19th century, mainly before the Civil War. Why?

The answer begins with an explanation of the temporal variance in the determinants of procedural change. The reason for such variance lies in the relationship between party and members' policy, electoral, and procedural preferences.[17] As my model of procedural change asserts, legislative rules bring greater precision to the prediction of policy outcomes (McKelvey 1976; Shepsle and Weingast 1987; Weingast 1989). As a result, members are intensely interested in shaping rules to promote policy interests—that is, they stack the deck (Cox 2000; Riker 1980). Extant studies of procedural change such as Binder's (1997) and Schickler's (2001) argue that party generally drives members' procedural choices, so partisan tussles determine procedural outcomes.[18] The argument is not really conditioned by time.

This work views procedural alteration in partisan terms for a simple reason: The two chambers of Congress are organized explicitly along party lines. Today, this organizational arrangement grants the majority party exclusive control of important congressional institutions. In the House, the Speaker is a partisan position; the Rules Committee is dominated by the majority; all other standing committee chairs are members of the majority; and in nearly every case, most members of each standing committee are from the majority party.[19] The Senate is organized similarly. Changes in existing procedures can therefore be thought of as benefiting one party or the other. Indeed Binder's (1997) and Schickler's (2001) dependent variables explicitly measure the strengthening of majority and minority party rights. As members of the majority or minority, legislators have assumed clear procedural preferences as they have learned what role procedural control can play in the determination of legislative outcomes. Members are acutely aware of how prospective changes to rules will affect their more fundamental interests. Since party members tend to share distinct policy and electoral preferences, procedural choice is also arranged along party lines. The two parties fight over procedures because some are more likely to bring about policy and electoral outcomes favored by the majority party, while others are more likely to bring about outcomes favored by the minority.

As the theoretical model presented in chapter 1 asserts, when applied to the floor, the congressional majority party prefers to decrease floor power and weaken floor rights—that is, it wants restrictive procedures. At least in a formal sense, the majority essentially has proposal and gatekeeping power. It sets the floor agenda. To ensure that legislative outcomes are at or close to its collective policy preferences, it wants a weak floor on which members have few rights so that bills cannot easily be changed or killed.

The minority party, conversely, desires to move procedures in a natural direction. A more powerful floor and greater floor rights would better allow it to block or alter the substance of majority proposals. The result is two parties competing to push procedures in opposite directions.

It is not axiomatic, however, that preferences about procedural change should fall neatly and predictably along party lines. It is not inevitable that the majority party should want restrictive procedures, the minority natural procedures. Indeed, two conditions must exist for such to be the case. First, there must be two main parties with perceptibly different policy preferences. If there is broad consensus on policy within a body, the legislative outcome is essentially predetermined, and procedural design matters little. If there is considerable heterogeneity of preferences but cleavages tend to cut across parties to form bipartisan policy coalitions, there will be little intraparty agreement on procedural design, and battles over organization are likely to occur not between parties but within them. Some members of the majority will continue to see their policy interests furthered by restrictive procedures, but others might prefer more natural ones.

It is rare that the two major congressional parties have not been distinguishable by policy differences, although between roughly 1815 and 1825 the federal legislature was essentially monopolized by one party, and there was widespread consensus on the important issues of the day. Moreover, the House has only really experienced two obvious intraparty procedural battles that stemmed from intraparty policy squabbles: the 1909–10 revolt against the intense centralization under Speaker Joseph Cannon (R-IL) and the reforms of the 1970s. In both cases, an insurgent group within the majority party—Republicans in the first instance, Democrats in the second—teamed up with members of the minority to naturalize procedures. In the first episode, the Speaker was stripped of power; in the second incident, standing committees and their chairs were stripped of much of their influence (Schickler 2001, 71–83; Schickler, McGhee, and Sides 2003).

Intraparty disagreements on policy are an indicator of party weakness—in the Binder measure I use and, if this heterogeneity is disproportionately large for the majority, in the Schickler measure, too. Both the 1909–10 and 1970s changes to procedure can, therefore, be thought of in the conventional partisan terms proposed by scholars such as Binder (1997) and Schickler (2000). Splintered and weak majorities allowed discontented members to win rules that enhanced, in the words of the existing scholarship, minority rights. In the language I use, relatively low levels of majority party strength resulted in a predicted naturalization of procedures.

The second condition required for the majority party to want to restrict procedures and the minority to want to naturalize them is that members of the majority occupy positions of authority—notably, the presiding officer and a majority of standing committees, members, and their chairs hail from the majority party. The majority party, in other words, clearly controls the floor agenda and directs the floor's proceedings. This second condition is always met in the modern Congress. A fundamental characteristic of congressional organization today is that the majority party dominates important institutions. Augmenting or reducing the power of institutions such as the House speakership, the House Rules Committee, the post of Senate majority leader, and standing committees has an obvious impact on the relative influences of the majority and minority parties.

Under current arrangements, the only time this second condition really might not be met is when, with the help of members of minor parties or majority party dissidents, the minority or a multiparty coalition organizes a body. If this occurs, it is presumably members of the minority or the multiparty coalition that want to restrict procedures and the rump of the majority that want them naturalized. A coup of this sort nearly happened in the House at the beginning of the 65th Congress (1917–19), when Democrats occupied only a plurality of seats. In this case, the party secured the election of Champ Clark (D-MO) as Speaker and control of standing committees by remaining unified and ensuring that Republicans would not win support of the smattering of minor party and independent members. Several deaths and illnesses in the months prior to the special opening session, as well as splits among the Republicans, helped. So did the polarizing effect generated by the issue of the country's entry into World War I. Democratic President Woodrow Wilson assiduously rallied his party away from neutrality, and even some progressive Republican members, like Thomas D. Schall (R-MN), argued that the United States needed Democratic control of the House on the eve of war (Margulies 1996, 166–67).

Minority organization of the chamber almost occurred at the beginning of the 68th Congress (1923–25) as well. At that time, about twenty progressive Republicans initially refused to vote for Frederick H. Gillett (R-MA), their party's formal candidate, and instead offered Henry Allen Cooper (R-WI) as an alternative speaker. Because only 225 Republicans held seats, it was plausible that a deep enough fissure might allow a Democrat to be selected. An agreement on a revision to chamber rules among Republicans ensured Gillett's victory, however (Galloway 1976, 50). Those two instances were just about the closest the United States came to having the majority or plurality party lose formal control of powerful House institutions in the 20th century.[20]

Party control of the Senate has been unclear on several occasions since the Civil War. Three Congresses provide particularly interesting examples. At the beginning of the 47th Congress (1881–83), the Senate was split with 37 Republicans, 37 Democrats, and 2 independents. One of the independents, David Dixon of Illinois, declared that he would vote with the Democrats to organize the body. Democrats fully expected the other, William Mahone, a Readjuster from Virginia, to follow suit, since the Readjusters were essentially a populist faction within their party. However, with the tie-breaking vote of Vice President Chester A. Arthur in their pocket, Republicans courted Mahone furiously, and in a dramatic turn of events, he cast his ballot for their leadership slate. Democrats retaliated by blocking a host of issues that required attention if the Senate was to organize fully. Democratic leverage was enhanced by the fact that the initial session of the Congress was a special one designed to approve executive appointments. The subsequent resignation of both of New York's Republican senators and the assassination of President James Garfield helped ease tensions. With the independent Dixon elevated to president pro tempore, the two parties agreed to the organizational arrangement forged immediately after the initial vote. The Republicans led the committees, while Democrats controlled the offices of secretary and sergeant at arms.[21]

The second example is the 83rd Congress (1953–55). In that case, the Republicans held the presidency and a one-seat advantage over the Democrats as the Senate convened. But during 1953 and 1954, nine senators died and one resigned, tilting the balance in favor of the Democrats on two occasions, and they could have taken control for much of 1954. Instead, they accepted Republican leadership, possibly because minority leader Lyndon B. Johnson (D-TX) understood how difficult orchestrating the ongoing investigation of Senator Joseph McCarthy (R-WI) might be.

As with the 83rd Congress, the Republicans had a tenuous hold of the Senate at the beginning of the 107th Congress (2001–3). There were initially 50 Republicans and 50 Democrats, allowing Vice President Dick Cheney to cast the tie-breaking vote on organizational matters. But Vermont senator James Jeffords's decision to leave the Republican Party and become an independent who pledged support to the Democrats changed control. Like the 47th and 83rd, therefore, the 107th Congress had a Senate in which members may have found it difficult to have clear and durable procedural preferences.

When both or either of the two conditions necessary for procedural preferences to be arranged along party are not met, there is reason to believe that procedural change will be generated by forces other than the relative strength of the majority party in its struggle with the minority. If no clear policy differences exist between the parties and the majority does not have unambiguous control of the floor agenda and floor proceedings, the parties are unlikely to have expressed clear procedural preferences and a list of internally agreed-upon procedural reforms. When such is the case, procedural change has other antecedents.

Party and Procedural Preferences: The Antebellum Congress

The first condition, that parties must have different policy preferences, was arguably not in full effect for much of the antebellum period. Two main parties separated by a cleavage based on substantive policy preferences emerged quickly in the first few Congresses (Aldrich 1995, 68–96). But the schism quickly closed. If there ever was a time that there was little discernible difference between the parties on policy, it was during the Era of Good Feelings that followed the end of the War of 1812 and lasted through the mid-1820s. This was a time of virtual one-party rule—the Federalists had just about withered away—illustrated most vividly by the unanimity of congressional approval for President James Monroe's decision to run for reelection in 1820. Monroe campaigned unopposed and eventually won 231 of 232 electoral votes. Poole and Rosenthal (1997, 93) have described this time as featuring "spatial collapse" in the range of legislator preferences.

For much of the rest of the antebellum period, both bodies were either dominated by a considerably more fractious Republican Party or split into three or more groupings with parties such as the Anti-Masons and Americans or Know-Nothings having at various times quite sizable numbers of seats, particularly in the House. Between the 18th (1823–25) and 39th (1865–67) Congresses, the lower chamber was marked by relatively large numbers of minor party members who were not formally allied with their Jackson/Democratic or Anti-Jackson/Whig/Republican colleagues in any meaningful governing or opposition group.

Binder (1997, 27–30) argues that the "antipartyism" of the period prior to 1830 did not preclude majority and minority parties and coalitions from recognizing and pursuing their procedural interests. But there is reason to believe otherwise—or at least that the differences between these two antebellum periods and the post–Civil War era are meaningful. From about 1812 to the mid-1820s, broad consensus on policy seemed to make procedural preferences largely immaterial. During and just after the Age of Jackson, policy preferences were more heterogeneous. But individuals' ideal points on important issues were not really organized into two clearly delineated party camps. As a result, members were uncertain about the policy consequences of pushing procedures in a restrictive or natural direction.

By the Civil War, the congressional party system resembled something close to the first condition and what we have recognized as commonplace for the past hundred years or so. Significant differences arose in the policy preferences of two dominant parties: By the 40th Congress (1867–69), differences in Democratic and Republican median first-dimension DW-NOMINATE scores resembled their levels in the partisan Congresses of the 2000s. The House parties were particularly cohesive immediately after the Civil War. The standard deviations of first-dimension DW-NOMINATE scores were frequently less than .1 for both parties, lower than they are today. Both bodies had few minor party members, although these numbers would be fairly large again in the 1880s and 1890s, particularly in the House. As Aldrich, Berger, and Rohde (2002) note, historically normal levels of conditional party government had been attained by the 1870s. Congressional party politics were characterized by the kind of interparty preference polarization and intraparty preference homogeneity that exists today.[22]

It is also difficult to make the case that the majority party controlled the floor agenda and floor proceedings of Congresses prior to the Civil War. The majority party did not always have a firm grip on key institutions that enabled it to exercise proposal and gatekeeping powers. It did not direct floor proceedings. The minority was not systematically excluded from influence over floor politics. Existing arrangements were not fully organized around the principle of party. The second of the conditions discussed earlier went unmet.

Not until after the Civil War and perhaps even 1900 did the House and Senate clearly become structured along the party lines we know today and procedural alterations come to be fought in the partisan fashion understood by congressional scholars. The 40th Congress (1867–69) is close to the beginning of what has been called the "third" or "Civil War" party system: the era in party politics brought about by a dramatic upheaval caused by slavery, sectionalism, and rebellion and to a lesser extent nativism and temperance (Burnham 1967; Key 1955; Sundquist 1983, 63–91). The 40th was also among the very first Congresses in which the majority party tightly and clearly controlled the selection of the Speaker and the composition of standing committees. As Stewart (1999, 49) writes, not until 1865 did the House settle on "a simple partisan organization of the body."

Prior to that time, members of the majority party frequently occupied formal positions of power and held a certain amount of control over the floor. But they clearly did not monopolize its agenda and tightly orchestrate its proceedings. Neither the selection nor behavior of chamber leaders and committees and their chairs was especially partisan.

The Antebellum Congressional Leadership

Today's speakership elections are essentially a two-part process. Each party internally selects a candidate and then, as its first order of business at the beginning of a Congress, the entire House votes almost cleanly along party lines. The process did not always take place this way. Stewart (2000, 8) argues that the 37th Congress (1861–63) represents the first of the current era, in which "control of the House has been effectively settled within the majority party prior to the House's convening."

In the antebellum House, members frequently voted for candidates of other parties, often by intentionally staying away from the caucus meetings at which a party pledged itself to a single candidate (Stewart 1999). Secret ballots, which existed until 1839, encouraged this behavior (Jenkins and Stewart 2003). On some occasions, more than one candidate from a single party ran. Fourteen of the 43 speakership elections before the 39th Congress (1865–67) took more than one ballot, including a contentious 22-ballot contest in 1820 that split Republicans along northern and southern lines and that eventually handed John W. Taylor (Rep-NY) the office; a chaotic 63-ballot, three-week process in 1849 that was characterized by numerous candidates and frequent vote switching by members; the 133-ballot marathon at the beginning of the 34th Congress (1855–57) that produced the only minor-party Speaker in American history, Nathaniel Banks of Massachusetts and the American Party; and the 1859 battle that consisted of 44 ballots in which the plurality Republicans were forced to jettison their first choice after 39 rounds and offer William Pennington (R-NJ), a freshman, who was eventually elected. On three occasions before 1861, the Speaker did not even come from the party that held the majority or plurality of seats: In 1795, Jonathan Dayton (Fed-NJ) was elected despite a Republican majority; in 1839, Robert M. T. Hunter (Whig-VA) was elected despite a Democratic majority; and in 1855, Banks received the body's nod.[23] As Young (1966, 120) writes, the early speakership contests were "repetitive, serious group bids for power *outside* a party system."

It also seems that prior to the 40th Congress, the Speaker frequently desired and was able to structure roll-call voting in a nonpartisan manner. This finding provides further evidence that although the speaker had power, speakership elections were not particularly about party. It also suggests that the speaker did not exercise his considerable powers in a particularly partisan fashion. Stewart (1999) has shown that for about two-thirds of the Congresses prior to the 37th (1861–63) the ideal point of the member who was the most frequent winner of roll calls was closer to the majority party median than the chamber median, providing evidence for the parties-as-cartels model of Cox and McCubbins (2005, 2007). But in a number of Congresses, Stewart (2000) also reveals a palpable "Speaker effect," or the ability of the coalition that supported the Speaker to change the voting behavior of its members beyond that which can be explained by party and member preferences. A Speaker effect is especially large in Congresses, such as the 30th (1847–49), 34th (1855–57), and 36th (1859–61), when the chamber's leader was elected after multiballot contests. Moreover, in every Congress but one between the 26th (1839–41) and 36th, even after controlling for party and preferences, supporters of the Speaker were on the winning side on roll calls more often than those who voted for the other candidates. The average size of this effect, at 5.3 percent when the average win rate was 62 percent, is not trivial (Stewart 2000).

Some observers have argued that a Speaker effect was present earlier, especially when the House was under the tutelage of Henry Clay (Rep-KY). Regardless of whether Clay was a critical agent and "great man" in the development of the House (Strahan 2002; 2007, 44–78; Strahan, Gunning, and Vining 2000) or a conduit through which the general membership's preferences were expressed (Jenkins and Stewart 2002; Stewart 2007), he did try to lead forcefully by stacking committees with members who held views close to his own and using his institutional position to forge majorities on policy issues, like the tariff and Missouri Compromise, that were important to him (Jenkins and Stewart 1998; Stewart 2007; Strahan 2002; 2007, 47–78; Strahan et al. 2000). As Gamm and Shepsle (1989) have written, the standing committee system that emerged in the House between 1811 and 1825 was, to some great extent, the product of Clay's attempt to control the House.

The selection of the Senate's presiding officer was also never a particularly partisan affair. Moreover, as I showed earlier in the chapter, the formal powers that came with the position did not provide the occupant with much authority. There were no formal party leaders and whips until just before World War I, so the vice president was not only the Senate's titular head but also ran the body. On the occasions when the vice president was absent, attending to executive responsibilities, the president pro tempore took over. This position was nearly always occupied by a member of the majority party, but the selected individual was not supposed to be partisan or ideological. As Senator George F. Hoar (R-MA) remarked in an 1886 debate over the president pro tem's role in presidential succession, the appointment was granted to a popular senior senator known "for his capacity as a debater and framer of legislation" (Erickson 2008, 57). Indeed, not until 1847 did the Senate assert that the vice president could not personally appoint his temporary replacement. Not until the 1880s did the Senate change its rules and state specifically that the body as a whole should choose its president pro tempore.

Committees in the Antebellum Congress

Party also does not seem to have been the main organizing principle when it came to the selection of officers for other institutions. Figure 3.4 reveals

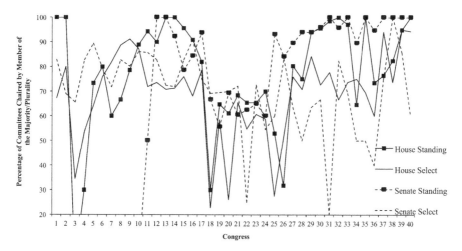

Fig. 3.4.   The percentage of committees chaired by a member of the majority/plurality party, 1st (1789–91) to 40th (1867–69) Congresses. (Data: author's calculations from Canon, Nelson, and Stewart 2002.)

the percentage of House and Senate select and standing committees that were chaired by a member of the majority or plurality party from the 1st through 40th Congresses. I use select committees because, at least before the 17th Congress (1821–23), the bodies consistently created a temporary or select committee to deal with individual pieces of legislation before it (Jenkins and Stewart 2002; Skladony 1985).[24] Issues were debated and general principles arrived at in the Committee of the Whole, then a select committee was appointed to shape these principles into a bill. The committees were forced to report, could make only minor changes in legislative language, and were dismissed as soon as their work was completed. Not all select committees were the same; the nature and importance of the legislation under consideration varied dramatically; some lived longer than the bills for which they were created; and some were referred more than one bill. I do not differentiate among select committees, however. In some circumstances, a member chaired a standing committee for only one session of the Congress. When this is the case and the position was divided among members of different parties, I split the observation accordingly.

Figure 3.5 shows the percentage of House and Senate standing and select committees in a Congress that had a majority of their members from the majority or plurality party. It is nearly identical to figure 3.4. In all cases

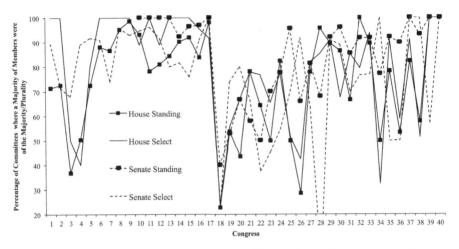

Fig. 3.5. The percentage of committees on which a majority of members were of the majority/plurality party, 1st (1789–91) to 40th (1867–69) Congresses. (Data: author's calculations from Canon, Nelson, and Stewart 2002.)

there are very few 100 percent scores. With the exception of the period before the 15th Congress (1817–19), when there were very few standing committees, the majority or plurality party monopolized chair positions on standing committees—that is, what always happens in the 20th and 21st centuries—only in the 32nd (1851–53) and 35th (1857–59) Congresses for the House and 31st (1849–51), 33rd (1853–55), 37th (1861–63), 39th (1865–67), and 40th (1867–69) Congresses for the Senate. The committee membership data also demonstrate that despite hefty majorities in both chambers between the 7th (1801–3) and 17th Congresses (1821–23), Jefferson's Republicans did not dominate committees the way governing parties do today. Indeed, not until the 39th Congress (1865–67) did the majority party systematically and consistently stack committees in both chambers with its members.

Both sets of data reveal three distinct periods. The first is prior to the 18th Congress (1823–25), the second between the 18th and the 26th (1839–41), and the third from the 27th (1841–43) to the 40th (1867–69). In the first and last periods, members of the majority or plurality party chaired a sizable proportion of standing and select committees. Members of this party tended to dominate committee rosters, too. In the middle period, majority or plurality party members chaired a much smaller number of standing committees and were less well represented on these panels.

Although members of the majority generally chaired standing and select committees up to the 18th Congress, it is difficult to make the case that
membership in the majority party was the critical determinant when deciding who should get these spots. The full Senate, not the parties, made
committee assignments during this period. In the House, a rule established
in the 8th Congress (1803–5) and renewed in the 9th (1805–7) and 10th
(1807–9) allowed standing committees to choose their own chairs if they
wished. As Cooper (1988, 40) notes, House committees took advantage of
this rule on only two occasions, but, as described earlier, speakers tended to
make appointments for reasons other than partisan fealty—perhaps partly
because they knew that committee members could influence the appointment process (Galloway 1976, 79). As for House select committees—of
which there were, with the exception of the 13th Congress (1813–15),
more than 100 per Congress before 1825—distributive and geographical
rather than partisan concerns seem to have motivated appointment procedures (Canon and Stewart 2001, 178). Many select committees dealt with
parochial issues such as local claims and petitions. In these cases, a disproportionately large number of chairs and members were from the same or a
neighboring state as the claimant or petitioner.

Perhaps more critically, the Republicans' general philosophy toward
standing committees attenuated partisan considerations. Jefferson's congressional allies believed in the sanctity of the Committee of the Whole
and argued that bills should initially be discussed there. They maintained
that when the Constitution "conferred certain powers and duties upon the
House of Representatives, it meant not a single member, nor a group of individuals, but the House itself, as an entity" (Harlow 1917, 211–12). This
view was reflected in the early legislative process. Bills were considered in-
choate law, and general principles were discussed on the House floor before going to committee. According to this philosophy, moreover, standing
committees were to be democratic and transparent and their membership
either expert or, if the jurisdiction was one of national policy, to consist of
at least one member from every state. In addition, the chair was to behave
as a moderator and be in favor of the bill (Cooper 1970, 22–23; Cooper
1988, 30–40). Since Republicans controlled both chambers for most of the
pre–1825 period, this philosophy assisted in arresting the development of
standing committees and prevented the majority party from exploiting
them for parliamentary advantage.[25]

Partisan affiliation was also unimportant to the appointment of rank
and file. In the earliest Congresses, House committees did not list mem-

bers by party, and Speakers generally picked committee members for reasons other than their party affiliation. Geographical diversity was among those reasons: only 22.5 percent of standing committees prior to the 20th Congress (1827–29) had more than one member from a single state.[26] As Alexander (1916, 67) writes of the original House committee appointment process, "Custom based on unwritten law obliged [Speakers] to recognize long service, peculiar fitness, party standing, and a fair division among States and important groups of men."

During the second period, 1825–41, standing and select committees were clearly not tools of the majority. Only for House standing committees in the 24th Congress (1835–37) and Senate standing committees in the 25th (1837–39) and 26th (1839–41) Congresses is the proportion of chairs from the majority or plurality party greater than 70 percent. The proportion of committees with most of their members from the majority or plurality party is greater than 80 percent in only one Congress for each body—the 24th for the House and the 25th for the Senate.

Many of these findings can no doubt be explained by the general consensus that pervaded the Era of Good Feelings and the resultant upheavals in the party system as old parties died and new ones were yet to mature. But the tremendous flux in the committee system probably played a significant role as well. In the 20th Congress (1827–29), the House employed only 23 select committees and had just about weaned itself off them. The House's fledgling standing committee system was getting to its feet—15 standing committees had been established over the previous decade—and the notion that committees could be quasi-permanent, deal with multiple bills, and have stable jurisdictions had just taken hold. Standing committees were forging links with their corresponding executive departments, and as interbranch consultation and executive agenda setting became routinized, so congressional business fractured along policy lines and the entrenchment of young committees deepened (Cooper 1970, 42–46). Jenkins and Stewart (2002) have made a series of arguments about what this transitional period meant for House procedures more generally, but it is clear that in the early years, governing parties did not exploit standing committees and their "antimajoritarian potential" (236). A similar story can be told about the Senate.

The third period, between the 27th (1841–43) and 40th Congresses (1867–69), had three important qualities, the last two of which were unique for the antebellum era. First, interparty policy differences widened to resemble those in the 1790s. Absolute differences in parties' median first dimension DW-NOMINATE scores increased in a roughly linear fashion—for the 20 years from the 26th Congress (1839–41) to the 36th (1859–61), they rose from .718 to .860 in the House and from .698 to .760 in the Senate—as an important underlying partisan difference on economic issues became apparent. By the 1850s, of course, slavery was the defining issue in congressional politics and, with the collapse of the Whigs and rise of the modern Republican Party, cleanly demarcated the two major parties (Poole and Rosenthal 1997, 91–100).

Second, interparty competition for control of the bodies became considerably more intense. With the exception of the 1st (1789–91), 2nd (1791–93), 5th (1797–99), and 6th (1799–1801) Congresses, supporters of Jefferson and Jackson—that is, members of the parties that became the Democrats—held majorities in the House continually through the 24th Congress (1835–37). For all of the post–1800 period, these majorities were quite large. Between the 26th (1839–41) and 40th (1867–69) Congresses, by contrast, party control of the chamber switched seven times, and in some Congresses—such as the 30th (1847–49), 31st (1849–51), 34th (1855–57), 36th (1859–61), and 38th (1863–65)—advantages were slim and often amounted to pluralities.

The pattern was less pronounced in the Senate. Federalists controlled the body exclusively until Jefferson's presidential inauguration in 1801. Jefferson's and Jackson's opponents subsequently held the Senate for only one Congress before 1842—the 23rd (1833–35). From the 26th to 40th Congresses, the upper chamber turned over just three times, and majorities—Democrats mainly until 1861, Republicans thereafter—remained quite healthy. Still, at least in the context of antebellum Senate history, this later period saw some volatility.

Third, whereas the previous 15 or so years had seen great upheavals in the standing committee system, the two decades or so prior to the Civil War marked a period of stability and entrenchment crucial to the establishment and legitimization of committee influence. The number of standing committees in the House remained at 34, basically unchanged between the 28th (1843–45) and 38th (1863–65) Congresses. By the 36th Congress (1859–61), House committees were appointed for the whole Congress, not just for a session. The average size of committees dropped slightly from 7.7 to 7.5 members during this period. Committee positions were, in turn, quite scarce—the aggregate number barely exceeded the total number of House members throughout the period—and important committees came with considerable prestige. Legislators responded by affixing value to committee slots. Jenkins (1998) has shown that Henry Clay's speakership was instrumental in creating a culture in which members viewed their positions on standing committees as "property rights" worthy of protection.[27]

Committee politics settled down in the Senate as well. Parties received the power to make appointments in 1846, even though their choices still required ratification by the full body. The Senate witnessed a net loss of just 2 standing committees in the two decades between the 28th and 38th Congresses, reducing the number of committees from 24 to 22. The average size of a Senate standing committee grew gradually from 4.8 to 6.2.

The stability of the period allowed for the anchoring of jurisdictions. Statutory jurisdictions at this time were incomplete, ambiguous, and of little importance because bills were referred to committees on motions from the floor. The fixedness of the standing committee system, however, facilitated the creation of "common law" jurisdictions—that is, jurisdiction by the precedent of previous referrals (King 1997, 34–41). Without the creation or abolition of many committees in the 1840–60 period, existing statutory jurisdictions stagnated, allowing common law to mature undisturbed. Although in the House there were occasions on which the referral of bills to committees was vigorously debated, the process was for the most part routine, uncontroversial, and consistent with precedent (King 1997, 91–92).

House committees slowly but surely began to acquire the power to report at all times. The Committee on Enrolled Bills was granted this authority in 1822, while the Engraving and Printing Committee received it in the 1840s. According to McConachie (1898, 174), other committees "occasionally exercised the privilege prior to 1850." Because of its limited application, this development is not of substantive significance. But it does illustrate the enhanced role of standing committees in the House during this third antebellum period.

More important, in 1837 the House changed its rules to alter bill introduction procedures, enabling individuals to introduce bills by requesting leave or permission to do so by motion (Cooper and Young 1989). As a practical matter, the rules change was used by standing committees to report bills on their own authority (Cooper and Young 1989).[28] The modern process in which committees filtered bills before they reached the floor was becoming apparent.

In the antebellum era, then, members were assigned to committees based largely on their expertise, the location of their district or state, and, toward the end of this period at least, whether they had served on the committee in the previous Congress. The standing committee system slowly began to mature and take on many of the characteristics it exhibits today, but committee majorities and chairs were not always from the majority or plurality party. In the Senate, leaders were not selected by members, and in the House, speakership elections were not always mundane party-line affairs. Once in office, moreover, leaders frequently used their institutional powers to further their own, not necessarily their party's, policy interests. Considerable evidence buttresses Stewart's (1999, 6) argument that before the Civil War, the parties "failed to formally control the comprehensive organization of the House." Such was also surely the case in the Senate. The second condition necessary for the majority party to quite unequivocally desire the body to move in a restrictive direction—the condition that it controls the floor agenda and floor proceedings—was not really present until the Civil War at the very earliest.

A Few Words on the House Floor of the Late 1800s

The analyses in chapters 2 and 3 suggest that majority party strength began to explain procedural change in the House on a consistent basis sometime between the Civil War and 1900. At some point in this period, party became the link between members' policy and procedural preferences. I am not particularly interested in nailing down the precise date that this fully developed, but two important procedural changes occurred in the last 20 years of the 19th century that placed control of the House's floor agenda and proceedings tightly in the hands of the majority party: the use of special rules issued by the Rules Committee and the adoption of Reed's Rules. From then on, procedural change would be clearly driven by partisan power struggles more than anything else. Cox and McCubbins (2005, 50–86) discuss the "primacy of Reed's rules" and argue that at this time, the House moved from a system in which the minority could block the agenda to a system involving a "procedural cartel" in which the majority monopolized it. Binder (2007) states that Reed's Rules established the "core partisan procedural regime" of the House that exists to this day.

The two developments only widened the existing procedural differences between the House and Senate. By the Civil War, members of the House, especially those in its majority, may not have fully understood or exploited existing rules to illuminate brightly the procedures that differentiated their body from the Senate, but such distinctions were plainly present. The two chambers had essentially parted ways, and their respective procedural paths were largely irreversible. By 1900 certainly, there was no going back. The House would be the more restrictive body; the Senate would remain more natural.

The Special Rules of the Rules Committee

As chapter 2 discusses, the special rule is a commonly used procedure by which bills are called up for floor debate out of their order on the calendars of the House. If adopted, the rule essentially determines how the bill will be treated on the floor. Until the 1880s, special orders, as they were known originally, could be approved only by unanimous consent or under suspension of the rules, a mechanism that required a two-thirds vote for approval. Moreover, the Rules Committee was thought to be charged solely with reporting new or revised standing rules. In 1883, Representative Thomas Brackett Reed (R-ME) called up, as a privileged question, a resolution reported by the Rules Committee declaring a disagreement with the Senate on a Republican-backed but minority-blocked tax bill and, as a consequence, a desire to go to conference (Alexander 1916, 202–4; Hinds 1907, sec. 3160, 194–95; J. M. Roberts 2010, 309–11). Democrats were outraged and protested Reed's action, arguing that the resolution was unrelated to the standing rules of the House and therefore that the committee had no authority to do such a thing. Speaker J. Warren Kiefer (R-OH) responded that he believed the resolution created a special rule that, although temporary and specific to the bill at hand, was no less a rule than a standing one. The Democrats submitted an appeal, but the House approved a motion to table it.[29]

Kiefer's decision created a significant precedent. The Rules Committee, which had only been promoted to standing status in 1880, became a filtering device for legislative business as it flowed from committee to floor. In 1886, the presiding officer ruled that the committee could take a bill from the calendar and give it a special order at a future date, hence enabling the committee to arrange the floor's business. The following year, it was ruled that all special orders had to go through the committee. By 1890, "Rules had been transformed, from a committee entitled only to propose general rules, to a committee entitled to propose special rules that would govern the order in which bills would be taken from the calendars (or sent to conference) and that could be adopted by simple majority vote" (Cox and McCubbins 2005, 58). Because special rules required only the approval of a simple majority, the governing party had effectively obtained even greater capacity to control the floor agenda. Coordination of Rules Committee and majority party strategies and preferences was largely assured by the fact that since 1858, the panel had been chaired by the Speaker.

These developments had partisan ramifications. They also seem to have had partisan causes. Because the initial use of special rules did not constitute a change in the chambers' formal rules, it does not make the list of changes in table 2.1. It does, however, make Cox and McCubbins's list and Schickler's list. For the 47th Congress (1881–83)—that is, the one in which special rules were born—a simple logit model of the Cox and McCubbins data containing just the ideological power balance variable provides a predicted probability of a restriction of the rules of 31.4 percent, while a change-in-workload-only variable provides a predicted probably of restriction of 23.0 percent; the mean is 25.5 percent. The predicted probabilities for the same outcome in the same Congress using the Schickler data are 45.7 percent and 31.3 percent, respectively, with a mean of 32.3 percent. From any perspective, it is very difficult to make a workload argument for the creation of special rules. Even the raw workload variable does not really increase prior to the 47th Congress.

The results of the quantitative analyses also complicate the case for chamber size. Still, the advent of special rules occurs in the Congress immediately prior to reapportionment. Members were presumably aware that the House, as was customary throughout the 19th century after a census, would grow. In the following Congress, 32 new seats were added, an 11 percent increase.

Reed's Rules

Cox and McCubbins (2005, 65) call Reed's Rules "the primary watershed in postbellum House organizational history." The story of the establishment of the rules in 1890 is a familiar one. At the beginning of the 51st Congress (1889–91), Speaker Thomas Bracket Reed, when considering Democratic objections to a Republican motion calling up a disputed election case from West Virginia, determined that nonvoting members were present. A quorum thus existed, and the Republicans could defeat the objection. Democrats had counted on the fact that by not voting, they could use the "disappearing quorum" device to block the motion. After Reed's ruling and despite an uproar from the minority Democrats, the disappearing quorum, an effective tool of obstruction, was dead. Its prohibition was put into the House's standing rules just under two weeks later.

The day after his ruling, Reed refused to hear any more appeals of his decision on the grounds that the House had definitively decided the question. He then told the body that he would not recognize any member rising to make a dilatory motion. The power of the Speaker to do so was incorporated formally into the chamber's rules at the same time as the disappearing quorum ban.

These changes greatly and permanently enhanced the Speaker's control over the conduct of floor debate.[30] The changes were, therefore, a tremendous boon for the majority.[31] After the adoption of Reed's Rules, Cox and McCubbins (2005, 65–73) have shown that policy outcomes in the House moved markedly in the direction of the majority party's preferences and that the minority party's roll rate—that is, the proportion of times a majority of members of the minority were on the losing side on a vote—increased.

Like the advent of special rules, moreover, Reed's Rules seem to have been the product of partisan politics, policy preferences, and the majority's procedural engineering (Den Hartog 2004). Indeed, the predicted probabilities of a restrictive rule being adopted in the 51st Congress for a change-in-ideological-power-balance-only model using the Cox and Mc-Cubbins and Schickler dependent variables are 32.1 percent and 47.2 percent, respectively. These numbers are much higher than for change-in-workload-only and change-in-size-only models.

However, Schickler (2001, 32–43) has suggested that Reed's Rules came about for reasons other than a strong majority party. He argues that the Republican majority was quite fractured, especially on the tariff, and Reed cleverly pulled members together to support these critical procedural changes by introducing his reforms on a disputed election case, an issue that generally stoked partisan ire and one that was taken up just before the House attended to its routine beginning-of-Congress evaluation of standing rules.

Schickler also argues that members were feeling the pressure of burgeoning workloads. In 1888 and 1889, for example, newspapers all over the country assaulted the House for failing to attend to national problems and blamed the rules that frequently tied it in knots (Schickler 2001, 36). Indeed, the raw measure I use to calculate the change in workload variable picks up palpably in the 50th Congress (1887–89), reaching its highest level to that point. In addition, and as Forgette (1997) and Peters (1997, 69) have argued, the House in the 51st Congress (1889–91) had a very large agenda—including the election's "force" bill, the Oklahoma Territories Act, the Sherman Antitrust Act, the McKinley Tariff, and the Sherman

Silver Purchase Act. It passed this legislation in large part because of the reforms instigated by Reed.

It is feasible that size was influential as well. The 51st Congress, like the 47th, was close to a reapportionment and scheduled expansion of the House. Between the 52nd (1891–93) and 53rd (1893–95) Congresses, the House grew by 24 members (7 percent).

Still, it is difficult to argue that the formal adoption of Reed's Rules was not explained largely by partisanship. The sectional and policy squabbling within the Republican majority may have made party members look quite heterogeneous, but Reed seems to have forced them to recognize the connection between procedural reform and their policy interests. Moreover, standard deviations of first-dimension DW-NOMINATE scores show the House Republicans of the era to have been more cohesive than their Democratic opponents and about as homogenous as any House party had been up to that time.[32]

Conclusion

This chapter fleshes out many of the findings presented in chapter 2. I have provided evidence that the causes of intercameral differences in specific individual procedures are consistent with those that explain variation in general procedural character. I have proposed an explanation of why measures of majority party strength explain procedural change in the 20th century but not in the 19th, or at least not before the Civil War. Whereas the House and Senate majority parties today have clear and formal control of the floor's agenda and proceedings, such was not the case in the antebellum Congress. The bodies' leaders were not selected in partisan elections and did not behave single-mindedly to further their parties' interests. Committees were frequently chaired by members of minority parties. Committee chairs affiliated with the majority often seemed to receive little direction from their party. Members of the chamber's majority often found themselves in select and standing committee minorities.

As a result, members' procedural preferences—or whether they would like to see the parent body move in a restrictive or natural direction—did not follow the partisan patterns we see so vividly today. Members of the majority did not reflexively favor restriction, even when the party was strong. Members of the minority did not always assume that naturalization would be good for them. Individual legislators were often uncertain about the potential effects of proposed procedural change on their personal policy and electoral interests, at least beyond the issue immediately at hand. Procedural alteration therefore came about when exogenous factors forced both those who largely controlled floor politics and those who did not to agree that restriction was required.

These factors included significant increases in the size of the body's membership and workload. The Senate responded in the same way the House did—and with regard to membership growth, it did so particularly when the body expanded above 70 members. But it just did not evolve like the lower body. The House grew by nearly 3.75 times from the 1st (1789–91) to the 39th (1865–67) Congresses, reaching 243 members; the Senate grew at a much lower rate, 2.08 times. By 1910, the House had reached 435 members and essentially stopped growing; it was 6.7 times bigger than it was in 1789. But the Senate was only 3.5 times larger in 1910 than when the 1st Congress met. The Senate also faced lighter workload demands. The House initiated legislation for the first 40 years of the Republic. The Senate's mean per-Congress increase in workload is lower than the House's in the antebellum era.

Because most of the critical procedural differences between the House and the Senate occurred prior to the Civil war and essentially all of them were in place by 1900, we can make a strong case that the bodies differ because of their respective sizes and workloads. The chapter reveals how a more rapidly growing membership and business load help explain why the House adopted certain important restrictive procedures that the Senate did not adopt. The House's adoption of the previous question in 1811 seems to be an exception, a rare moment of policy and procedural partisanship.

The House Rules Committee's authority to promulgate special rules and the body's abolition of the disappearing quorum and dilatory motion also had partisan roots. By then, the cleavages on procedural and policy preferences were falling along the same plane. The very different procedural trajectories of the House and Senate were also fixed.

The House and Senate have very different procedures, and their members engage in very different practices. The Senate is a perceptibly more natural body; its floor is more powerful in its legislative process, and senators clearly have stronger floor rights than their colleagues in the lower chamber. The House has more restrictive procedures. The determinants of these differences have been the focus of this first part of the book.

I have tested three hypotheses about what causes these differences. Analyses of the history of House and Senate procedures and practices reveal evidence consistent with all of these expectations. When memberships and workloads grow and majority parties get stronger, both the House and Senate tend to move in a more restrictive direction. I also show that electoral shocks, particularly in the form of member turnover, have pronounced effects on procedures and practices.

Prior to the Civil War, the House's more rapidly growing membership and workload pressured members as a class to create procedures that weakened the floor and floor rights. Members' policy preferences did not generally explain change because they were not fused with procedural preferences. Members were unsure of how procedural alteration would affect their policy and electoral interests. A burgeoning membership and greater societal demands forced the House to adopt more restrictive procedures so that it would continue to function effectively. Organized opposition to this decision was diluted, and those with little influence over the floor agenda and its proceedings withheld resistance. Under these conditions at least, they believed that restriction was consistent with their personal goals.

Between 1865 and 1900, parties coupled members' policy and procedural preferences. Not only did the Democrats and Republicans have distinct policy positions, but members of the majority party began to realize that weakening the floor and the rights of members on it expedited the transformation of their positions into law and furthered their collective electoral interests. As a result, when the majority party strengthened—it grew in size, became more ideologically homogenous relative to the minority, and found itself closer to the chamber median—it tended to push for restrictive procedures and exercise restrictive practices. These efforts frequently succeeded.

This story is critical to an understanding of intercameral procedural differences. By 1865, the rules that differentiate the two chambers today, with the important exceptions of Reed's Rules and the establishment of special rules in the House and Rule XXII in the Senate—a reform that moved the upper chamber in a restrictive direction and therefore toward the House anyway—were solidly in place. The effect of a growing antebellum membership and workload was to forge a House that was procedurally distinct from the Senate, a body that was not exposed as much to these pressures.

Change since that time has been considerably less dramatic. The two chambers' procedural trajectories have been heavily constrained by their pre-1900 choices. I have suggested what other scholars show more definitively (Binder 1997; Binder and Smith 1997; J. M. Roberts and Smith

2007): that these trajectories have been path-dependent.[33] By 1865, the House had a previous question motion, whereas the Senate did not. The House had a germaneness provision for floor amendments; the Senate did not. The House had a stronger presiding officer and more vigorously protected the prerogatives of its committees. No amount of majority or minority party strength could overcome these basic procedural characteristics. Most procedural change in the 20th century concerned issues that do little to move the chambers very far along the natural-to-restrictive continuums. In the House, for example, numerous battles have taken place over the number of signatures required for a discharge petition. In the Senate, members have fought over the precise size of the supermajority of votes needed to invoke cloture.

Having addressed the issue of intercameral differences in procedures and practices that affect the floor in Congress, I now turn to floor proceedings themselves. Motivated by a belief that what happens on the House and Senate floors is vital to a healthy legislature, chapters 4 and 5 test two pieces of conventional wisdom on the subject.

PART II

Floor Proceedings

4 · The Quality of Floor Proceedings I

Concepts, Measures, and Data

"And now, Mr. President, instead of speaking of the possibility
or utility of succession, instead of dwelling in these caverns of
darkness, instead of groping with those ideas so full of all that is
horrid and horrible, let us come out into the light of day; let us
enjoy the fresh air of liberty and Union; let us cherish those
hopes which belong to us; let us devote ourselves to those great
objects that are fit for our consideration and our action; let us
raise our conceptions to the magnitude and importance of the
duties that devolve upon us; let our comprehension be as broad
as the country for which we act; our aspirations as high as its
certain destiny; let us not be pigmies in a case that calls for
men. Never did there devolve, on any generation of men,
higher trusts than now devolve upon us for the preservation of
this Constitution, and the harmony and peace of all who are
destined to live under it. Let us make our generation one of the
strongest, and the golden chain which is destined, I fully
believe, to grapple the people of all the states to this
Constitution for ages to come."

—DANIEL WEBSTER to the U.S. Senate, March 7, 1850

"You stand there and say we are increasing spending, but we are
cutting spending. I do not know whether you cannot add or
subtract. I do not know what your problem is. But I can tell you
this, and you can be cute, you can be smart, and you may even
pull this off son, but I can tell you one thing, you are young
enough, you are going to have to live with it. You are putting a
tax on the next generation that they cannot pay and they cannot
repeal it, and you are going to have to live with it.

Do not ask for my time because I will not yield.

I can tell you this: you are going to suffer the consequences just like everybody else in the next generation and those to come thereafter. And I cannot believe you have the audacity to come to this floor with this assault on women and children and try to portray it, as this other Howdy Doody–looking nimrod said, that he wanted to talk about family values and values. That is unprecedented in this House."

—MARION BERRY to the U.S. House of Representatives, November 17, 2005

These two passages are representative of popular impressions about the quality of floor proceedings in Congress. The first, part of revered orator and lawyer Daniel Webster's (Whig-MA) famous speech on the Constitution and the Union, is eloquent and melodic, although it may not have been made quite as it was recorded. It is about issues fundamental to the country. The speech was delivered in an era renowned for its floor debates and in the prestigious upper chamber, where statesmen carefully deliberated on the important topics of the day. It surely exemplifies what *should* happen on the floor. The man who delivered the second speech, Arkansas Democrat Marion Berry, also is no intellectual slouch. He was a special assistant to President Bill Clinton on domestic policy and at the time was in his fifth term in the U.S. House. Like the first, this segment is about an important—if not quite as important—issue, the size of the federal government. But the passage is indelicate and grating, reflecting an era of partisan rancor and petty attacks and a chamber inhabited by unexceptional politicians unaccustomed to weighty discourse. It strikes us intuitively as an example of poor floor proceedings.

These passages, in other words, communicate two stylized and common notions that we can form into working hypotheses. The first is that floor proceedings are better in the Senate than in the House (the *Senate-superior* hypothesis). The second is that floor proceedings used to be better than they are now—or, more precisely, that they have generally deteriorated over time (the *worsen-over-time* hypothesis). In this and the following chapter, I test these hypotheses empirically, systematically, and quantitatively.

I am thus embarking upon a journey into relatively unexplored territory. Only a few studies of the content of floor proceedings in Congress have been conducted. Taylor and Rourke (1995), for example, analyze the use of Munich agreement and Vietnam War analogies in the Gulf War debates of 1991. Niven (1996) also evaluates debate prior to this conflict. These studies provide rigorous analyses of just a single case, however. Strahan, Gunning, and Vining (2006) thoroughly examine the floor contributions of just a single member—the Speaker of the House. Other scholars have undertaken more systematic studies of congressional floor proceedings. Hill and Hurley's (2002) study of symbolic Senate speeches; Lehnan's (1967) examination of 51 Senate bills in 1961; and Harris's (2005), Maltzman and Sigelman's (1996), Morris's (2001), and Rocca's (2007) examinations of one-minute and special-order speeches in the House are good examples. But these scholars are largely interested in why members participate rather than in the substance of the proceedings.

More normative analyses of floor debate are, conversely, largely theoretical (Lascher 1996) and, when empirical, not particularly systematic or comprehensive. Bessette (1994), for example, qualitatively analyzes 29 case studies of bills between 1946 and 1970. Steiner et al. (2004), in what is largely a comparative study of national legislatures, look at debates on crime, minimum wage, and partial-birth abortion from the late 1980s until the mid-1990s. Connor and Oppenheimer (1993) examine deliberation in just three Congresses. Mucciaroni and Quirk (2006) look at debates on three bills in the 1990s—welfare reform, estate tax repeal, and telecommunications deregulation. Wirls (2007) examines four debates in the 19th-century House and Senate—those on the Missouri Compromise, the Gag Rule that suppressed resolutions about slavery, the declaration of war with Mexico, and the Kansas-Nebraska Act. One project uses computer programs to analyze the frequency and use of words in the *Congressional Record* (see, for example, Quinn et al. 2010). It will have many applications in legislative studies and can be used for extensive systematic study of floor debate. As of now, however, it remains in its infancy.

The Senate-Superior and Worsen-over-Time Hypotheses

Whence do the impressions that help form these hypotheses come? After all, both chambers have a colorful and rich history of churlish argument and even bloody brawls—that is, one assumes, bad floor proceedings. As early as 1798, a beating occurred on the House floor when Representative Roger Griswold (Fed-CT) responded to being spat on by Representative Matthew Lyon (Rep-VT) by hitting him repeatedly with a cane. In 1856, there was the famous incident in which Representative Preston Brooks (D-SC) stormed into the Senate chamber and bludgeoned antislavery Senator Charles Sumner (R-MA) after Sumner had insulted Senator Andrew Butler (D-SC), a relative of Brooks. South Carolina's Democrats were at it again in 1902 when the state's senior senator, "Pitchfork" Ben Tillman, punched his junior colleague, John McLaurin, in the face after McLaurin had accused Tillman of lying. This incident led directly to Rule XIX, which limits what senators can say about one another. A general melee broke out on the House floor in September 1841 after President John Tyler vetoed a bank bill. The next year, Representative Laurence M. Keitt (D-SC) initiated a scuffle between dozens of members as they debated Kansas's admission into the Union. In 1850, Senator Henry Foote (D-MS) drew a pistol as Senator Thomas Hart Benton (D-MO) approached. Much of the boisterousness of the mid-19th century was probably fueled by snuff and switchel—a mix of molasses, ginger, water, and Jamaica rum that many members imbibed on the floor (Moore 1895, 253). According to Alexander (1916, 265), "Before the Civil War it was not unusual for members to bear concealed weapons," so disputes on the floor were often taken outside. Floor incidents prompted some famous duels, including an 1838 skirmish between representatives Jonathan Cilley (D-ME) and William Graves (Whig-KY) that cost Cilley his life.[1]

But considerable anecdotal evidence is consistent with my hypotheses. Observers of Congress have noted intercameral differences in the quality of floor proceedings for many years. Indeed, as historian Joseph West Moore (1895, 143) shows in quoting a 1791 Philadelphia newspaper, the dissimilitude was on display as early as the 1st Congress: "Among the Senators is observed constantly during the debates the most delightful silence, the most beautiful order, gravity and personal dignity of manner. . . . The Senators, in their courtesy present a most striking contrast to the independent loquacity of the Representatives below stairs, most of whom persist in wearing, while in their seats and during debates, their ample cocked hats, placed 'fore and aft' upon their heads." William Maclay, a great observer of the inaugural Congress, agreed (Freeman 2004). The difference continued to be seen in the Jacksonian period. Alexis de Tocqueville (2004, 229) reported in the 1830s that "when you enter the chamber of the House of Representatives in Washington, you are struck by the vulgar appearance of that 'august' assembly. . . . In a country where education is almost universal, it is said that not all of the people's representatives are capable of writing correctly." By contrast, "among the senators," Tocqueville wrote, "are eloquent attorneys, distinguished generals, clever magistrates, and well-known statesmen. Every word uttered in this assembly would do honor to Europe's greatest parliamentary debates" (229).[2]

Tocqueville may have been writing at a time when the Senate was held in its greatest esteem. This was, after all, the Golden Age, an era when the institution, informally led by the Great Triumvirate of John C. Calhoun (D/Nullifier-SC), Henry Clay (Whig-KY) and Daniel Webster (Fed/Adams/Anti-Jackson/Whig-MA), consummated "the Whig ideal of a great deliberative body, at once solid and brilliant, dedicated to preserving liberty and self-government from tyrannical executive power" (Peterson 1987, 234–35). But a higher level of proceeding in the upper chamber has been detected in other periods as well. Historian Alvin M. Josephy Jr. (1979, 234–35) did not think much of the Senate's proceedings in the Gilded Age but found them markedly better than those conducted in the House, where "members visited with each other, walked around aimlessly, read newspapers, puffed on cigars, slammed their desk lids, shouted for pages, cleared their throats nosily, spat at pink and gold china spittoons, and called out to each other while one or two Representatives tried to carry on debate above the din and confusion."

Bicameral differences seem to be on display today. Systematically examining a series of floor debates on crime, minimum wage, and partial-birth abortion bills from the late 1980s through the mid-1990s, Steiner et al. (2004, 125–28) provide some harder evidence for greater deliberation in the Senate. They also show that greater civility exists in the Senate's proceedings. Ornstein (2000) confirms this view in his analysis of the Clinton impeachment process, and Froman (1967, 7) writes that the most marked difference between the two chambers is "the apparent confusion and impersonality in the House chamber contrasted with the relatively more informal and friendly atmosphere in the Senate." Mucciaroni and Quirk (2006) argue that debates in the Senate generally represent an improvement on those in the House because speakers in the upper chamber better substantiate their claims and more frequently find their unsubstantiated charges rebutted. The Senate is, after all, still popularly known as the world's greatest deliberative body.

If anything, a more thorough reading of congressional history furnishes even more evidence, anecdotal again though it may be, for the worsen-over-time hypothesis. By way of example, many congressional scholars' personal who's whos of the ten greatest debaters might include Representative/Senator John Quincy Adams (Fed-MA), Senator Thomas Hart Benton (D-MO), Calhoun, Clay, Representative/Senator Stephen Douglas (D-IL), Senator Robert Young Hayne (Jackson/Nullifier-SC), Representative/Senator Robert La Follette (R-WI), Representative/Senator Henry Cabot Lodge (R-MA), Representative Thaddeus Stevens (Whig/R-PA), and Webster. Not only is this list extremely heavy with senators, it is made up almost exclusively of members from the early to mid-19th century. To be sure, Representative/Senator James G. Blaine (R-ME), Representative Joe Cannon (R-IL), Representative Newt Gingrich (R-GA), Representative/Senator Lyndon B. Johnson (D-TX), Representative Sam Rayburn (D-TX), Representative Thomas Brackett Reed (R-ME), and Senator Robert Taft (R-OH) would be high on anyone's ranking of all-time great members. But these individuals are generally remembered as policymakers, power wielders, and superior strategists rather than wonderful orators and brilliant debaters.

In a similarly unscientific way, congressional historian Robert Luce (1922, 303–29) sketched out a story of general decline in congressional oratory. Senator Robert Byrd's (D-WV) (1994) listing of great post-1833 Senate speeches made on the floor consists of 19 from the 67 available years of the 19th century and only 16 from the 94 available years of the 20th—and 4 in the latter category are by Byrd himself.[3]

The early to mid-19th century congressional galleries were often full of spectators eager to see skillful debate. This was the "Golden Age of American Oratory" (Parker 1857). In the words of one historian, "Men and women flocked to the Capitol to hear [Clay, Webster, and Calhoun]; all across the country their speeches were read as if the fate of the nation hung on them" (Peterson 1987, 234). After the Civil War, however, observers began to criticize what they witnessed on the House and Senate floors, despite the redesign of the House chamber during the 35th Congress (1857–59) to replace the desks with benches so that members would sit close to one another and "perforce participate more generally in the discussions and proceedings of the House" (Fuller 1909, 134). James Parton observed in 1870 that "not more than one speech in five was written out and read" fifteen years earlier, "but now four in five are" (Luce 1922, 245–48). Woodrow Wilson (1981, 69) noted rather sarcastically that House members displayed an "entire absence of the instinct of debate" and an "apparent unfamiliarity with the idea of combating a proposition by argument." The future president lamented that the House floor had delegated meaningful debate to its committees. Writing just before the United States entered World War I, famous House historian De Alva Stanwood

Alexander (1916, 289) noted that debate in the lower chamber was frequently "dreary" as speeches were too often "recited from memory or read from manuscript in a monotonous tone." He added, "One set speech follows another and, although recognition alternates from one side to the other, the answering speech seldom bears directly on the points of the preceding speaker."

Moments of great debate have occurred since the Civil War, of course. In 1910, the *Nation* (1910, 155) observed that "when large matters are up and free play is given to intellect, there is as much [quality debate] available in Congress as in any place we know." George Rothwell Brown (1922, 282) argued that "one finds nothing in the great discussions over slavery and succession exceeding in power and majesty the debates of the Senate at the close of" World War I. The general feeling, however, is that the quality of debate has gone and continues to go downhill. By the 1920s, Luce (1922, 254–55) was criticizing the paltry attendance on the floor. Today, members seem to spend even less time there. The House and Senate chambers are nearly always empty with the exception of presiding officers, floor managers, and those actually speaking. Journalist George Packer (2010, 39) has called the Senate chamber "an ornate room where men and women go to talk to themselves for the record." Proceedings are characterized by a series of addresses read by members from "one-pagers" or a list of "talking points" provided by staffers. While on the floor, members do not listen to one another but instead are working on their own speeches or communicating electronically with their offices. Debate is compartmentalized, as its managers distribute small speaking slots to colleagues.[4]

All in all, Mucciaroni and Quirk (2006, 181) conclude that contemporary congressional floor debate is "somewhat disappointing." In the House, floor time has also been set aside for special order and one-minute speeches that allow members to talk on topics of their choosing—including "Twinkle Twinkle Kenneth Starr," a ditty about the independent counsel written and performed by Representative Michael Pappas (R-NJ) in July 1998.[5] There is, as a result, very little interaction and deliberation. As characterized by journalist Ronald Elving (1993), contemporary floor proceedings "compose a picture of inactivity, disorganization and delay—with intermittent outbreaks of rancor and rhetoric leading to interminable votes on incomprehensible motions." To former House majority leader Richard Gephardt (D-MO), floor proceedings are fractured into "small units of time in which statements are read and no real debate or dialogue occurs" (Joint Committee 1993a, 2:36). For Mann and Ornstein (1992, 49), general debate in the House "has become a time of reading prepared statements by the floor managers and is widely considered a filler time between adoption of the rule and voting on amendments during which members can leave the floor for other activities." Representative Bill Thomas's (R-CA) remarks during the House's discussions on the North American Free Trade Agreement in the early 1990s nicely describe another quality of contemporary floor debate: "Bear with us folks. We have only about two hours to go. Everything that needs to be said has been said just not everybody has had a chance to say it" (*Congressional Record*, November 17, 1993, H9999). Whatever constitutes good proceedings, this is not it.

Similar criticisms are leveled at the upper chamber. As former senator Nancy Landon Kassebaum (R-KS) (1988) has put it, in the Senate "serious policy deliberations are a rarity" and " 'great debate' is only a memory." Instead, she notes, "Floor debate has deteriorated into a never-ending series of points of order, procedural motions, appeals and waiver votes, punctuated by endless hours of time-killing quorum calls." Senator Robert Byrd (D-WV) proclaimed in the 1990s, "Senate debate is dying as a legislative art" (Senate Rules Committee 1993, 6). Senators, he argued, no longer "perceive that time spent on the Senate floor, debating the issues of the day, as the best way in which to use their always-limited time." Even the upper chamber's discussion about the 1991 Gulf War, a supposed paragon of congressional debate, was not, in the words of Senate historian Donald Ritchie, "a debate per se." On the contrary, Ritchie argues, it was "a series of speeches" (Victor 2004).

There is also a pervasive sense that today's congressional debate is not only vacuous but often uncivil. Recent episodes, such as Representative Randy Neugebauer's (R-TX) "baby killer" comment made as Representative Bart Stupak (D-MI) discussed the health care reform bill on the House floor in March 2010, reinforce this notion. It is also the conclusion of a series of recent academic and journalistic studies of deliberation in Congress. Observers such as Ahuja (2008) and Eilperin (2006) have provided numerous examples of unsavory language uttered and personal attacks unleashed on the floors of the Senate and particularly the House. These accounts tend to blame heightened partisanship.

The two hypotheses have strong theoretical foundations. The proposition that the Senate enjoys floor proceedings of greater quality than does the House is the product of a number of formal intercameral differences derived from the Constitution. The first of these is size. Larger bodies are not predisposed to good floor proceedings because they require procedures that, among other things, constrain speaking time. The 435-member lower chamber cannot afford lengthy deliberation and full participation in floor debate because with them it would reach gridlock and be unable to pass bills. In the words of Framer James Wilson, procedural imperatives mean that smaller chambers are "fittest for deliberation," more numerous ones "for decision" (Farrand 1966, 1:544).

Along similar lines, James Madison wrote in Federalist 55, "In all very numerous assemblies, of whatever characters composed, passion never fails to wrest the scepter from reason" (Hamilton, Madison, and Jay 1961, 342). This loss of reason—a critical element of healthy proceedings, according to the Framers—occurs because, Madison continued in Federalist 58, the bigger the assembly, "the greater will be the proportion of members of limited information and of weak capacities" and the more likely "ignorance will be the dupe of cunning, and passion the slave of sophistry and declamation" (360). A breakdown in order and civility led newspapers to characterize the House of the 27th Congress (1841–43) as a "bear garden" and the Whig-led Congress to pass the 1842 Apportionment Act that reduced the size of the lower chamber from 242 to 223 (Shields 1985).

Second, related to Madison's point, senators and the manner in which they are selected provide the body with more distinguished members capable of superior proceedings. Such was especially the case before 1913, when the 17th Amendment was ratified. State legislators rather than the uninformed and passionate public elected senators. The minimum requirements that members be thirty years old and nine years a citizen ensured that in the early days senators, at least according to Madison in Federalist 62, had a "greater extent of information and stability of character" than their colleagues in the House (Hamilton, Madison, and Jay 1961, 376). But even today, the case can be made that senators are better equipped for floor proceedings of a higher level. The Senate is a more prestigious body, and many members of the lower chamber aspire to join the upper house: Thomas Hart Benton believed the Senate to be "composed of the pick of the House of Representatives, and thereby gains doubly—by brilliant accession to itself and abstraction from the other" (Haynes 1938, 2:1002).

Members' six-year terms are a third reason to believe that the Senate has superior floor proceedings. Lengthy terms were established to furnish senators with the critical experience and knowledge many Framers believed to be requisite to enable legislators to engage in quality proceedings (Bessette 1994, 23–24), extended discussions of difficult issues, and "look forward and deliberate with each other—an impossibility if every moment is spent looking over the shoulder at the home constituency" (Malbin 1987, 195). Long terms also weaken constituents' grip on elected officials, allowing senators to, as Hamilton phrases it in Federalist 71, utilize the "time and opportunity" brought by their long tenure to engage in "cool and sedate reflection" (Hamilton, Madison, and Jay 1961, 432). Put succinctly, the six-year terms "foster and secure the independent judgment of legislators that was [viewed as] indispensable to sound deliberation" (Bessette 1994, 25).

In addition to the incentives created by the Constitution, the Senate has made procedural choices that, theoretically at least, nurture quality proceedings. In 1811, five years after the Senate dropped the previous question, the House decided to reinvigorate its version of the procedure and since then has employed it to limit floor debate. Without a previous question motion, the Senate established a tradition of unlimited debate that meant "dignity and courtesy prevailed and senators depended upon the logic and eloquence of forceful speeches to persuade their colleagues and the country to accept their views" (Byrd 1991, 161).

The worsen-over-time hypothesis has numerous theoretical undergirdings as well. An increasing and excessive workload is one. Luce (1922, 305) noted that the decline in the quality of oration he observed in the early part of the 20th century could be directly attributed to "the change in the nature and volume of parliamentary business." The December 1993 report on congressional procedures by the Joint Committee on the Organization of Congress described how "intensified policy demands" and the "increasingly demanding requirements of representation and campaigning" incentivized shorter workweeks in Washington and additional committee assignments (1993b, 2:35). For various reasons—including the federal government's involvement in more policy areas, the introduction of many more bills, larger constituencies, a greater ease with which voters can contact their elected officials, and augmented partisanship—work, deliberation, and important policy decisions have been increasingly devolved from the floor to committees and party caucuses. Indeed, most of the recent influential theoretical work on congressional organization views the efforts of both committees (in the case of gains-from-exchange [Weingast and Marshall 1988] and informational [Krehbiel 1991] models) and parties (in the case of the parties-as-procedural-cartels [Cox and McCubbins 1993, 2005] and conditional-party-government [Aldrich, Berger, and Rohde 2002] models) as consuming tremendous amounts of members' time and making critical policy decisions. As a result, according to responses to the Joint Committee's 1993 survey, 41.9 percent of House members and 54.2 percent of senators spent "only a little time attending floor debate or watching it on television" (Joint Committee 1993b, 2:276). Floor proceedings have, in turn, suffered.

Greater transparency is offered as another reason for deteriorating floor proceedings. Increased transparency is an important dimension of good proceedings because it educates the public about policy and the political process and helps hold members accountable. But some congressional scholars and observers have argued that although the public should be able to witness what is happening on the floor, openness has had deleterious effects on the quality of debate and deliberation. As early as the 1880s, for example, Woodrow Wilson (1981, 70–76) complained that press coverage of the floor had led members to do most of their important work in committee. In more recent years, live televised floor proceedings have been considered especially bad.[6] Smith (1989, 62–69) has discussed how television invokes petty partisanship. Zelizer (2004, 206–32) explains how televised proceedings and cable news encourage members to be dramatic and controversial rather than deliberative and reasonable. Tip O'Neill (D-MA), the Speaker at the time the House began its use of television, called coverage a "disaster" and believed that it encouraged grandstanding for constituents and long and vacuous speeches (Garay 1984, 138). "Once television was in place," former House parliamentarian Charles Johnson has added, "members were less willing to take on their opponents and to potentially be embarrassed, preferring, instead, to have prescripted speeches and then sit down" (Remini 2006, 461). Mixon, Hobson, and Upadhyaya (2001, 2003) argue that the presence of C-SPAN cameras has brought about showboating and filibusters in the Senate. Other observers believe that television encourages members to stay off the floor, which, in turn, means that the personal relationships necessary for good debate are not fostered (Robinson 1981). Indeed, Cook (1988) has argued that press secretaries urge their bosses to pursue media attention strategies off the floor since effective opportunities abound—and he was writing in the days before the Internet and ubiquitous 24-hour cable news.

Concepts and Data

I focus here on the potentially varying quality of floor proceedings. By floor proceedings, I mean the words spoken, for the record, on the floor of the House and Senate. I am not interested in written remarks submitted for the record, committee proceedings, or what members say outside of the halls of Congress, however important these actions may be.[7] I do more than just analyze words uttered in the context of debate—that is, members' spoken contributions to floor discussions about a particular legislative measure. I am interested in what happens on the floor more broadly. I also talk of proceedings rather than debate because I consider "debate" a distinguishable behavior and an attribute of desirable proceedings rather than something in which members automatically engage whenever a bill is brought up.

To detect intercameral and longitudinal variation in the quality of floor proceedings, I analyze two distinct groups of data. The first, macrolevel data, come from observations of the floor proceedings of entire congresses. In my analysis of some measures, for example, I examine the number of times all House and Senate members participated in floor proceedings in every fifth congress from the 32nd (1851–53) to the 107th (2001–3). I begin with the 32nd Congress because that is when floor proceedings were first provided in a form that is close to verbatim. I choose every fifth congress to give us a comprehensive taste of floor proceedings in every subsequent decade.

The second group of data is microlevel. Here I examine, in considerable detail, specific proceedings across time in three issue areas. For the most part, the issues provide meaningful comparisons across chambers and time because the way they have been framed has remained largely unchanged. All three are deemed important to members and the country; therefore, we ought to care that they furnish examples of quality floor proceedings.

The first issue is presidential impeachment and trial. I look at the House debates on impeachment and the Senate trials of Andrew Johnson in 1868 and Bill Clinton in 1998–99.[8] There had long been talk about impeaching Johnson because of his Reconstruction policy—indeed, the full House defeated an impeachment resolution brought against the president in November 1867—but Johnson's attempted ouster of secretary of war Edwin Stanton and consequent perceived violation of the Tenure of Office Act directly precipitated the House's action of February 1868. Radical Republicans—those who wished to subject Confederate states to harsh Reconstruction—had passed the bill to protect their supporters in the administration and to check what they saw as increasingly treasonous behavior by Lincoln's former vice president. Johnson's perceived flagrant disregard for the law incensed them, and the House indicted him on eleven counts. He was impeached on all of them.

Clinton was charged with four counts and impeached on two because of testimony he gave, in connection to a sexual harassment suit, about his affair with a White House intern, Monica Lewinsky. As with Johnson, Clinton's defenders felt the attempt to remove him from office was politically motivated. The Senate acquitted both presidents, although the body fell one vote short of the two-thirds needed to convict Johnson on three separate counts. These are the only two cases of presidential impeachment and trial, but they are certainly significant events that should have provoked floor proceedings of quality.

Comparing the Johnson and Clinton impeachments and trials is valuable for another reason. In 1999, the Senate reached back to the Johnson episode as it designed procedures for its trial of Clinton. The use of House managers, the process by which senators submitted questions and motions, and the prerogatives of the president's counsel were all facsimiles of procedures employed in 1868. Direct comparison thus is even more pertinent.

Second, I look at declarations of war and a series of analogous decisions authorizing the president to use military force. Again this is a crucial issue that grips the country and should engage members of Congress. I use six cases: the War of 1812, the Mexican-American War, the declaration of war against Germany in 1917, the Tonkin Gulf Resolution, and congressional authorizations of the presidential use of force against Iraq in 1991 and 2002. The criteria used to admit cases were that the president asked for and received a declaration of war or permission to use military force and that the congressional action initiated significant American military involvement. The first rule led me to reject cases where calls for military action were initiated by Congress, such as the Coudert-Taft Resolution about Korea in 1951. The second rule led me to the exclusion of cases such as actions against the Barbary Pirates in the first two decades of the 19th century and presidential requests for action in Lebanon in 1958 and 1982. The declarations of war against Spain in 1898 and Japan, Germany, and Italy in December 1941 are conspicuously missing because the congressional debates were extremely short and very few members participated. In 1898, moreover, the Senate debate took place in closed executive session.[9]

Finally, I examine House and Senate proceedings concerning critical trade legislation. Trade is an issue with which Congress has dealt more often than impeachment and war. Moreover, it has been continuously important and had similar meaning throughout American history. Although some observers have viewed trade as distributive policy (Lowi 1964), many others see it as continually controversial (Bensel 2000; Hiscox 2002; O'Halloran 1994). According to this second group of scholars, although divisions have been at various times partisan and sectional, trade and the tariff have generally been discussed in the same way. The issue has been a contest between liberalization and protectionism. This consistent frame, along with the fact that it has been a crucial part of the business of many Congresses, differentiates trade from another subject central to the American experience, race. Race appears less often on the congressional agenda, and debate surrounding it changes dramatically. Where, for example, were the discussions about it in the Congresses of the first half of the 20th century? How should we compare congressional floor proceedings on slavery with those on desegregation or affirmative action? We might make a meaningful comparison of debates on the 1875 and 1964 Civil Rights Acts and the 1890 federal elections rights or "force" bill and the 1965 Voting Rights Act, but these measures provide us with observations of only two periods.[10] Trade, by contrast, provides us with 31 observations, 29 that I take from Hiscox's (2002) work on trade policies in Western democracies and 2 that I added to extend the time series closer to the present and incorporate cases under recent Republican majorities.[11] The first 6 of Hiscox's observations occur too early for verbatim coverage, although I do provide some rudimentary analyses of these episodes.

To construct measures that allow for meaningful analysis of the data, I need to conceptualize proceedings comprehensively and define precisely what constitutes good and bad floor proceedings. I start by identifying five fundamental and broad principles that good floor proceedings should display. The first of these is *accountability*. In functioning democracies, legislatures should provide the electorate with the ability to make informed decisions about the quality of their representation. Voters should be able to see and comprehend what the body and its members are doing. The second principle is the *education* of the electorate. Mayhew (2000) argues that Congress should provide critical information to the public about important problems facing the nation and the proposals that compete to solve these problems. In turn, what happens on the floors of both chambers of Congress should be instructional and even part of a dialogue with citizens inside what political theorist Jürgen Habermas (1989) has called the "public sphere." For Woodrow Wilson (1981, 71), "the enlightenment of public opinion" was the "chief, and unquestionably the most essential, object of all discussion of public business." In this sense, then, floor proceedings should not only be seen by the public but also should inform and influence.

The third principle is *representation*. Lawmakers should represent the interests of their constituents, regardless of whether they have a delegate or more Burkean view of representation. This is no less true for members' participation in floor proceedings than it is other legislative behavior.

The fourth and fifth principles are what Bessette (1982) calls *debate* and *deliberation*. Debate involves the vigorous advocacy of a formed point of view and its defense in the face of an opposing argument. It is salubrious because it forces thorough analysis of policy proposals yet, because arguments and proposals are formed prior to the proceedings, helps expedite consideration of alternatives. Debate on the floor essentially constitutes competition between and justification of previously hardened positions. Debate sometimes will sway legislators who have soft preferences but it is more often a way to legitimize policy proposals—something that is more than just window dressing in a democracy—and to generate public support for them. Smith (1989, 238–42) has observed that the House's floor is more predisposed to debate than the Senate's.

Deliberation, conversely, is characterized as "reasoning together about the nature of a problem and solutions to it" (Smith 1989, 238–39). It is a thorough search for various options to societal problems. Deliberation involves the formation, not just the competition, of policy proposals. Deliberation is healthy because it assists members in their search for superior policy outcomes and provides procedural legitimacy for a final decision. It also forces lawmakers to educate themselves about policy and helps nurture a greater sense of collective rather than individual interest (Bessette 1994; Lascher 1996).[12] Rawls (1997, 772) views "deliberative legislative bodies" as one of the "three essential elements of deliberative democracy," along with public reason and the public's willingness and ability to follow this reason. As Bessette (1994, 151–65) and Smith (1989, 239–40) show, deliberation can occur in congressional forums other than the floor, not least because the process is so time-consuming. Still, because it is a uniquely inclusive institution, the floor should be as deliberative as possible.[13]

These five principles yield eight characteristics of high-quality floor proceedings. This additional level of understanding—or concreteness—is required because the basic principles are somewhat abstract and not directly observable. These characteristics, however, are. The presence of relatively high amounts of the characteristics is indicative of the presence of one or more of the principles. The characteristics allow us to spawn measures that can be applied to the data.

The first of the characteristics is *quantity*. Superior debate, deliberation, representation, and education take time; floor proceedings, therefore, should be long. As Alexander Hamilton put it while discussing the presidential veto in Federalist 73, "The oftener a measure is brought under examination, the greater the diversity in the situation of those who are to examine it, the less must be the danger of those errors which flow from want of due deliberation" (Hamilton, Madison, and Jay 1961, 443). In an analysis of congressional proceedings, Connor and Oppenheimer (1993) use time as a measure of deliberation.

Second, both deliberation, as a thorough search for policy options, and debate, if the authoritative decision is to be deemed legitimate, require widespread *participation* in floor proceedings. In his seminal work on deliberative democracy, Fishkin (1995) argues that broad engagement is requisite for deliberation. Lascher (1996) also points to participation in his attempt to lay the foundations for an empirical analysis of legislative deliberation. He believes that floor proceedings need to be well attended to be deliberative. Broad participation, moreover, is necessary for effective aggregate representation.

The third characteristic is directly related to the second. The amount of participation should, especially for purposes of deliberation and representation, be even across members. There should be *equality* in participation. Both Fishkin (1995) and Lascher (1996) believe this characteristic to be essential. Gabardi (2001, 551) identifies equality as a "key feature" of deliberative democracy.

The fourth characteristic, *interaction*, is designed to indicate the presence of debate, deliberation, and presumably education. Quality floor proceedings consist of give-and-take. According to Lascher (1996, 506), "The extent to which legislators engage each others' arguments" is an appropriate measure of deliberation. Fishkin (1995, 40–44) sees "thinking through the issues together" as an essential part of his mass deliberative democracy.

Debate, deliberation, and education also require the presence of the fifth and sixth characteristics, *civility* and *reasoning*. Civility, as Uslaner (1993, 6) writes, is essential to both debate and deliberation: "Serious discourse demands that we exchange views with adversaries and give them the respect that we demand of our own ideas." Steiner et al. (2004, 22) argue that respect is central to deliberation and that "the capacity and willingness to listen to others" are critical. Contemporary legislators also seem to think that incivility hinders quality proceedings. The House Rules Committee has held several hearings on the topic, and bipartisan retreats have sought to elevate discourse. In the cause of civility, Representative Joe Wilson (R-SC) was reprimanded for calling President Barack Obama a "liar" during a joint session of Congress in September 2009.

Reasoning occurs when participants explain their positions rather than purely state them (Bessette 1994; Lascher 1996). Reason was an important concept to the Framers of the Constitution, in Federalist 10, Madison writes that the passion inherent in political factions is the enemy of reason (Hamilton, Madison, and Jay 1961, 77–84). Moreover, Steiner et al. (2004, 20–21) argue that a "logical justification" of the speaker's argument is inherent to deliberation. Mucciaroni and Quirk (2006) concur. I do look at reasoning a little in the next chapter, but the definitional and coding issues involved with its measurement are immensely intimidating and cause enough problems to deter systematic observation and analysis.

The seventh characteristic was also important to the Founders. As he notes in Federalist 10, Madison felt that majority factions worked to the detriment of the public good as well as reason (Hamilton, Madison, and Jay 1961, 77–84). To the Founders, the public or common good was more than just the aggregation of the self-interest of all of society's individual members. The community or nation had its own discernible interest that required protection from the myopic and often conflicting personal and parochial interests of its members. Such an act of guardianship is a central part of deliberation and is portrayed on the floors of Congress when members couch arguments in terms of the public good (Bessette 1994; Gabardi 2001; Lascher 1996). Steiner et al. (2004, 21) also believe that deliberation consists of "a sense of empathy or solidarity that allows the participants to consider the well-being of others and of the community at large." I call this characteristic *commonweal*.

Finally, floor proceedings, as I stated earlier, should provide accountability and educate voters. They cannot do so if the public cannot see, hear, or read about them. The final characteristic, therefore, is *transparency*. Notwithstanding the deleterious by-products of live television coverage discussed earlier, the public should have access to what happens on the floor.[14] Moreover, and as Mucciaroni and Quirk (2006) argue, misleading and extreme claims occur more often when members' remarks are not subject to close scrutiny. Waldron (2009, 337–40) has gone as far to say that transparency is the "first virtue" of legislatures.

Specific Measures

With these principles and characteristics in hand, we can now create measures to analyze the data. Each measure is designed to reveal the extent to which a characteristic is present in the observed chamber at the observed time. Table 4.1 shows the indicators, the characteristics that they measure, and the principles that high levels reflect. It also shows the data to which they are applied, which I evaluate in the next chapter.

I utilize five measures in my examination of the macrolevel data—that is, the panoramic observations of phenomena from a sample of or continuous series of entire Congresses. Quantity is measured as the cumulative length of a Congress's sessions minus recesses in days and hours. Transparency is measured through various chunks of quantitative data and a qualitative analysis of how floor proceedings and congressional life more generally have been recorded. The rationale here is that more comprehensive record keeping and greater amounts of media coverage make floor proceedings more visible. Civility—or incivility, to be more precise—is measured borrowing from data presented by several scholars. These data contain requests and rulings to have "words taken down"—a formal response to members transgressing the rules of debate and decorum. Some of it also comes from newspaper coverage.

Measures of participation and equality are taken from comprehensive examination of floor proceedings in every fifth Congress from the 32nd (1851–53) to the 107th (2001–3). As stated earlier, I begin with the 32nd Congress because before this time, floor proceedings were reported in the *House Journal,* the *Senate Journal,* the *Annals of Congress,* the *Register of Debates in Congress,* and the *Congressional Globe* in summary or incomplete form. In 1851, the *Congressional Globe* presents what is considered close to a verbatim record of what happened on the floor.[15] I use every fifth congress to select a random sample of 16 congresses from the mid-19th century to the current period. The Congresses used are the first of every decade from the 1850s to the 2000s.

Combing indexes of all sessions, including special ones, of a Congress, coders counted the number of remarks made by each member on the floor.[16] Written remarks and materials added to the record were not included.[17] Although index terms change slightly over time, coders counted separate references to each member's "remarks on," as was the case in the early Congresses covered by the *Congressional Globe,* or "remarks by, on," as was the case in the more recent congresses covered by the *Congressional*

TABLE 4.1. The Quality of Floor Proceedings: Principles, Characteristics, and Measures

Measure	Data Applied To	Characteristic Measured	Principle(s) Reflected
Number of days/hours of Congress's sessions	Macro—all Congresses for days, 80th–107th for hours	Quantity	Education, Representation, Debate, Deliberation
Various quantitative and qualitative measures of record keeping and media coverage	Macro—analysis includes Cook 1989, Hess 1991, Swift 1996	Transparency	Accountability, Education
Words ruled out of order	Macro—analysis includes Uslaner 1993, Jamieson and Falk 1998	Civility	Debate, Deliberation
New York Times articles on incivility	Macro—Dodd and Schraufnagel 2007	Civility	Debate, Deliberation
Mean number of remarks per member	Macro—all members' remarks in entire Congress, every fifth Congress from 32nd to 107th	Participation	Representation, Deliberation
Coefficient of variation of number of remarks per member	Macro—all members' remarks in entire Congress, every fifth Congress from 32nd to 107th	Equality	Representation, Deliberation
Cumulative number of columns in record of debate	Micro—impeachment, war, trade bills	Quantity	Education, Representation, Debate, Deliberation
Percentage of chamber's membership that contributed to debate	Micro—impeachment, war, trade bills	Participation	Representation, Deliberation
Coefficient of variation of members' individual cumulative columns in record of debate	Micro—impeachment, war, trade bills	Equality	Representation, Deliberation
Number of colloquies per 100 columns in record of debate	Micro—impeachment, war, trade bills	Interaction	Education, Debate, Deliberation
Times speaker yielded when asked per 100 columns in record of debate	Micro—impeachment, war, trade bills	Interaction	Education, Debate, Deliberation
Percentage of those who participate who mention phrases like "public good"	Micro—impeachment, trade bills	Commonweal	Deliberation
Quality of arguments made in debate	Micro—impeachment	Reasoning	Education, Debate, Deliberation

Record.[18] I am unconcerned by the length of the remark—either in printed columns or time—but use the number of separate mentions of remarks made. Each observation constitutes a "remark."[19] Participation is measured as the mean number of remarks per member in a chamber for an entire Congress. Equality is the coefficient of variation—that is, the standard deviation divided by the mean—of remarks per member in a chamber for an entire Congress. This approach allows us to compare equality across chambers and Congresses that vary considerably in the average number of remarks made per member.

Seven measures are used in analysis of the microlevel data (the presidential impeachments, war declarations or resolutions authorizing the presidential use of force, and the trade bills). I coded debate on the original passage of the bill, including amendments, the motion to recommit, and, in the case of the House, on the special rule—debate set aside for this generally focuses on the substance of the legislation. Where applicable, I coded debate on the motion to proceed in the Senate. Only remarks made by members are coded. I do not include remarks made by members about the bill outside of this time—for example, during one-minute or special order speeches or in "extensions of remarks." I also do not code comments made by and explicitly to the presiding officer.

The first measure, quantity, is indicated by the cumulative number of columns, measured in quarter-sized increments, of proceedings on each impeachment, war, or trade item in each chamber. Column lengths are not ideal, because there are slight changes over time in their average length and some have more words than others for formatting reasons.[20] Still, even a perfunctory glance at the *Congressional Globe* of the 1850s and 1860s reveals column size and typeset to resemble those of the modern *Congressional Record*. And for many of the debates, especially in the early Congresses, accurate measures of time are not available. Column inches are, therefore, a blunt but acceptable measure of quantity.

Participation can be more precisely measured. It is the percentage of the entire chamber's membership that contributed at least once to the proceedings on the bill or resolution. Wirls (2007) uses this measure in his analysis of four great antebellum debates. Equality is the coefficient of variation for individual members' cumulative contributions to the proceedings measured in column amounts.

I use two measures of interaction. These are the number of colloquies— literally conversations between members—in the debate per one hundred columns of text and the number of times members yielded to a colleague when asked to do so by that colleague per one hundred columns of text. An individual colloquy is counted as a distinct interaction between any two members, excluding the presiding officer. These can be of any length—they can be as short as one remark from each participant—and begin when two members interact and finish when one or both stop talking directly to each other. Colloquies frequently involve three or more members. In these cases, I count each pairing where it is clear that the two members are addressing each other as a colloquy. A three-member colloquy is, therefore, three separate colloquies if all the participants are addressing one another.

A yield occurs when a member turns the floor over to a colleague. Since members generally do so for the purposes of a question or statement that necessitates a reply, a yield nearly always leads to a colloquy. A member may yield to more than one request from the same colleague in a single colloquy, however. The number of yield requests granted seems to be a good measure of members' willingness to engage in interaction and, in turn, deliberation. I count only explicit requests to yield made by and of any member except the presiding officer. In the Senate, I include instances of acquiescence that are accompanied by the member's assertion that he or she retains the right to the floor.[21]

Commonweal is measured as the percentage of all members who participated and who mentioned the public good at least once in the debates on impeachment and trade—contributions to the war and use of force debates seemed almost universally framed in terms of the nation's interest. Members needed to discuss their position or desired outcome of the proceedings as enhancing the public good or their opponents' views as being harmful to it.[22]

Reasoning, as mentioned previously, is particularly tricky to measure. I gauge it only during the debates surrounding presidential impeachment in the House and then in an impressionistic manner. I also apply it only to the worsen-over-time hypothesis. I attempt to make a judgment about the overall quality of the argument made by presidential accusers and defenders.[23]

Conclusion

The conventional wisdom about floor proceedings in Congress is that those of the Senate are superior to those of the House and that in both bodies they have worsened over time. Armed with a set of principles, characteristics, and measures, I test these hypotheses on the macro- and microlevel data in the next chapter.

5 ◆ The Quality of Floor Proceedings II

Analysis

I am testing two hypotheses: (1) Floor proceedings are better in the Senate than in the House (Senate-superior); (2) floor proceedings have deteriorated across history (worsen-over-time). To reject the null of the first hypothesis, we should see appreciable differences revealing better Senate proceedings when contrasting intercameral observations of the macrolevel data taken from the same Congresses and microlevel data taken from proceedings on the same bills or resolutions. Such differences should be detected in most of the measures for most of the time. To reject the null of the worsen-over-time hypothesis, we need to see a widespread deterioration in both chambers' proceedings over time. We should have no real expectation of the pattern that such deterioration will take, however. It may be fairly linear or perhaps even zigzag on a generally downward trajectory. There may be dramatic decline followed by stability or a long period of stasis and then a rapid descent in more recent years. In any event, contemporary floor proceedings must be demonstrably worse than early ones.

I test the hypotheses together by analyzing the macro- and microlevel data separately. Within the examination of each type of data, I treat the eight characteristics individually. I first evaluate the macrolevel data and the indicators derived from looking systematically across chambers and time.

Macrolevel data

Quantity

Figure 5.1 displays how long the House and Senate were in session, in days, from the 1st to 107th Congresses. The data are taken from records

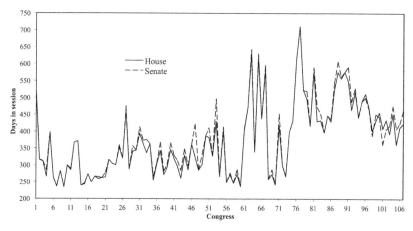

Fig. 5.1. The number of days the House and Senate were in session, 1789–2002. (Data: author's calculations from U.S. Senate, http://www.senate.gov/reference/ Sessions/sessionDates.htm.)

kept by the U.S. Senate and exclude recesses but include weekend days within sessions when the bodies may not actually have been meeting.[1] This measure of the quantity of floor proceedings seems somewhat blunt—the number of hours a chamber is in session during a day fluctuates wildly, and some practices, like waiting through quorum calls, are not really what we would consider useful floor activity. Still, it certainly gives us a broad historical overview.

At first blush, little intercameral difference seems to exist in the quantity of floor proceedings. In many Congresses during the 19th century, for example, House and Senate sessions were identical in length. Passing laws requires both bodies to be in session, and in the age before rapid transportation it was very difficult to recall members to the Capitol on short notice. The only times House and Senate sessions differed perceptibly was when a special session of the Senate was called, frequently by presidential proclamation. These sessions generally coincided with the inauguration of the president on March 4 for the purpose of having the Senate conduct executive business, principally the confirmation of presidential nominations. In the beginning, the special Senate sessions were a day or so, though they later became longer. During the 47th Congress (1881–83), there were two such extraordinarily long sessions lasting a total of 98 days. Both were largely the result of problems organizing the closely split chamber. In the first, the minority Democrats tried to take advantage of Republican vacancies brought about by the appointment of three of the opposition's senators to new president James Garfield's cabinet. A flurry of reappointment activity in state legislatures and complex and drawn-out maneuvering between the two parties lengthened the session. So did a Democratic filibuster undertaken to exploit the resignations of the two Republican members from New York, Roscoe Conkling and Thomas C. Platt, who had been involved in a dispute within the New York Republican Party that essentially mirrored the more national Stalwart versus Half-Breed spat. The conflict flared up when Garfield appointed a Conkling nemesis, Half-Breed William H. Robertson, as collector for the port of New York. The two senators believed that after resigning their seats, they would be reselected and, in turn, vindicated and strengthened. They were not (see Schiller and Stewart 2004, 9–13). The first special session ended with a fragile peace in which Thomas F. Bayard Sr. (D-DE) remained president pro tempore and Republicans chaired committees. In the second session, in October 1881, the Republicans were ready to lead after the New York legislature had appointed two Republican replacements for Conkling and Platt. The Democrats, however, readily understood that the Senate president pro tempore position had taken on added significance because Garfield had been assassinated in July. Bayard was now statutorily designated as the immediate successor to the new president, Chester Arthur. After protracted negotiations, Conkling and Platt's successors ultimately were sworn in and an independent, former Lincoln confidant and Supreme Court justice David Davis, was made president pro tempore.

Over the entire data series, the House was in session an average of 374.9 days per Congress, the Senate for 383.8 days. The difference is statistically significant at the $p < .01$ level. At least as far as quantity is concerned then, this provides some evidence for the Senate-superior hypothesis. Some of the difference is attributable to the special Senate sessions—themselves perhaps a reflection more of constitutional and statutory rules and responsibilities than quality floor proceedings. Even after the 20th Amendment effectively ended the special sessions in 1933, however, the Senate was still seated for more days than the House—an average of 483.3 to 475.0. The difference in chamber means for the 74th (1935–37) to 107th Congresses (2001–3) is statistically significant but at the $p < .02$ level.

The worsen-over-time hypothesis must be rejected. Indeed, if anything, a dramatic increase has occurred in the number of days Congress has been in session. Again, splitting the data using the 20th Amendment is instructive. The pre-74th Congress average for the House is 328.3 days, for the Senate it is 337.5, 146.7 and 145.8 days fewer, respectively, than the 74th–107th Congress figures. Before 1910, it was rare to have a Congress experience more than 400 days of session; prior to the 63rd Congress (1913–15), the 1st Congress (1789–91) was the longest, at 519 days for both chambers, but representatives spent a significant portion of this time waiting for colleagues to arrive in New York, and senators had to sit tight anticipating the preservation of House-passed bills.

There are several plausible reasons for this counterhypothetical finding. The 20th Amendment is obvious because it fundamentally restructured when Congress met. Prior to its ratification, Congress was forced to meet at least once a year on the first Monday in December. As a result, members put off their first full gathering for about thirteen months after they had been elected, effectively wasting about a year of potential floor time. Beginning with the 74th Congress, the federal legislature was forced to meet at the beginning of January every year and as a result began to convene almost continually through the two years with the exception of frequent and often lengthy recesses. Still, the cumulative length of these recesses was inevitably shorter than the time members missed under the old rule.

Another reason for longer sessions was that it became easier for members to get to and from Washington. Workload—both legislative and representative—also increased. The number of bills introduced in each chamber of Congress reached about 1,000 during the Civil War. By the 1970s this figure had mushroomed to between 12,000 and 15,000, although it has subsequently dropped off considerably, not least because the House changed its rules about cosponsorship. Congresses that experienced procedural battles have been particularly long. Examples of these include the 27th (1841–43), in which the Senate experienced its first continuous filibuster over the national bank, and the 51st (1889–91) and 53rd (1893–95), when the Republicans controversially ratified Reed's Rules and then, after being forced into the minority, began to exploit the same opportunities for obstructionism they had vehemently criticized two Congresses earlier.

Jet travel, larger and more informed constituencies, and parliamentary shenanigans do not necessarily translate into what we would think of as quality floor proceedings. But anecdotal analysis also suggests that the treatment of important issues lengthens sessions. There are discernible upward spikes during the preliminaries, declaration, and initial conduct of the War of 1812 (12th and 13th Congresses, 1811–15), the Mexican-American War (31st Congress, 1849–51), World War I (65th Congress,

1917–19), and World War II (75th and 76th Congresses, 1937–41). There were also lengthy sessions in Congresses that produced a lot of domestic policy. The 640-plus-day 63rd Congress (1913–15) under Woodrow Wilson made much in the way of economic policy, creating the Federal Reserve, overhauling the tariff, and passing sweeping antitrust legislation, among other activities. Mayhew (2005, 34–99) detected a "bulge in the middle" in his study of the number of important laws passed per Congress in the post–World War II era. This bulge coincides with long Congresses. The 87th (1961–63) through 93rd Congresses (1973–75)—the era of the Great Society, civil rights, sweeping regulation, and large expansions to New Deal programs—were all, save one, longer than 500 days. The 104th Congress (1995–97) of the Republicans' Contract with America was also significantly longer than the several before or since it. Mayhew (2005) sees the 104th as particularly productive—it passed 15 important laws, more than any other Congress in the 1990s. Discussing the gravity of war and numerous important domestic matters seem to be what we want out of floor proceedings.

Days in session is a necessarily blunt instrument by which to measure the quantity of floor proceedings across congressional history. We do have a sharper instrument, however, in the form of hours in session. Reliable data on session lengths in hours are only available since World War II, but they do allow a test of the hypotheses, especially the Senate-superior one. Figure 5.2 reveals the cumulative number of hours the House and Senate were in session from the 80th to the 107th Congress (1947–2003). The data are from the *Congressional Record*.

The data clearly vindicate the Senate-superior hypothesis. The average number of hours per Congress the Senate has been in session since World War II is 2,163. The figure for the House is 1,572, only 73 percent of that of the upper chamber. In some Congresses, particularly in the 1950s and 1960s, the Senate was in session for nearly twice as many hours than the House—indeed, in the 86th Congress (1959–61), the Senate's hours more than doubled those of the House. Sinclair (1989) asserts that Senate sessions expanded as younger, liberal, and less deferential members entered a body as it met a more pervasive media and complicated issue environment. An increased heterogeneity of policy preferences, greater electoral pressures, and new values converged to elevate amending activity and facilitate the exploitation of the Senate's tradition of unlimited debate.

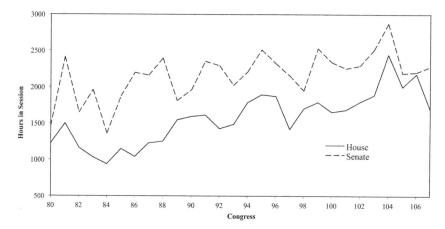

Fig. 5.2. The number of hours the House and Senate were in session, 1947–2002. (Data from *Congressional Record* [various months], "Resume of Congressional Activity.")

Transparency

Transparent floor proceedings are revealed by accurate and public record keeping and extensive coverage by an accessible media. With regard to the former, it is difficult to disprove the null of the Senate-superior hypothesis. Both chambers were instructed to keep journals of their proceedings and have done so either separately, in the *House Journal* and *Senate Journal*, or together, in the *Register of Debates*, the *Congressional Globe*, and the *Congressional Record*. The same conclusion should be drawn for the worsen-over-time hypothesis. Indeed, if anything, record keeping has improved. Not until 1851, for example, did the *Congressional Globe* provide a close-to-verbatim transcript of floor proceedings.

Evaluating intercameral differences and longitudinal fluctuations in media coverage of congressional floor proceedings is a little more complex. To gain some purchase on the subject, I examine congressional press coverage utilizing snippets of available quantitative data and the few detailed studies of the topic we have.

Analysis of the bodies' accommodation of the media suggests that there is little to the Senate-superior hypothesis. In fact, the House at first seemed to be considerably more transparent than the Senate. The upper chamber, replicating the practice of the Continental Congress, met behind closed doors for the first few years. The original decision to keep the public out does not seem to have been conspiratorial. As Kerr (1895, 39) writes, the policy "was provided for by no rule and seems to have been entered upon without debate and without question." But it soon provoked numerous state legislatures to call for transparency, and the Senate began to split over the policy. Three open-door motions were defeated until Federalist opposition to public access withered under Republican attack. The chamber's doors were finally opened in December 1795.[2]

The House and Senate later generally adopted policies in tandem. Both chambers recognized the press's right to cover proceedings by admitting stenographers in 1802. In 1827, the House put reporters on the floor to avoid errors in coverage, and the Senate followed suit eight years later. To keep out meddlesome opposition papers like the *New York Express*, Senate Jacksonian Democrats including Vice President Richard M. Johnson and Connecticut's John M. Niles altered the rules in 1838 so that only reporters for Washington-based papers could access the floor (Marbut 1971, 56–60). The same year, the House forced reporters to declare in writing their employers, and, presumably with this information in hand, permitted the Speaker to prohibit any individual stenographer's access to the floor. In the late 1850s, when both bodies moved into their new chambers, they ordered the construction of new and permanent press galleries. Between the 1860s and 1880s, both bodies had allowed the Associated Press direct access to the floor and had forced their presiding officers to relinquish complete control of the press galleries. By World War I, both allowed the press itself to govern policies regarding the galleries. In 1939, both invited radio reporters in; two years later, both accepted magazine reporters. Live gavel-to-gavel television coverage—brought to the public today via C-SPAN and C-SPAN 2—was established in the House in 1979 and the Senate seven years later.

In addition, the Senate, and by inference its floor, has not received a sizable majority of press coverage. Indeed, the press coverage of early Congresses clearly favored the House. Swift (1996, 122–23, 166–68) shows, for example, that newspapers such as the *National Intelligencer* focused most of their nonelection congressional reporting on the lower chamber.[3] This was the case through the second session of the 20th Congress (1827–29), when Swift calculates that there was nearly three times more coverage of the House than the Senate. Not until the 23rd Congress (1833–35) did parity arise in press treatment of the two bodies.

The pattern in the post–World War II period is different, but the Senate does not dominate. Blanchard's (1974) survey of 96 congressional correspondents in the early 1970s shows that most of their time spent covering Congress was devoted to the Senate. Stephen Hess (1991, 5), who has extensively studied media coverage of Congress, claims that "the national news reporters lean toward Senate stories." But his systematic analysis of local television coverage of Washington in the early 1980s shows that although a slight majority of the coverage of congressional institutions may have favored the Senate, House members were more likely to be on television in their constituents' media markets than were senators (39–59).

Such measures of transparency lead us to reject the worsen-over-time hypothesis with greater certainty. The few systematic longitudinal analyses of the quantity of media coverage generally show upward trends. These analyses do not directly concern the floor, but they are instructive. Swift's (1996, 122–23, 166–68) analyses reveal increased newspaper treatment of both bodies through the first half of the 19th century. To be sure, evidence exists that television news stories about Congress as an institution decreased precipitously between Watergate and the 1994 Republican Revolution (Lichter and Amundson 1994, 133–35). But Cook's (1989, 59–62) study of the number of House members mentioned on the network television nightly news shows a steady increase from 1969 through 1986: In the early years, about one in four members was mentioned; by the early 1980s the figure was nearly one in two. Many of these mentions no doubt included discussions of members' floor activity. Harris (1998) reveals dramatic increases in the number of references to the Speaker of the House over the 1969–96 period on the network nightly news and House party leaders on NBC's Sunday morning *Meet the Press*. Malecha and Reagan (2004) show that media coverage of the majority party leadership has increased spectacularly over the past decade or so as well.[4]

More indirect measures tell the same story. M. J. Robinson's (1981) data from the period between the late 1950s and late 1970s show both an increase in the use of House radio and television studios by members and a rise in the number of journalists credentialed for the press galleries.

Civility

Measuring general levels of civility or identifying specific incidents of incivility are not easy things to do.[5] Still, what measures we have of these phenomena in Congress tend to provide little evidence to support the worsen-over-time hypothesis. Uslaner (1993, 40–41), for example, argues that incivility "reached a fever pitch in the antebellum period." Forty percent of all instances of what he calls "breaches in comity" during the 1790–1956 period occurred in the 30 years leading up to the Civil War.[6]

In a 1998 report for the House undertaken by the Annenberg Public Policy Center, Jamieson and Falk (1998) examined instances of demands that words be ruled out of order and rulings by which these demands were met. Words are ruled "out of order" when a member complains about what a colleague has said on the floor and the chair agrees. The ruling prevents a member from speaking again on the same day unless he or she is allowed to do so by motion or unanimous consent and may—again, if the action is approved by motion or unanimous consent—result in the violators' words being expunged from the *Congressional Record*. The report showed that the House of the late 1990s, a time when members' heightened sensitivity to discourtesy had driven them to call for precisely this kind of study into their behavior, was really no less civil than the body of the World War II and Cold War eras.

The same case is made by Dodd and Schraufnagel (2007). They measure incivility by examining articles written about Congress in the *New York Times* and *Washington Post* and then reporting the proportion of these articles that deal with matters such as courtesy, respect, and other types of expressed conflict. They reveal that levels of incivility have been marginally higher in the past 20 years than they were for the rest of the post–World War II period but are now appreciably lower than they were in the last 30 years of the 19th century.

The evidence is also murky when it comes to the Senate-superior hypothesis. Uslaner's (2000) comparative study of the House and Senate seems to suggest that since "Senate rhetoric is generally not as shrill" as House rhetoric (40), there is more incivility in the lower chamber. He argues that procedures also necessitate greater civility in the upper chamber. We do not, however, have any hard data to verify the assertion.

Participation

For the next two measures, I gather data from remarks spoken on the floor by members of the House and Senate in every fifth Congress from the 32nd (1851–53) to the 107th (2001–3). I describe how remarks are identified in the previous chapter. Participation is revealed by the mean number of remarks per member per Congress: The higher the score, the greater the participation. Figure 5.3 displays the data.

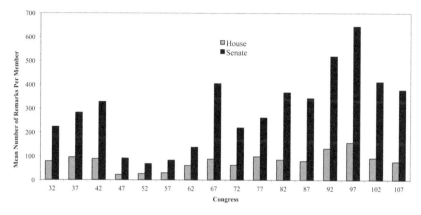

Fig. 5.3. Mean number of remarks per member per Congress, every fifth Congress from the 32nd (1851–53) to the 107th (2001–3). (Data from author's calculations.)

The data clearly vindicate the Senate-superior hypothesis. In every Congress, the average number of remarks made per senator is more than double—and frequently more than three times—the average number of remarks made per House member. The differences in the chambers' sizes and the Senate's tradition of unlimited debate seem to be obvious candidates as causes. The data do not, however, provide support for the worsen-over-time hypothesis. In the Senate in particular, this participation score has generally, if not entirely smoothly, been moving upward. No doubt this is a direct result of increasing session lengths that are mitigated only a little by increases in chamber size.

The relatively low scores in the 47th (1881–83), 52nd (1891–93), 57th (1901–3), and 62nd (1911–13) Congresses are difficult to explain. It is possible that unidentifiable changes occurred in indexing protocols during this period. The Senate score in the 67th Congress (1921–23) is unusually high. This is the first Congress in the data set after the establishment of the 17th Amendment and the direct election of all senators. Members may have felt an increased need to be heard by constituents.

The House scores are generally flatter, a phenomenon that also provides for rejection of the worsen-over-time hypothesis. However, for both chambers, the data spike for the 97th Congress (1981–83). I do not think too much should be made of an outlier in a sample, but it is interesting this was the first Reagan Congress and a time of fervent debate about the country's ideological direction. It seems as though members exploited nu-

merous opportunities to speak on the floor about the great policy tussles
of that time.

Equality

Figure 5.4 reveals the coefficient of variation of the total remarks made per
member in the same Congresses. Here, higher scores—that is, the standard deviation is larger in relation to the mean—reveal greater inequality.

The Senate-superior hypothesis again finds some corroboration. In
every Congress except the 107th (2001–3), there is greater equality in the
Senate than in the House. Senate floor proceedings generally become
more egalitarian after the 77th Congress (1941–43), although the range in
the upper chamber, from .73 in the 97th (1981–83) and 102nd (1991–93)
Congresses to 1.05 in the 77th (1941–43), is not particularly broad. The
trend in the House is more spectacular. Inequality, if anything, rises
slightly before the 62nd Congress (1911–13), then spikes and then drops
off dramatically after the 72nd (1931–33), so that in the past 30 years, floor
proceedings in the lower chamber are nearly as equal as they are in the
Senate.

How do we explain the more striking House findings? An intuitively
plausible story line is that they are driven by changes in formal rules. The
Senate, with its tradition of unlimited debate and smaller size, has always
been able to accommodate equality. If there is a great amount of time available to talk about things, more members will be able to contribute. When
time is limited, a circumscribed group of powerful and designated members will consume most of it themselves. Changes in House rules to limit
or extend debate ought to influence equality in that chamber, this reasoning goes. But a procedural story is not particularly compelling here. We
might conjecture, for example, that the revolt against the speakership and
rise of the caucus in the 1910s and 1920s would result in greater equality.
These events do not. Moreover, an institutional explanation cannot account for the dramatic decline in inequality that takes place in the 1930s
and that continues in a considerably more gentle fashion to the 1980s. No
institutional reforms of note took place at the beginning of this period, and
although there is some longitudinal fluctuation in the number of special
rules issued by the Rules Committee restricting proceedings, standing
rules governing the length of floor debate have essentially remained the
same since the turn of the 20th century.

A better explanation is provided by the rise in careerism and the per-

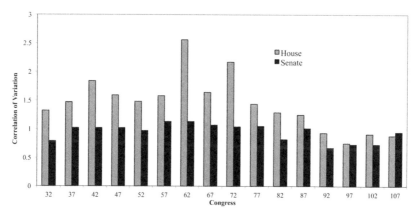

Fig. 5.4. Coefficient of variation of remarks per member per Congress, every fifth Congress from the 32nd (1851–53) to the 107th (2001–3). (Data from author's calculations.)

sonal vote. The most dramatic reduction in the House's turnover rate comes at the turn of the 20th century, just as the seniority rule was making lengthy careers in the House attractive (Price 1977). But another appreciable decline occurs during World War II. Before the war, about one in four new members in a Congress was a freshman, a figure that subsequently dropped to about one in six. Average House terms lengthened discernibly at this time as well. By the 72nd Congress (1931–33), the mean number of terms served was nearly 4.5, but this was an aberration. The figures for surrounding Congresses were generally in the 3.75–4 range. After the Roosevelt landslide claimed many legislators, members again began to accrue long careers, and the 76th Congress (1939–41) was the last one in which the average tenure of a sitting House member was less than eight years (Bullock 1972; Polsby 1968, 145–48).

Of course, earlier rises in careerism had not brought about equality. In fact, the 1895–1905 period seems to coincide with rising inequality. But after World War II, members' desire to make careers in the House was infused with the knowledge that their personal behavior could directly affect their electoral prospects.[7] Voters began to look beyond party labels when selecting House members. The percentage of House districts that were carried by a presidential candidate of one party and a House candidate of the other hovered around 14 percent during the FDR years before topping 21 percent in 1948, and that number was 19 and 30 percent in

1952 and 1956, respectively. The rise of radio and television allowed individual members to become better known to their constituents. Other changes encouraged members to work somewhat selfishly to secure their reelections. In the 73rd Congress (1933–35), for example, 54 members were not from single-member districts; a decade later, their number had dropped to only 13.

As a result, the House provided assistance as members sought to secure reelection with little help from the parties. The Legislative Reorganization Act of 1946 strengthened committees' control over legislative product. Members' committee assignment requests were increasingly shaped by electoral considerations, accommodated by panels of appointers, and protected by seniority and the property right norm that, once on a committee, a member could not be removed. Between 1935 and 1947, the number of personal staff in the House nearly doubled, to about 1,500 (Ornstein, Mann, and Malbin 2002, 128).

Members were motivated to exploit the floor as part of a general strategy to advertise, claim credit, and take positions (Mayhew 1974). The Rules Committee often worked against this effort by preventing bills from coming to the floor and sometimes prohibiting amendments to those that did. Rank-and-file members chafed at these restrictions and were patchily successful at getting around the committee with the establishment and reestablishment of the 21-day rule in 1949 and 1965, the expansion of the Rules Committee to 15 members in 1961, and the stripping of the committee chair's power in 1967. But the committee could not interfere with members' ability to participate in floor debate. The House had long since developed the norm that the presiding officer should allow floor managers to control debate within the basic parameters of the special rule.[8] Floor managers—generally the chair and ranking member of the committee that reported the bill—were free to parcel out their half of the debate time as they saw fit. Since they had little need to associate themselves further with the bill—voters presumably understood that the chair and ranking member of a standing committee had considerable responsibility for legislation within the panel's jurisdiction—committee leaders realized the benefits of dividing time into small increments so that as many grateful members as possible could speak.

My guess at the causes of relative inequality in the House prior to the 77th Congress (1941–43) is more speculative. Formal procedures played at best a small role. Debate was largely unlimited prior to the 1880s, but there was also little demand for floor time. Many members did not pursue congressional careers, and others realized that the fortunes of their party were the principal determinant of their own success. This phenomenon, in turn, was a function of the party ticket system (Bensel 2004, 14–17)—the Australian ballot was not generally adopted until the early 1890s (Katz and Sala 1996; Kernell 1977; Rusk 1970)—and the aggressiveness of party agents at the polls (Bensel 2004). The absence of the direct primary exacerbated matters.

Moreover, in a heterogeneous and segmented country in which the federal government had considerably less power than it does today, members frequently had little interest in what was being debated on the floor. The paucity of media and the relatively uneducated public likely also led many legislators to believe that their constituents were too ignorant to know and understand what happened in the Capitol. If there were direct representational demands, they were probably more often in the form of patronage requests and private bills than attention to broad policy matters.[9] And although most members were well educated by the 1850s, a few undoubtedly still felt unequipped to participate in debate.[10] Over the 32nd Congress (1851–53), for example, the inappropriately named Representative John Schoolcraft (Whig-NY), a man who had received limited education, participated only seven times. Wirls (2007) has shown that the college educated were disproportionately represented among those who contributed to the great debates of the antebellum period.

For those who wanted successful careers in Washington, conversely, frequent participation in floor debate was considered de rigueur. Ambitious members realized that they could impress their colleagues with intellect and oratory rather than with large campaign war chests and frequent appearances on national television. Furthermore, of course, some members wished to express strong positions on issues. Debate, therefore, was taken up by those who had something to say and who were comfortable saying it. Representative Thaddeus Stevens (R-PA), a great rhetorician who was later to chair Ways and Means and lead the House managers at President Andrew Johnson's impeachment trial, was highly educated and cared deeply about slavery. With little competition for floor time in the 37th Congress (1861–63), he participated 1,066 times. In the 32nd Congress (1851–53), Alabama Unionist Democrat George Smith Houston participated 884 times. Measured in space consumed in the *Congressional Globe*, he also spoke for 672 columns. Indeed, the coefficient of variation for the number of columns in the *Globe* covering each House member's remarks is 1.67 for the 32nd. The few who spoke also spoke for a long time.

The relative equality of floor proceedings in the 19th-century Senate is consequently the product of several critical differences between the two chambers of that period. Handpicked by state legislators, senators were truly the elite of society. They represented heterogeneous states, and those who selected them were highly attentive. They had, therefore, a tremendous incentive to involve themselves in the making of all types of legislation. The demand for floor debate was widespread. The Senate's tradition of unlimited debate accommodated these requests, and members participated freely.

Microlevel Data

Presidential Impeachment and Trial

The Constitution describes two separate and very different roles for the House of Representatives and Senate in the impeachment process. It grants the House the authority to impeach certain public officials for "treason, bribery, or other high crimes and misdemeanors." Officials who are impeached face Senate trials; if convicted by at least two-thirds of members present, they are removed from office. As a result, the House and Senate dealt differently with the two presidential impeachments of American history. The House held what amounted to conventional debates on impeachment resolutions, while the Senate conducted trials, presided over by the chief justice, in which members acted as jurors. Senators were permitted to make remarks, offer motions, and ask questions of counsel, but the proceedings were filled largely by the presentation of evidence by the defense and prosecution. In both cases, the latter group consisted of "House managers" who had brought impeachment charges in the lower chamber. Because senators were greatly restricted in what they could say, I apply measures of interaction and commonweal only to the House. Because of the fundamental formal differences in House and Senate proceedings, these cases are not particularly useful in our evaluation of the Senate-superior hypothesis. Instead, I will use the Johnson and Clinton impeachments and trials to assess only the worsen-over-time hypothesis.

Quantity

Figure 5.5 reveals the quantity of floor proceedings in the Johnson and Clinton impeachments. The House figures are the cumulative number of columns in the *Congressional Globe* and *Congressional Record* consumed by

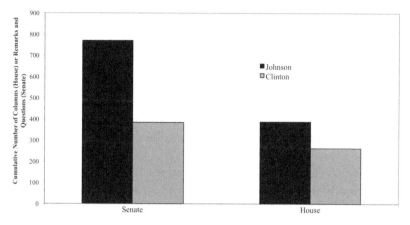

Fig. 5.5. The quantity of floor proceedings in the Johnson and Clinton impeachments and trials. (Data from author's calculations.)

members as they discussed the impeachment resolutions. The Senate figures are the cumulative number of remarks made and questions posed by senators. Senators were permitted to make remarks only after the trials had been formally completed.

The data show a discernible decrease in the quantity of proceedings, especially in the Senate. The Johnson trial covered about twice as many columns as did the Clinton trial and lasted 15 days longer (35 days compared to 20). Why? First, Johnson was charged with 11 counts, and the House reported articles of impeachment on all of them. Clinton was charged with 4, and 2 were dropped by the lower chamber. In addition, the Senate outcome was in considerably more doubt during 1868. Johnson was acquitted on the 3 articles the upper chamber fully considered by just one vote. In Clinton's case, the Senate seemed to be going through the motions and never looked likely to secure the votes of the two-thirds of its membership necessary for conviction. Still, even accounting for some differing circumstances, some evidence supports the worsen-over-time hypothesis. Although aggregate floor proceedings were fewer in the 19th century, Congresses of this era may have intentionally allocated more time to big issues such as this one.

This argument is corroborated by the Senate's resolution condemning President Andrew Jackson in 1834. As a reprimand without an express constitutional basis, such formal criticism of the president, often called censure, differs qualitatively from impeachment. There is also no verbatim record of the Jackson rebuke. Nevertheless, it does provide an interesting data point. In December 1833, the Senate convened for a "panic session" to respond to economic crises that the president's critics argued had been precipitated by the firing of treasury secretary William J. Duane and the removal of government deposits from the Second Bank of the United States by his successor, Roger B. Taney. A resolution was introduced on December 26 and was passed on March 28, after months of impassioned debate, by a vote of 26–20.

The Jackson incident is of additional interest because it evinces the intuitive appeal of the worsen-over-time hypothesis in other ways, such as interaction and reasoning. Reports and analyses of the debate are striking on account of the eloquence and intellect of the participants—Thomas Hart Benton (D-MO), Henry Clay (Whig-KY), John Tyler (Whig-VA), Daniel Webster (Whig-MA), and William Wilkins (D-PA) played especially large roles.[11]

Participation

A quick reading of the participation data suggests that we should reject the worsen-over-time hypothesis. Figure 5.6 shows the percentage of members who participated in the impeachment debates and trials. The Senate data are split into remarks made by members and questions offered by them. In both chambers, although especially when it came to questions in the Senate, more legislators were actively involved in the process affecting Clinton. This can be explained not so much by a pervasive intensity of feeling but by increased representational demands on members. For example, the country was transfixed by the events of 1867 and 1868—the galleries were constantly full and the press followed proceedings closely—but members certainly did not receive as much explicit direction from the public as their counterparts did during the Clinton episode. During 1998, for example, the House e-mail system frequently crashed because of the volume of advice members were receiving from constituents (P. Baker 2000, 222–23).

Equality

Figure 5.7 shows the coefficient of variation for the number of times members participated in the Johnson and Clinton impeachment and trials.[12] As with the macrolevel data, the worsen-over-time hypothesis is not supported. There was greater equality in the Clinton proceedings than the Johnson proceedings, although the temporal differences are explained en-

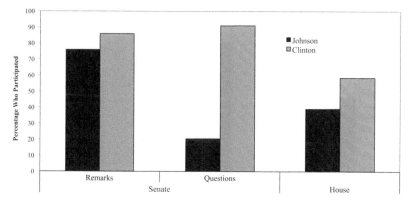

Fig. 5.6. The percentage of members who participated in the Johnson and Clinton impeachments and trials. (Data from author's calculations.)

tirely by the Senate. Differences in the certainty of outcomes may explain the intercameral variation in equality, as well as participation. In Johnson's case, it seemed clear that the House would impeach, but there was tremendous uncertainty about conviction. For Clinton, the House's decision was harder to predict than the Senate's. So as to send unambiguous signals and try to convince colleagues with softer positions, leaders and those with intense preferences about the outcome are likely to demand disproportionately more floor time when it is uncertain. As a result, the doubt surrounding the House's decision on the Clinton impeachment likely mitigated the general historical trend toward greater equality and participation detected in the macrolevel data, while the certainty about the outcome of the Senate trial accentuated it.

Interaction and Commonweal

Figure 5.8 shows the performance of the interaction and commonweal measures for the Johnson and Clinton impeachment data. There were nearly three times as many colloquies in the Johnson impeachment proceedings per one hundred columns as there were for Clinton. There were more yields in the earlier episode. However, the high number of yields in the Johnson impeachment does not necessarily indicate greater agreement among members. Eighty percent of yield requests were granted in the Clinton case, compared to only 55 percent for Johnson. Still, at least when it comes to interaction on presidential impeachment, an essential part of

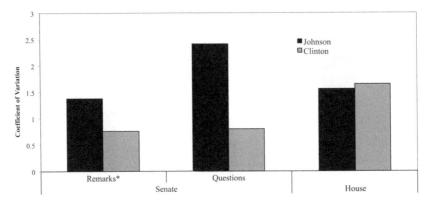

Fig. 5.7. The equality of participation in the Johnson and Clinton impeachments and trials. (Data from author's calculations. The remarks score for Clinton excludes remarks made by Majority Leader Trent Lott. Lott made 38 remarks pertaining to parliamentary procedure.)

deliberation and education, some evidence corroborates the worsen-over-time hypothesis.

I do not think it is a stretch to say there was greater meaningful deliberation in the Johnson case. During the Clinton impeachment, members seemed much more interested in giving speeches than in engaging colleagues. Although the House was divided in both instances, members exploited the opportunity to state and justify their positions for constituents more in 1998. The Clinton proceedings were more disjointed as members stepped forward to make prepared remarks rather than respond to those made immediately prior. It would be hard to claim that the 1868 debate constituted great floor proceedings, but House members in that case were more keen to tussle directly with colleagues and presumably more engaged with the arguments of opponents.

Reasoning

As I noted above, I do not want to put too much stock in my measure of reasoning. But reasoning is an important element of deliberation, debate, and education, and I should at least tip my hat to it. Consequently, I have attempted to gather evidence about the arguments House members made in both episodes. I do not analyze the upper chamber because senators only made statements after the trial. This situation likely encouraged after-the-fact rationalization rather than reasoning.

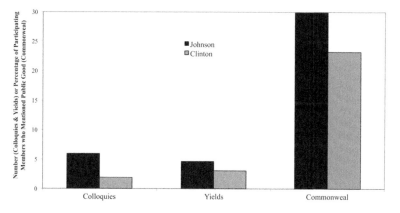

Fig. 5.8.   Interaction and commonweal in the House floor proceedings in the Johnson and Clinton impeachments. (Data from author's calculations.)

Similarities exist between the two debates. In both episodes, presidential accusers honed a multifaceted and complex legal argument to make their case, while defenders corralled a greater variety but less cohesive set of points to make theirs. In the Clinton case, for example, Republicans referred constantly to how the president's testimony to a grand jury constituted perjury and obstruction of justice. Democrats, for their part, explained that the charges were an extension of what minority leader Richard Gephardt (D-MO) called "the politics of smear and slash and burn," that Clinton's behavior was personal, that the public was opposed to impeachment, and that impeachment supporters wished to overturn an election.[13] Clinton's supporters also resorted to arguments concerning procedure. The impeachment debate, several asserted, should be delayed because the United States had launched cruise missiles against Iraq a day earlier. Others claimed that censure was more appropriate and that impeaching Clinton would trivialize an important constitutional process.

In the Johnson instance, Republican detractors asserted that the president had clearly violated the Tenure of Office Act, that presidential power to remove officers was limited, and that the Senate was justified in overruling Johnson's dismissal of Stanton. Johnson's supporters argued that his crime was one of political disagreement, that dangerous ideological extremists had taken over the Republican Party, that impeachment was part of a Republican strategy to get blacks to vote, that removing the president would cause deep political harm and be tantamount to reversing an election, that public opinion sided largely with Democrats, and that the Committee on Reconstruction's report that precipitated the proceeding was improperly presented because it sat while the House was in session without special leave to do so.

As with the interaction data, however, greater engagement between members is noticeable in the Johnson impeachment, perhaps a product of different circumstances but also suggesting a higher level of reasoning. Republican accusers directly addressed their opponents' claims. They talked a great deal, for example, about the president's blatant disregard of legislative prerogatives, his defiance of the legacy of brave Union soldiers, and the fact that the Civil War repudiated Democratic Party politics in the eyes of the American people. Similarly, Democratic defenders confronted the legal case against the president. Many of them made an intricate argument that the firing of Stanton did not violate the Tenure of Office Act, especially since it allowed for the removal of executive personnel one month after the expiration of the appointing president's term (Lincoln had tapped Stanton for the War Department) and that a reading of the act's legislative history, the Constitution, and existing statutes provided the president with the right to sack cabinet members. The two sides were forced to take on one another on a broader intellectual expanse. A clear distinction exists between the two cases. Its exact magnitude defies quantification, but I believe a difference exists.[14]

War and Authorizing the President to Use Force

Unlike presidential impeachment and trial, the cases of war declaration and the authorization of the presidential use of force are treated the same in both the House and Senate. There is debate surrounding an identical or nearly identical resolution. These cases can, therefore, be used to test the Senate-superior hypothesis as well as the worsen-over-time hypothesis.

Quantity

Figure 5.9 reveals the cumulative number of columns devoted to floor proceedings surrounding four of the cases—World War I, the Tonkin Gulf, the Gulf War, and the Iraq War. We do not have a verbatim record of the declarations of war on Britain in 1812 and Mexico in 1846, so I do not include these cases here. There are two occasions where the House's proceedings are longer than the Senate's and two when the opposite is the case. This is inconsistent with the findings from the macrolevel data and

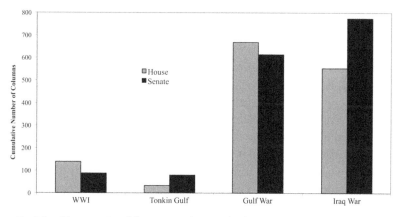

Fig. 5.9. The quantity of floor proceedings in the decisions to go to war or authorize the presidential use of force. (Data from author's calculations.)

leads us to rebuff the Senate-superior hypothesis. Furthermore, there is a dramatic increase in the quantity of proceedings over time that forces a rejection of the worsen-over-time claim.

Why is there such a huge increase in the quantity of proceedings? One explanation is that the authorizations of the presidential use of force prior to the Gulf and Iraq Wars were, at the time, more controversial than the decisions to enter World War I and respond to North Vietnamese aggression. Indeed, the Spanish-American War and World War II are not in my data set precisely because broad consensus in favor of U.S. entry greatly truncated the proceedings surrounding those declarations. The Senate passed the resolution declaring war on Germany in 1917 by a vote of 82–6; the House passed it 373–50. The Tonkin Gulf Resolution of 1964 famously received unanimous support from the House members who voted on it and passed 98–2 in the upper chamber—only Senators Ernest Gruening (D-AK) and Wayne Morse (D-OR) opposed it.

But Congress also traditionally did not like to dwell on such matters. The Mexican-American War, declared during the middle of what has been considered an era of splendid floor proceedings, passed the House by a 174–14 vote after just two hours of debate. The considerably more contentious War of 1812 was debated in the House for just one day. Led by Speaker Henry Clay (Rep.-KY), southern and western "war hawks" railed at the British for their attack on the U.S. *Chesapeake*, impressment of American seamen, seizure of American ships, blockade of American ports, incitement of Indian attacks on the frontier, and 1807 orders in council that barred trade with France by third parties. Congress rushed to war at the expense of floor deliberation. That the House debate over the 1812 war resolution was conducted entirely in secret—and that part of the Senate's debate took place behind closed doors as well—does not assist the worsen-over-time hypothesis with regard to transparency either.

The floor debates on declarations of war with Britain and Mexico provide some vindication for our expectation that the Senate is superior, however. Despite being approved by a 40–2 vote, the Senate resolution was debated over two days in 1846 as members argued about whether they should provide President James K. Polk with the authority to prosecute the war vigorously rather than merely recognize that it existed. In 1812, the Senate debated for five days before declaring war on June 18 by a vote of 19–13.

Participation

As was the case with the macrolevel data, we see the expected intercameral differences in the area of participation. As figure 5.10 shows, a larger proportion of Senators than House members participated in all four floor proceedings. Again, the upper chamber's propensity for unlimited debate is a likely cause. Senate participation was also greater in the proceedings surrounding the declaration of war with Mexico. Although we lack a verbatim record of the debates, the *Congressional Globe* reports that 43.1 percent of sitting senators participated, compared to only 16.2 percent of House members.

As with impeachment and trial, however, we must reject the worsen-over-time hypothesis. A general upward trend in participation exists. Given the scrutiny paid the prologues to the two conflicts with Iraq and the importance of the personal vote in congressional elections, members likely felt the need to put their thoughts on the most formal of records. On several occasions in 1991 and 2002, legislators mentioned that this was the most important debate in which they would participate over their careers. But it is still interesting that the quantity and participation scores for the wars with Iraq should be so high. The current era is purportedly one in which Congress is tremendously deferential to the president on issues of national security.

Equality

In contrast with the findings from the macrolevel analysis, the Senate-superior hypothesis is not corroborated by the equality data. The worsen-over-time hypothesis must also be rejected, just as it was in the assessment

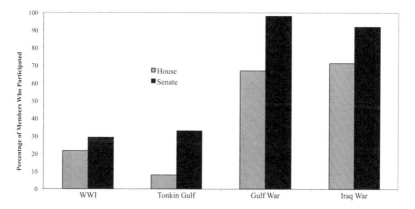

Fig. 5.10.   The percentage of members who participated in the decisions to go to war or authorize the presidential use of force. (Data from author's calculations.)

of the macrolevel and impeachment data. Indeed, as figure 5.11 shows, there is some evidence of increasing equality over time.

The macrolevel data revealed a dramatic increase in equality in House floor proceedings after World War II. With the very conspicuous exception of the Tonkin Gulf Resolution, which was uniquely uncontroversial, equality increased here, too. I hesitate to make too much of this observation, but I think it is instructive to contrast the equality of House floor proceedings surrounding the declaration of war against Germany in 1917 and those that led to the authorization of presidential force against Iraq in 1991 and 2002. There is no doubt that members had strong feelings about the U.S. entry into World War I. Proponents were outraged by the sinking of the *Lusitania* and the Zimmerman note and energized by President Woodrow Wilson's call to arms.[15] Opponents—generally midwesterners—spoke of British duplicity and construed American interests more narrowly by arguing that the country should keep out of European affairs. At one stage during the House debate, the sergeant at arms approached Representative John Burnett (D-AL) with the mace after the congressman excitedly accused his fellow Alabama Democrat, Representative Tom Heflin, of being a British stooge. Despite the importance of the issue and strength of preferences, however, many members did not feel compelled to speak.

This situation contrasts starkly with the 1991 and 2002 debates on resolutions authorizing the presidential use of force against Saddam Hussein, in which large majorities of members participated. Again, the reasons seem

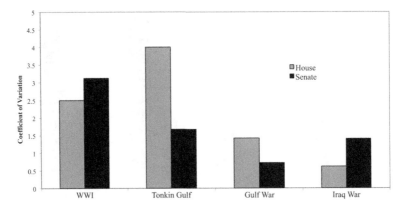

Fig. 5.11. The equality of participation in the decisions to go to war or authorize the presidential use of force. (Data from author's calculations.)

electoral—as I have explained before, the personal vote, greater transparency, and heightened representational demands seem to have motivated legislator contributions to floor proceedings.

In fact, with regard to important debates about war and peace, this contemporary notion of equality seems to have developed from a need, through a norm, and, recently at least, into a procedure. For example, during a February 2007 House debate about President George W. Bush's policy of increasing troop levels in Iraq by 20,000—the "surge"—each member formally received the opportunity to speak for up to five minutes.

This general finding about equality is confirmed by the proceedings surrounding the declaration of war against Mexico. The coefficients of variation for the number of times each member of the chamber participated—not the length of participation—are quite high, at 2.97 for the House and 1.78 for the Senate.

Interaction

Figure 5.12 shows that the data on yields and colloquies somewhat corroborates the worsen-over-time hypothesis. This finding is consistent with the analysis of presidential impeachment and trial and is strengthened if we consider the Senate results for the Tonkin Gulf Resolution to be outliers. The scores in those proceedings suggest very high interaction, but they can be largely attributed to members on each side of the debate yielding and conversing with allies. For example, the two naysayers, Gruening and

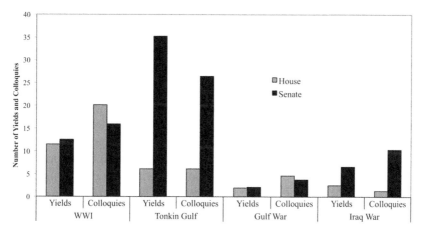

Fig. 5.12. Interactions in the decisions to go to war or authorize the presidential use of force. (Data from author's calculations.)

Morse, consumed a large proportion of the proceedings, engaging in a sort of tag-team exercise. In reality, little interaction occurred in either chamber in 1964. By contrast, the 1917 proceedings displayed a great deal of interaction uncontaminated by obsequious dialogue. Only 47 percent of yield requests were granted in the House, 78.6 percent in the Senate. Ninety percent of such requests were granted during the Senate debate on the Tonkin Gulf.

The Senate-superior hypothesis is more difficult to substantiate, especially if we take out the Tonkin Gulf proceedings. The 2002 Iraq resolution, however, displays markedly greater interaction in the Senate. The deep partisan split on the issue and clamor to participate may explain why House members did not want to give up any of their floor time to colleagues. With fewer limitations on their freedom to speak, senators probably felt more comfortable yielding.[16]

Trade

I use the trade bill proceedings to test both hypotheses, and because of the larger number of observations, I can do so a little more systematically. Since verbatim records of debate are not available before 1857, I split the time series into two parts. I examine the 6 1824–46 bills separately from the 25 1857–2002 measures. Comparisons across the two sets of proceedings are, therefore, difficult to make.

Quantity

Figure 5.13 displays the number of days the trade bills of 1824, 1828, 1832, 1833, 1842, and 1846 were debated on the House and Senate floors. Figure 5.14 reveals the total number of columns consumed by floor debate on the 25 bills since 1857. The patterns are certainly complex and take time to discern; however, after some study, they reveal little evidence to confirm the Senate-superior hypothesis. Indeed, in the early years, proceedings were much longer in the House, a finding consistent with the notion that the lower body gathered information and the Senate behaved as a sort of House of Lords by either approving or rejecting bills written by the other chamber. By the turn of the 20th century there is greater quantity of floor proceedings in the Senate. Some of this growth can probably be attributed to the upper body's embrace of the more equal and symmetrical bicameralism we witness today. Much is also likely the result of members' exploitation of the chamber's practice of unlimited debate, something that had essentially been eliminated in the House by that time. The Senate's treatment of the 1930 Smoot-Hawley Tariff, for example—which consumes the most columns of those proceedings in the data set, 4,183.5—was subject to an energetic and obstinate filibuster by members from agrarian states.

The post–World War II pattern is mixed. But it is clear that since the early 1990s, the Senate again spends considerably more time on trade proceedings than the House. Procedures probably help explain this result as well. Since trade bills are reported by the Committee on Ways and Means, they are subject to closed special rules. In recent years, these rules have not only barred amendments but also been stingy on the amount of time set aside for debate—for example, the rule on the 1994 General Agreement on Tariffs and Trade bill allowed for four hours, while the resolution providing further consideration of the 2000 bill to create permanent normal trade relations with China only three.

Analysis of the worsen-over-time hypothesis is no easier. Figure 5.13 clearly illustrates that the debates of the 1820s were longer than those of the 1840s but figure 5.14 shows a rather bell-shaped pattern, with debates from the 1880s to 1930s much longer than those before or after. Procedural issues likely account for much of this bulge. Soon after the House Rules Committee began to issue special rules, it used them to restrict trade proceedings. Chastened by the lengthy and raucous debate on the 1888 Mills Bill, the Republican majority, led by Speaker Thomas Brackett Reed

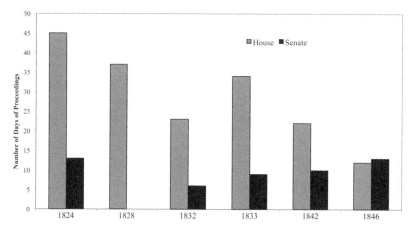

Fig. 5.13.   The length of floor proceedings on major trade bills, 1824–46. (Data from author's calculations.)

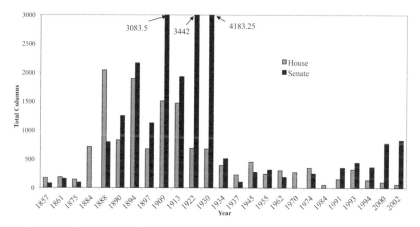

Fig. 5.14.   The length of floor proceedings on major trade bills, 1857–2002. (Data from author's calculations.)

(R-ME), forced the adoption of a restrictive rule during general debate on the 1890 McKinley Tariff. Although House treatment of trade bills continued to consume many columns of the *Congressional Record*, the majority slowly began to constrain floor debate on the issue to the point that today, such measures are granted a closed special rule as a matter of convention.[17]

The explosion in the number of issues dealt with by the federal government has undoubtedly suppressed the amount of floor time devoted to trade bills as well. Trade remains a crucial issue for the American economy, but members of Congress are consumed by many more problems and policies now than was the case prior to the New Deal.

All in all, the worsen-over-time hypothesis only has real merit if we compare the proceedings of the modern era with those of the end of the 19th century and beginning of the 20th. If we test the hypothesis on the entire expanse of congressional history, the results are considerably more ambiguous.

Participation

Figure 5.15 displays the percentage of members who participated in these proceedings, beginning with the 1857 bill. For only one bill, the 1888 Mills Bill, the proportion of House members that took part in the debate exceeds that of the Senate, and then only marginally. For all the bills in the 1824–46 period, a greater percentage of lawmakers participated in the Senate than in the House.[18] The evidence quite clearly corroborates the Senate-superior hypothesis. Indeed, in most cases, especially since 1930, Senate participation rates are much higher. An educated guess again suggests that procedural and size differences generate the disparity. The small Senate's open procedures allow a greater percentage of members to participate.

There is a little evidence to reinforce the worsen-over-time hypothesis on the Senate side, especially because participation rates drop off a bit after 1930. I think it is fair to say, however, that the House data are quite consistent with the hypothesis, although the contentious 1993 debate on the North American Free Trade Agreement (NAFTA) is a conspicuous exception. Again, the restrictive procedures that come about after the 1880s and the time pressures of a sizable and growing agenda are likely causes.

Equality

Once more, the Senate-superior hypothesis is confirmed. As figure 5.16 displays, on all but three pieces of the more modern legislation—the 1888 Mills bill, the 1894 Gorman Tariff, and the 1955 Reciprocal Trade Agreement extension—the House's coefficient of variation is larger than the Senate's. This is the case for all the bills prior to 1857. On trade bills, at least, debate in the Senate is considerably more equal than in the House.

The worsen-over-time hypothesis must be rejected for the Senate. There really is no temporal pattern here. There is some evidence consistent with the expectation within the House data, however. It does seem as though proceedings in the lower chamber have become less equal since

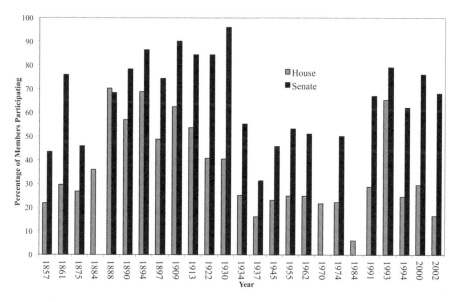

Fig. 5.15. The percentage of members who participated on major trade bills, 1857–2002. (Data from author's calculations.)

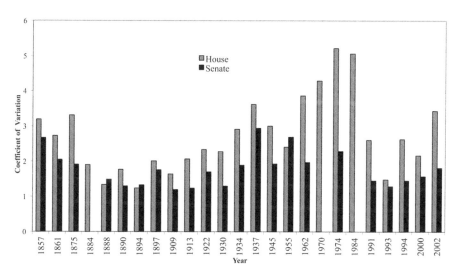

Fig. 5.16. The equality of participation on major trade bills, 1857–2002. (Data from author's calculations.)

World War II, at least until the 1990s. The relative equality during the late 19th and early 20th century occurs when many amendments on trade bills were still permitted and large numbers of members felt compelled to come to the floor to defend or promote the direct commercial interests of their constituents. After that date, amending activity was restricted and members likely believed the fate of their parochial economic concerns turned, if member preferences on the legislation were not already determined, on broad arguments about the bill that many of their colleagues would make.

The inequality of later proceedings is also likely a function of the prominence of standing committees in the era between 1945 and the post-reform Congress (Deering and Smith 1997; Fenno 1973). The norms of policy specialization and deference to these institutions meant committee members were looked to for leadership and management of floor proceedings on the bills their panels reported. Members of Ways and Means, therefore, were supposed to participate on trade bills more than colleagues who were not on the committee. In 1962, for example, the cumulative contributions of Ways and Means' members as a proportion of all contributions was 5.16 times larger than the committee's membership as a proportion of the size of the entire body. In 1970 and 1974 these figures were 7.37 and 8.11. This compares with scores of 3.93, 5.33, 2.94, 7.25, and 4.45 for 1888, 1890, 1894, 1897, and 1909.

Note the rising inequality of debate in the House during this period is counter to the trend we see in the macro data presented in Figure 5.4. The apparent contradiction fits with a procedural "committee government" argument in which the House agenda is large and diverse and all committees report bills. The result is that in the aggregate proceedings are relatively equal, but proceedings on individual bills are not. It contrasts with the period from roughly 1880 to 1930 when participation on individual trade bills is relatively, but not completely, equal but there is no compensatory equalizing effect on the aggregate data because certain members contribute more than their colleagues to proceedings on all types of bills. For example, during the 67th Congress (1921–3) House members who contributed most to the entirety of floor proceedings also tended to be those who spoke most on the 1922 Fordney-McCumber tariff. Reps. Thomas L. Blanton (D-TX) and James R. Mann (R-IL), for example, were in the top five in total contributions in that Congress and were among the most talkative of participants in the Fordney-McCumber debate. Neither of them sat on Ways and Means. Indeed, Blanton participated most in the Congress (1,364 mentions) and spoke for the longest time in the tariff debate (21.5

columns). It also seems as though floor leaders took their responsibilities seriously and gave much to floor treatment of bills on all sorts of issues. Reps. Finis Garrett (D-TN), acting minority leader during Fordney-Mc-Cumber, and Frank Mondell (R-WY), majority leader for the entire Congress, were also in the top five by total numbers of aggregate contributions in the 67th Congress and occupied a lot of floor time during the trade bill proceedings. Again, neither was a member of Ways and Means.

This contrasts with 2002, the year of the trade promotion authority bill. In the 107th Congress (2001–3) only Rep. Bill Thomas (R-CA), chair of Ways and Means, was both a top twenty contributor to aggregate floor proceedings and particularly prominent in the debate on the trade bill itself.

Interaction

Figures 5.17 and 5.18 reveal the number of colloquies and times members yielded when requested to do so per 100 columns for the post-1857 trade bills. These data are used to test the hypotheses on the interaction characteristic. Note two very different patterns. The colloquies data reveal a rather steady decline over time, the yield data sketch out a bell-shaped curve. What do we make of the worsen-over-time hypothesis in light of this? My sense is that there has been a rather dramatic decline in interaction over the time series as the colloquy data display. There are a small number of yields in the 19th century because the culture of Congress at the time permitted more free-wheeling debate in which members regularly interrupted one another without securing permission to do so. By 1900, however, formal requests to yield had become the norm and lawmakers interacted with one another by acquiescing. It is not that pre-20th century proceedings were all models of give-and-take. The 1884 House debate on the Morrison bill, for example, is characterized by members' long speeches and unwillingness to engage their colleagues in any sort of interaction. But on reading the proceedings of the pre-1960 period, one gets a real sense of what superior debate and deliberation should be. Members respond to one another's arguments directly and are quick to allow colleagues to join the discussion.

It is clear that by 1970 there is little interaction in House and Senate floor proceedings on trade. Both the colloquies and yields data reveal the current practice of members coming to the floor, delivering prepared speeches, largely respecting each others' desires not to be interrupted, and leaving after their remarks with the effect that they are not around to engage colleagues when it is time for others to participate.

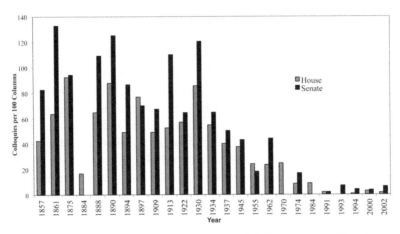

Fig. 5.17. The number of colloquies on major trade bills, 1857–2002. (Data from author's calculations.)

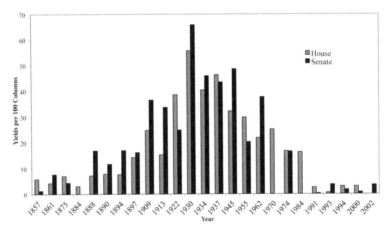

Fig. 5.18. The number of yields on major trade bills, 1857–2002. (Data from author's calculations.)

The interaction data make it a bit more difficult to make a judgment about the Senate-superior hypothesis. On the whole, Senate proceedings on individual bills tend to have more colloquies and yields than their House equivalents, presumably because senators need not covet floor time as much as do House members, who have many more colleagues and operate under greater restrictions. Still the difference is not spectacular. Indeed, in recent years, despite enjoying more open procedures than their counterparts in the lower chamber, senators really interact with each other no more than do members of the House.

Commonweal

Figure 5.19 reveals the proportion of participating members who appealed to the collective interest during their contributions to the floor proceedings on trade bills. Its most striking feature is its flatline quality. Generally between one in seven and one in three members use language that frames their case as one in the national interest. There is no real up or down trend. There is certainly little here to confirm the worsen-over-time hypothesis, and although more senators generally use commonweal terms to justify their position than do House members, the differences are negligible and probably largely attributable to the longer contributions to proceedings made in the upper body.

A close reading of debates readily illustrates that many legislators have utilized arguments other than those that their position promotes the general welfare. The points made have changed over time, but their roots in economic self-interest and partisan, ideological, procedural, and interbranch conflict have not. Members have come to the floor to promote vigorously the positions, among others, of the oil, shoe, sugar, tobacco, watch, wool, and whiskey industries. Trade proceedings have been ground zero in geographic tussles (most notably between southerners and members from New England) and sectional battles (most notably between manufacturing and agriculture and since 1900 at least between business and organized labor). The proceedings frequently involve issues other than trade policy. Procedural issues have come into play: The 1890 and 1955 House proceedings were characterized by minority party members bemoaning the use of Gag Rules to restrict the offering of amendments, for example. There are continual complaints about the growth of executive power as well, since bills have frequently incorporated an authorization for the president to negotiate trade agreements or agencies to set tariff levels, especially after Smoot-Hawley. Some proceedings have been immersed in the politics of their particular era. These arguments are generally framed as promoting broader interests. The 2002 Senate proceedings on Trade Promotion Authority (TPA) involved much talk of the Israeli-Palestinian conflict. Many contributions to the 1974 Senate proceedings on the Trade Reform Act focused on the Jackson-Vanik provision and its implications for human rights and the Cold War. In the mid-19th century, slavery was frequently discussed by southerners and New Englanders, and prior to the

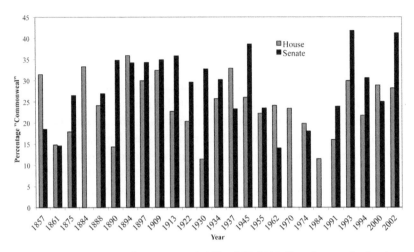

Fig. 5.19. Commonweal on major trade bills, 1857–2002. (Data from author's calculations.)

creation of the direct income tax in 1913, discussion repeatedly centered on public finances because tariff proceeds were so important to general revenues. In fact, the Underwood Tariff Bill reinstituted the federal income tax. The basic sense these data provide, however, is one of constancy rather than change.

If anything, we could argue that members have been invoking public interest arguments a bit more frequently in the past two decades. The 1993 NAFTA and 2002 TPA proceedings have some of the highest instances of commonweal, especially in the Senate. Yet, even if one accepts the premise that general welfare arguments have been employed more recently, this development may not necessarily be positive. Legislators today seem to present rather emotive and vacuous appeals to country, a habit that I think contrasts with earlier, more thoughtful arguments using similar language. To be fair, this fluffiness might not completely be the fault of the participants. I would hazard a guess that procedural constraints—the restrictive special rules in the House and unanimous consent agreements (UCAs) in the Senate—have forced legislators to discuss bills succinctly and in their entirety. Before about World War II, the capacity of the rank and file to offer amendments on even the most narrow of provisions forced members to understand and construct arguments from the complex technicalities of trade and the American economy. The debates from about 1930 illustrate that many members had an amazing grasp of policy details.

On just about all of these characteristics, the debates between the 1880s and 1930s show themselves to be of the highest quality. They are of greater quantity, enjoy more widespread and equal participation, and display a tremendous amount of interaction. This phenomenon is hard to explain, although high levels of partisanship and procedural restrictions—that is, the kinds of qualities that many observers accuse of undermining congressional floor proceedings today—existed for much of that time as well.

Conclusion

This section of the book represents a first attempt to test systematically two hypotheses, built on both anecdotal evidence and theory, about the quality of congressional floor proceedings. Table 5.1 summarizes the findings, which, it must be noted, are not completely unambiguous.

TABLE 5.1. Testing the Senate Superior and Worsen-over-Time Hypotheses: A Summary of the Findings

Characteristic	Senate Superior Hypothesis			
			Micro-Level Data	
	Macro-Level Data	Impeachment	War	Trade
Quantity	+	NA	•	+/•
Participation	+	NA	+	+
Equality	+	NA	•	+
Interaction	NA	NA	•	+/•
Civility	•	NA	NA	NA
Commonweal	NA	NA	NA	•
Transparency	•	NA	NA	NA

Characteristic	Worsen-over-Time Hypothesis			
			Micro-Level Data	
	Macro-Level Data	Impeachment	War	Trade
Quantity	–	• (Hse), + (Sen)	–	+/•
Participation	• (Hse), – (Sen)	–/• (Hse), – (Sen)	–	+ (Hse), +/• (Sen)
Equality	– (Hse), • (Sen)	• (Hse), – (Sen)	–	+/• (Hse), • (Sen)
Interaction	NA	+/•	+	+
Civility	•	NA	NA	NA
Reasoning	NA	+/•	NA	NA
Commonweal	NA	+/•	NA	•
Transparency	–	NA	NA	NA

Source: Calculated by author.

+ denotes that the hypothesis is corroborated, – that the opposite is found, • that there is no discernible finding either way. NA denotes that the characteristic was not measured using that particular data set. Note that in some cases findings are equivocal—that is, the findings are different for each chamber or they straddle two different outcome types.

There is some clarity, however. First, the Senate-superior hypothesis has stronger claims than the worsen-over-time hypothesis. Plus signs greatly outnumber minus signs in the top half of the table; this is not the case in the bottom half. I have previously suggested a number of explanations for why floor proceedings are of higher quality in the Senate than the House. The size and heterogeneity of Senate constituencies have compelled members of the upper chamber to take greater interest in a wider variety of policy areas. House members represent constituents with narrower concerns. Over time, the House has decided—with, for example, its previous question, special rules, and intolerance of dilatory practices—to restrict floor proceedings. The Senate, conversely, has rules and conventions that allow essentially unlimited debate, permitting greater quantity and participation. To a lesser extent, these practices also lead to enhanced interaction, since senators do not have to worry about yielding scarce floor time to colleagues.

Second, the worsen-over-time hypothesis has a kind of dual quality. Although the post–World War I trade data constitute an exception, we should probably reject the hypothesis with regard to quantity, participation, and equality. Greater aggregate quantity, participation, and equality in the modern era are likely the result of the decline of parties and the rise of candidate-centered campaigns and the personal vote. These developments generate pressure on members to speak on the floor and take positions, claim credit, and avoid blame. In turn, the chambers have established practices and procedures that facilitate broader participation in an orderly and fair manner.

However, considerable evidence corroborates the worsen-over-time hypothesis in the area of the substance of proceedings, or how members deal with each other and opposing arguments. Measures of interaction, reasoning, and to a lesser extent commonweal tend to decrease over time. Important indicators of debate and deliberation do seem to experience temporal decline.

Why? Again the most likely cause is electoral interests and resultant facilitative procedures. As congressional life has become more transparent and the media more attentive to legislators' behavior, members have a greater incentive to go to the floor for the purposes of impressing an external audience—most notably, their constituents. At the same time, however, the floor has been losing its importance in the legislative process. The fate of policy is generally decided in committees, party caucuses, and leadership meetings. What happens in these forums has a significant effect on congressional careers as well. Although ambitious members interested in accumulating power on the Hill or moving up to higher office are acutely aware of the spotlight on floor proceedings, they understand that the sophisticated audiences—congressional leaders and colleagues, party activists, media pundits, and engaged citizens—that largely determine policy and electoral outcomes also scrutinize loyalty to the party, committee behavior, intellectual ability, organizational talents, campaigning, newspaper op-ed pieces, and numerous other activities in which members engage off the floor.

As a result, the floor is viewed as a place for show rather than for work. The many other demands on members' time mean that they cannot be on the floor much or even follow debate on television. They cannot, therefore, tailor their remarks to what colleagues have said. Members also shun debate and deliberation because they consume time that might be more efficiently spent. Both activities require significant preparation and eat up floor proceedings that could be used to allow legislators to advertise positions. They would reduce participation and equality, two characteristics most treasured by the general membership these days. To make matters worse, with greater transparency the floor has become a show for a broad audience, much of which is quite uncultivated when it comes to politics. Debate and deliberation complicate the delivery of simple and clear arguments and emotive messages that appeal to many voters because superior debate involves the construction of a multifaceted case and superior deliberation a direct response to critics. These qualities have become liabilities.

The new politics of floor proceedings have been institutionalized and reinforced by formal rules changes and the emergence of informal norms. To allow for greater participation and equality, floor managers divvy up floor time into small parcels. This practice contributes to disjointed proceedings and provides less opportunity for members to engage in debate and deliberation. The House has also been setting aside increasing amounts of time for one-minute and special order speeches (Schneider 2003a, 2003b). Established by the Speaker's policies and unanimous consent, these speeches allow members to discuss nonlegislative matters of their choosing—they are conducted when there is no bill on the floor—at the beginning and end of the day. For special orders, members apply to be recognized in advance. In both practices, they read from prepared remarks.[19] Political scientists have shown that participation in these activities is related to electoral security, minority party status, and ideological extremism, findings that fit with the story here (Maltzman and Sigelman

1996; Morris 2001).[20] Members, especially those who find it relatively difficult to secure time during regular debate, want to use the floor to signal simplistic and emotive positions to constituents. Such members have been accommodated by leadership and formal rules because floor time is cheap compared to a role affecting the substance of policy. The proliferation of one-minute and special order speeches, in turn, contributes nothing to debate and deliberation.

Something similar has happened in the Senate. As demand for floor time and obstructionism rooted in heightened partisanship and ideological polarization have increased, so the upper chamber has had to order its floor proceedings. It has largely done so through UCAs that restrict amendments and the amount of time floor managers control (Ainsworth and Flathman 1995; Evans and Oleszek 2000; Smith and Flathman 1989). Floor proceedings have consequently become increasingly choreographed and disjointed. In other words, they exhibit less debate and deliberation.

The explanations for the patterns I see are not rigorously tested, and some may seem a little speculative. But there is little doubt from this exploratory effort to test systematically and empirically basic assumptions about the quality of congressional floor proceedings over a long time series that a sizable amount of the evidence validates the two hypotheses, even if it is quite a bit less than impressionistic evaluations would have us believe.

Conclusion

A Future for the Floor

"My legislative home is here on the floor with you, and so is my heart."

—SPEAKER DENNIS HASTERT to the U.S. House of Representatives, January 6, 1999, breaking with tradition by giving his first remarks as Speaker from the floor rather than from the Speaker's chair on the dais

This book provides a systematic analysis of the floor. It is a topic crucial to an understanding of what makes a good legislature because the kinds of bodies we should want have powerful floors where members exercise robust rights and engage in proceedings of the highest caliber. More specifically, the book answers two critical questions. I first explored the causes of the profound bicameral differences in floor power and rights—the House is clearly more restrictive, the Senate more natural. I proposed and tested three hypotheses. I showed that House and Senate floor power and floor rights generally weaken when the chambers experience growth in membership and workload and their majority parties strengthen.

I concluded, however, that although the House and Senate are clearly pushed in a restrictive direction when majority parties are strong, the distinctiveness of the two bodies' floors is largely attributable to differences in size and workload. Most of the critical procedures that make the House more restrictive were put into place before members' policy and procedural preferences were fused together by party, and majority party legislators realized that manipulating the floor agenda and rigorous control of floor debate were beneficial to the advancement of their policy and electoral interests. The House and Senate accrued most of their critical procedural differences prior to the Civil War, diverging on such matters as the power of presiding officers and committees, the previous question, and germaneness of amendments. By 1900, the bifurcation was largely complete.

In the antebellum era, it was unclear which party controlled the floor agenda and proceedings. When the bodies' memberships and workloads grew, a broader agreement to restrict procedures was more likely to materialize. By the dawn of the 20th century, potential changes in procedures and practices could be readily gauged in partisan terms, and members were assured of the kind of changes that would benefit both themselves and their party. Since then, the strengthening of the majority party has been a more reliably robust determinant of the bodies' organizational development. The House and Senate were essentially locked into their procedural trajectories, however. As others have noted previously (Binder 1997; J. M. Roberts and Smith 2007), the Senate, not least because of its tradition of extended debate, found it impossible to move much from its comparatively natural state. The House remained more restrictive.

The answer to the second question incorporates a test of the Senate-superior and worsen-over-time hypotheses. I find some considerable confirmatory evidence for them, especially the Senate-superior hypothesis. At least in the aggregate, however, floor proceedings have not deteriorated unambiguously over time. There has been appreciable erosion in the standard of debate and deliberation, but contemporary floor proceedings exhibit greater participation, equality, and transparency than those of the 19th century.

My examination clearly shows that the House and Senate floors are not what they might be. Both could be better legislative bodies. The House floor in particular has lost a great deal of power in the chamber's legislative process. The Speaker and standing committees have accrued strong proposal and gatekeeping powers. Floor rights in Congress have weakened too, even in the Senate, where revisions to Rule XXII continue to move the body away from its natural state. And floor proceedings have changed over time. Debate and deliberation have deteriorated. Speeches today are made with little regard to opponents' arguments, and viewed collectively, members' contributions are disjointed. This phenomenon is surely to the detriment of Congress and to public life more generally.

In the remainder of this conclusion, I suggest reforms that can improve the floor, both by naturalizing the two chambers—or giving the floors greater power and invigorating the rights exercised on them—and improving floor proceedings. All of these changes are realistic and reasonable. I do not suggest, for example, that we go back to the 1st Congress or the days of Calhoun, Clay, and Webster or erase Rule XXII from the Senate's books. I also shy away from some obvious but dramatic reforms suggested by my analysis. I do not call for changes that could radically undermine majority party strength, such as reforming the redistricting process to create greater heterogeneity of policy preferences within the House parties. To be effective, such changes would require concerted action across time, institutions, and jurisdictions.

Some of my recommendations are novel; others have been discussed before. But all, I argue, have some value. For reasons I have discussed throughout this book, a good floor is important. It is an integral part of a good legislature.

Reforms That Naturalize the House and Senate

For normative reasons I sketched out earlier, the generally restrictive nature of procedural change in the House and Senate over the past 200-plus years is cast negatively. But decreasing the power of the floor and weakening the rights exercised on it are traded off against certain procedural benefits. Restrictive procedures do not just facilitate the transformation of a cohesive and assertive majority's policy preferences into law. They provide important efficiency gains and help prevent Congress from becoming gridlocked, as many members of recent Senate majorities would readily attest. Indeed, as we saw in chapters 2 and 3, procedural change in the antebellum era often seemed geared explicitly toward overcoming obstacles to legislative productivity. During that period, high workloads and large increases in chamber membership tended to move procedures in a restrictive direction.

Furthermore, the U.S. House and Senate are not, in a cross-sectional comparative sense, particularly restrictive. The data on national legislatures I discussed in chapter 1 reveal that the Senate is 1 of only 10 bodies that have the most naturalized debate termination procedure. The House is 1 of 18 that have the second-most-natural of the three debate termination rules. Taylor (2006) has shown that many national legislative bodies have more restrictive floor amendment procedures. The chambers of Congress also do not have particularly restrictive procedures when compared to American state bodies. While the House's previous question procedure is by far the most commonly used at the state level, the Senate's 60-vote threshold to terminate debate is more natural than that of all but 20 of the 99 state bodies. Only 24 state chambers require fewer members to discharge a committee than the Senate's rule of a simple majority of members present and voting.[1] Only 40 chambers require fewer members than the House's simple majority of members elected.[2]

Still, congressional procedures could be naturalized without undermining efficiency too much. One frequently discussed possibility involves lengthening the congressional workweek so that the House and Senate can spend more time in session. Jet travel and the pressures of candidate-centered campaigns have furnished the capability and will for members to spend considerable time in their states and districts, meeting with constituents. Today the House's "Tuesday-Thursday Club"—the name given to members who limit their time at the Capitol to those three days of the week—is an entrenched institution that dictates the floor schedule. Leaders have also inserted numerous extended "district work periods" that are clustered around holidays and in the late summer. By the 109th Congress (2005–7), the House was in session for only 226 days, about 100 fewer than had been the case 30 years earlier.[3] The new House Republican leadership instituted a "two weeks on, one week off" schedule at the beginning of the 112th Congress in January 2011.

A call for longer sessions is nothing new. Influential Congress-watcher Norman Ornstein (2006) has recommended that Congress commit to spending at least 26 weeks working full time. The new House Democratic majority in the 110th Congress pledged a five-day workweek with members expected at the Capitol by 6:30 P.M. on Monday for votes and to stay until legislative business was finished sometime early Friday afternoon.[4] The House was in session for 283 days in that Congress and 286 in the next. A "three weeks on, one week off" schedule has been proposed elsewhere.[5] Longer sessions—for example, at least 130 days or 26 complete weeks a year—would allow the floor greater time to examine and discuss the legislation brought to it. It would mean greater information for members and in turn more power for the floor. It might also improve civility, as members would be forced to spend more time together. Mayhew (2006, 227) has written that what he calls "communality"—a quality nurtured by intimacy and consisting of strong relationships between members—can improve congressional performance. And, indeed, more floor time is something members seem to want. A 1993 survey of legislators by the Joint

Committee on the Operation of Congress revealed that 60 percent would like to have more opportunities to attend floor debate or follow it on television (Joint Committee 1993a, 275–80).

Of course members do not spend too little time on the floor because they are lazy. There are tremendous demands on their time. They must meet with constituents, staff, and representatives of organized interests; they need to attend to electoral concerns; they have considerable committee work; and they are supposed to keep up with an avalanche of legislation and policy issues. Furnishing greater floor time is more easily said than done. It may make sense to alleviate some of these competing pressures in addition to mandating longer sessions. The demands to be in the district, for example, could be diminished by giving members larger staff budgets. Assistance with fund-raising might help, too, although I am not convinced that Mucciaroni and Quirk's (2006, 207) proposal for public financing of congressional elections as a way of increasing floor time is practicable (or indeed desirable). Cutting committee and subcommittee assignments would likely force legislators' attention to the floor when they are on the Hill (Mann and Ornstein 1992; Mucciaroni and Quirk 2006, 207; G. B. H. Solomon and Wolfensberger 1994, 364).

I also recommend a series of reforms to address the majority party's stranglehold on scheduling and amending activity in the House, powers that weaken the floor and dilute floor rights. I do not propose that the House try to replicate Senate procedures in this regard, but the body could be naturalized a bit. First, the House could institute a supermajority requirement for the acceptance of restrictive special rules written by the Rules Committee. Smith (1989, 248) has suggested that three-fifths of members be needed to approve most types of restrictive rules. Given the narrow majorities of recent history, at least some members of the minority party would have to support the restriction of floor amendments. Such a move is unlikely to result in an avalanche of open rules, since members understand the efficiency value of restrictive ones. But the Rules Committee would have to be more sensitive to members' floor rights. I believe that the reform would force bargaining between Rules Committee members and principal opponents of the bill in question. The former would trade floor rights, the latter support for the special rule.

Second, I suggest a designee of the minority party have the right to offer a first-degree amendment or an amendment in the nature of a substitute to every bill that comes to the floor with a special rule. If adopted without revision, a first-degree amendment replaces part of the bill under consideration, one in the nature of a substitute the entire bill. Such amendments must be germane under standing House rules. One way this could be done is by guaranteeing a motion to recommit with instructions and an order for the committee to which the bill is recommitted to report "forthwith." Current House rules protect the right of the minority leader or his or her designee to offer a motion to recommit with or without instructions.[6] An approved motion to recommit without instructions essentially kills the bill. A motion with instructions directs the committee of jurisdiction to report the bill back to the floor with the requested changes, but in reality the committee does not do so, and the bill dies when this procedure is used. When these instructions direct the committee of jurisdiction to report "forthwith," the mover is essentially amending the bill consistent with the instructions so that the bill would not really leave the floor (Cox, Den Hartog, and McCubbins 2007; Oleszek 2011, 207–10).[7] If passed, the chair of the committee of jurisdiction immediately offers the bill as amended.

If this expanded right to recommit were incorporated into House rules, it would ostensibly provide a right for the minority to propose some kind of alternative to the bill under consideration. Currently, however, the right to recommit with instructions is only subject to 10 minutes of debate unless the special rule provides otherwise. As a result, if the House were to change its rule and establish and protect the right to recommit with instructions forthwith, it ought to increase the amount of time set aside for debate on the motion.

The minority would surely be tempted to use this expanded right for political advantage. Its leadership might not be particularly interested in affecting the substance of the bill but instead might be motivated to put certain members on the record about a controversial iteration of the issue at hand.[8] Regardless, the reform would wrestle away House majority party leaders' near-total control over the agenda and allow the floor to debate a different version of bills under review. It would do so without opening the floodgates to amendments and undermining legislative productivity. Smith (1989) has written extensively about how members used permissive special rules to slow down the legislative process with an avalanche of dilatory amendments in the 1970s and 1980s.

Third, floor power would increase greatly if members were given more time to consider legislation before they were scheduled to debate it. The Rules Committee often issues special rules waiving the requirement that committee reports be made available to members for three business days before the House can take up the related bill. As a result, members are sometimes forced to read and digest legislation that is hundreds of pages long in a matter of hours. This is often the case for conference reports that make considerable changes to bills. The 1,073-page, roughly $800 billion economic stimulus package passed in February 2009 was voted on by both chambers less than a day after the conference report had been finalized.

That practice has now ended. In 2009, just after the stimulus legislation passed, Representatives Brian Baird (D-WA) and John Culberson (R-TX) offered a resolution that required all bills, reports, and conference reports be posted on the Internet at least 72 hours prior to floor consideration. Nicknamed "Read the Bill," the measure gained 217 cosponsors in the 111th Congress and was subject to a discharge petition initiated by Representative Greg Walden (R-OR) that garnered more than 180 signatures. A national grassroots campaign endorsed by a variety of good-government groups accompanied the effort. Republicans incorporated the measure into House rules at the beginning of the 112th Congress. It is hoped that members will use the extra time to prepare themselves thoroughly for the floor.

One especially egregious violation of the principle of plenary review is the earmark, a provision within a bill that sets aside spending for a specific project or program, usually within a single congressional district or state. The use of earmarks has escalated spectacularly over the past dozen or so years as members have discovered the technique is a useful way to take spending decisions out of the hands of executive branch officials—bureaucrats who are constrained in their distribution of funds by formulaic procedures embedded in existing statute and agency rules. The Congressional Research Service estimates there were 6,073 earmarks in congressional bills worth $29.6 billion (in 2005 dollars) in FY 1994, but 15,877 worth $47.4 billion in FY 2005, a high-water mark and a 285 percent increase in number and 60 percent increase in value from 11 years earlier.[9] Earmarks are heavily criticized for many reasons, not least because they furnish opportunities for corruption and add to fiscal problems. But they also undermine the floor's ability to deal adequately with legislation. First, earmarks are often added late in the legislative process, sometimes during conference in a process called airdropping. Members consequently have little opportunity to scrutinize them. Crespin, Finocchiaro, and Wanless (2009) estimate that on average 16 percent of earmark dollars between FY 1995 and FY 2006 were added in conference. Second, as parts of larger bills that frequently contain more costly or important provisions, their merits are not discussed.[10] Third, they are sometimes placed in endnotes or reports that are appended to bills and therefore cannot be amended or removed.

Congress's decision in early 2007 to clamp down on earmarks empowers the floor, although the effort ostensibly took place as a direct response to ethical concerns.[11] The new standing rule dictated that earmarks and narrowly targeted tax benefits and their proposers be specifically listed by the reporting committee or in a conference report. Members could also bring a point of order against an earmark, making it debatable. A little later, President George W. Bush ordered federal agencies and departments to ignore earmarks contained in endnotes and appendixes. Yet even though earmarks declined a little, observers estimate that approximately 9,000 of them were contained in the $555 billion omnibus appropriations bills that passed Congress in December of that year (Hulse 2007a).

In early 2009, the House moved to restrict earmarks further after a $410 billion FY 2009 omnibus appropriations bill was rather embarrassingly deemed full of them—Taxpayers for Common Sense estimated that the measure contained 8,750 earmarks costing $7.7 billion. The Democratic leadership was forced to adopt new rules subjecting earmarks to executive review and those granted to private for-profit entities to competitive bidding (P. Baker and Herszenhorn 2009). The next year, House Democratic leaders announced a complete ban on earmarks to for-profit entities, and Republicans in the body imposed an outright prohibition on earmarks originating from their members (Lichtblau 2010a). Legislators of both parties in both bodies pushed for a public database on earmark requests (Singer 2010). Most recently, lobbyists and public interest groups have begun their own efforts to attenuate the connection between earmarks and campaign practices (Lichtblau 2010b). Republicans began a discussion of a broad self-imposed earmark ban immediately after the 2010 elections (Hook 2010; Hulse 2010b). These efforts are all to be commended, and it is to be hoped that the reform impulse will continue.

Another way in which the floor's power has been reduced in recent years is by aggressive manipulation of the intercameral bill reconciliation process. Ironing out the differences between House and Senate versions of a bill has become a process controlled directly by the majority party leaders of both chambers who consult with one another before presenting their bodies with a take-it-or-leave-it proposition (Jansen 2009).

Differences between House and Senate passed bills are frequently resolved in conference committees. These committees have tremendous power because they may exercise an ex post veto and kill bills passed by the floor. They can also alter indelibly the substance of legislation because their revisions must be either accepted or rejected by the floors—conference reports cannot be amended. These powers have been on prominent display in recent years. Important and sprawling legislation has been changed radically in conference and then presented to the floor with little opportunity for members to read and understand its content. Today, conferences often operate in secret, and minority party members, especially in the House, have been increasingly shut out of their proceedings. Taibbi (2006) reports one recent episode in which Representative Charles Rangel (D-NY), the ranking member on the House Ways and Means Committee at the time, ran around the Capitol looking for a conference meeting. Having found it, he knocked on the door of the room in which it was being held. The conference's chair, Representative Bill Thomas (R-CA), the head of the Ways and Means Committee, cracked open the door and told Rangel, "This meeting is only open to the coalition of the willing." The opacity continued under Democratic control (Hulse 2007b) with the conspicuous exception of the televised coverage of the conference proceedings on the 2010 financial regulatory reform bill (Dennis and Brady 2010).

There are several ways that the amount of power conference committees have could be reduced. At the beginning of the 110th Congress, the House changed its rules to ensure greater openness in conference proceedings.[12] Among other things, the new regulation forces leaders to notify all House conferees of committee meetings and prohibits the addition of provisions after conferees have signed off on a final product. The reform could be taken further to make conference committees as transparent as standing committees. Other changes could naturalize procedures by constraining conferences themselves. As Mann and Ornstein (2006, 233) have argued, floor power would be increased if conferees were prohibited from adding items that were never discussed on the floor and revising provisions on which the House and Senate were in agreement. These are all steps in the right direction.

Finally, the Senate could do away with the enigmatic privilege all members have to "hold" bills, resolutions, or nominations—in other words, the capacity to prevent them from coming up for debate. This would obviously strengthen the floor. In 1999, majority leader Trent Lott (R-MS) and his counterpart in the minority, Tom Daschle (D-SD), informed their colleagues that they would no longer protect the anonymity of those who held legislation, hence greatly assisting members who wished to push matters to floor consideration (Oleszek 2011, 200–202). Lott and Daschle's policy was never really executed, but in 2007, Congress passed a package of ethical and procedural reforms that included revision of the hold. The provision forced the disclosure of holders' motives and names in the *Congressional Record* six days after the hold had been placed.

This constituted movement in the right direction. But the hold survives. In March 2010, Senator Jim Bunning (R-KY) single-handedly and rather dramatically blocked disposition of legislation extending unemployment benefits until he was granted a floor vote on a measure that would pay for them. Bunning relented under considerable pressure from senators of both parties (Hulse 2010a). The episode illustrated how one senator could prevent, at least for a time, floor consideration of a bill supported by a sizable majority of colleagues—the measure ultimately passed by a 78–19 vote.

In September 2010, Senate majority leader Harry Reid (D-NV) planned to attach an outright and formal ban on the hold to the defense reauthorization bill that was wending its way through the body. His attempt was, however, blocked by the Republican minority, largely because the bill accommodated controversial provisions on immigration and the Pentagon's "Don't Ask, Don't Tell" policy (Barnes, Bendavid, and Entous 2010). At the beginning of the 112th Congress, Senators Susan Collins (R-ME), Charles Grassley (R-IA), Claire McCaskell (D-MO), and Ron Wyden (D-OR) introduced a stand-alone resolution to end the hold. Twenty-six Democrats sponsored a different reform package to eliminate it.[13] In the end, the body agreed to reduce the time until the holder's identity is disclosed to two days. It remains to be seen whether senators have the appetite to abolish the practice or at least curtail it in a more meaningful way.

Reforms to Improve Floor Proceedings

Guided by the analysis in chapters 4 and 5, I also suggest a number of reforms to improve House and Senate floor proceedings. These suggestions are designed largely to elevate the principles of debate and deliberation, since the characteristics of interaction, civility, reasoning, and to a lesser extent commonweal are largely missing from the contemporary floor.

The first reform is to institute what are generally called Oxford Union–style debates. In these forums, a small group of members would debate a general policy issue by presenting arguments and then rebutting and critiquing their opponents. The focus would not be a particular bill but a broad and significant societal problem, and members would talk about the strengths and weaknesses of various solutions. The debates would enhance deliberation by forcing members to address and respond to opponents' positions. Moreover, as Mayer and Canon (1999, 153) have argued, such debates would help members perform their public education responsibilities.

This is not an original idea. In 1993, the Joint Committee on the Organization of Congress recommended that the House and Senate experiment with the approach. As House Rules Committee chair Joe Moakley (D-MA) remarked at the time, these occasions would offer "a useful vehicle for conducting thoughtful, substantive, and balanced debate on important national issues" and "would allow for a meaningful exchange of ideas between members" (Joint Committee 1993a, 63). Kathleen Hall Jamieson testified to the House Rules Committee in April 1997, "In Oxford debate, strong partisanship would be the rule, but in an environment in which the debate structure increases the likelihood that one arbitrates evidence and doesn't engage in personalities" (U.S. House of Representatives, Rules Committee 1997). A number of other scholars have encouraged Congress to use them (Evans and Oleszek 1998; Mayer and Canon 1999, 153), and in the spring and summer of 1994, the House had three Oxford Union–style debates, one each on health, welfare, and trade.[14] Four participants from each party faced off against each other. The authority for the debates came from unanimous consent.

Others have proposed similar types of forums that would enhance deliberation. Connor and Oppenheimer (1993, 329) suggest that the full House and Senate debate critical issues at the beginning of a Congress's first session, before formal bills are even considered in committee. Doing so would allow members to think broadly about the important issues facing that Congress and to begin to evaluate different solutions in general terms. A central goal would be to inform bill sponsors and members of committees of jurisdiction as they shape legislation.

Another alternative is the Lincoln-Douglas debate style. These devices are more structured and have rules similar to those used in recent debates between presidential candidates. That they allow for cross-examination makes them particularly salubrious. As Mucciaroni and Quirk (2006, 209) state, cross-examination forces members to address others' claims and substantiate their own contentions. In November 1993, the House experimented with this approach in a debate involving five members, with one acting as a moderator. The debate's resolution was, "Shall the United States Adopt a Single-Payer Canadian-Style Health Care System?"[15]

A fourth option along the same lines is a general debate on the issue du jour. Other legislative bodies hold these regularly—the German Bundestag, for example, frequently schedules hour-long debates on matters of topical interest, and the British House of Commons sets aside twenty days each session for the two main opposition parties to bring up issues of current concern. Again, adopting these practices would encourage deliberation. The debates could be sprinkled through the congressional calendar and called for by designated members—perhaps the majority and minority leaders—at certain times. In fact, the Senate has undertaken general debate on issues of the day on a couple of recent occasions. In September 2003, Senators John Kyl (R-AZ) and Byron Dorgan (D-ND) orchestrated a debate on Social Security. It was permitted during morning hour by unanimous consent.[16] To highlight Democratic intransigence on President Bush's judicial nominations, majority leader Bill Frist (R-TN) organized an all-night debate on the process by which the Senate confirms judges in November of the same year. He did so by moving that the Senate go into executive session to discuss pending business—the stalled nominations of three judges to circuit court positions. Although Frist's strategy was political—he wanted to break Democratic filibusters of the three nominees— the result was an interesting general debate about an important issue.[17]

Finally, the weekly colloquy between members of the House majority and minority leaderships could be formalized and extended and the focus shifted from the upcoming floor schedule to policy. In recent years, the practice has been exploited for political advantage (Dennis and Kucinich 2010), but with some tweaking, it might become a substantive debate about the House's legislative agenda between the heads of the two parties—perhaps something along the lines of the Prime Minister's Question Time in the British House of Commons.

There are ways proceedings on bills themselves could be improved. Members should, for example, be encouraged to pool time yielded to them under unanimous consent agreements or by floor managers with colleagues on the other side. They could then engage in deliberative colloquies. This already happens, particularly in the Senate, but the practice could be increased in the lower chamber if the House created "banks" where, prior to debate, floor managers deposited time to be withdrawn later specifically for this kind of interaction.

Civility might be increased if presiding officers received the authority to allow members to respond, if they so desired, when they are named, questioned, or referred to by colleagues. Currently, requests to yield in these instances are granted as courtesies by the member who holds the floor. Although she did not recommended this as a formal rules change,

Jamieson (1997) suggested that members be encouraged to do so in a late 1990s report on civility in the House.

Some changes to the Senate's Rule XXII might assist deliberation in that chamber. Three in particular seem worthy of additional exploration. First, and most radically, the number of votes needed to invoke cloture could be reduced over time. In early 2010, for example, Senators Tom Harkin (D-IA) (a perpetual critic of the filibuster) and Jeanne Shaheen (D-NH) proposed maintaining the current 60-vote threshold for two days but then allowing cloture to be invoked with fewer votes, in increments of 3 down to 51, as time passed.[18] Second, the motion to proceed and motion to go to conference might be made nondebatable or at least immune to filibuster (Ornstein 2010b; Stevenson 2010). Third, it may be worth forcing "real" filibusters and requiring members to obstruct bills by "going to the mattresses" in old-fashioned Mr. Smith style (Koger 2010, 197–99; Ornstein 2010b; Smith 2010). This might be done by eliminating the tracking system. The elimination of the filibuster on motions to proceed and the requirement that members remain present on the floor to maintain their filibusters were part of a much-discussed rules package introduced at the beginning of the 112th Congress by Harkin and Senators Tom Udall (D-NM) and Jeff Merkley (D-OR).[19]

These reforms would clearly sacrifice Senate floor rights in favor of efficiency and the expedited disposition of bills. But they protect the principle of extended debate. They might also encourage members to consume floor time with debate on the merits of legislation rather than a choreographed series of discussions and votes on procedural matters.

A final set of reforms would increase transparency. A significant proportion of votes in every Congress are cast viva voce. Most of these oral votes involve uncontroversial matters, but a surprisingly large number of votes to pass bills of historic significance have been by voice—that is, they went unrecorded (Clinton and Lapinski 2008). Forcing more recorded votes would provide constituents with additional information about representatives' behavior and policy preferences. The public would also know whether members were actually on the floor at the time a particular vote was undertaken. Making it harder to vote by voice ought, therefore, to increase attendance at floor proceedings. Such a change might involve a constitutional amendment, because, as Article I, Section 5 states, "The Yeas and Nays of the Members of either House on any question shall, at the Desire of one fifth of those Present, be entered on the Journal." But the idea merits consideration.

Congressional floor proceedings are as open to scrutiny as they have ever been, but public comprehension of what legislators do on the floor prior to voting seems minimal. In 1993, for example, 84 percent of members who responded to a survey undertaken by the Joint Committee on the Organization of Congress "strongly agreed" that the "public's understanding of Congress" was a problem for the institution. Citizens have a hard time penetrating the fog of congressional life and perceive that laws are getting thicker and floor procedures more complicated (Mayhew 2006, 225–26).

In the House, sophisticated special rules make legislative action particularly difficult for even the most seasoned observer to follow (Oleszek 2011, 155–62). The complexity is quite intentional. Deception is generally the goal. Over the past decade or so, we have seen King- and Queen-of-the-Hill rules that allow several substitute amendments but that make the vote on only one of them meaningful (Oleszek 2011, 158–60). The House majority has also repeatedly written byzantine special rules for resolutions raising the debt limit. In fact, prior to its revocation at the beginning of the 112th Congress, the "Gephardt Rule" permitted the debt limit raise to be bundled with the budget resolution as a matter of general practice, hence circumventing a separate vote on the former. The goal was to avoid putting members on the record as fiscally irresponsible (Wolfensberger 2010a). In June 2010, a seemingly simple measure to fund continuing operations in Afghanistan and Iraq was placed into an exceedingly complex and quite novel rule with spending provisions on education and summer jobs programs for youth (Wolfensberger 2010b). In March 2010, the House Democratic leadership seriously contemplated a self-executing rule that would essentially allow the body to approve the Senate version of the historic health care reform bill without a direct vote. Instead, the rule for a different and much narrower bill correcting unpopular parts of the Senate legislation would have included a provision simply deeming the main bill passed by the House (Montgomery and Kane 2010).

One way to make legislating more comprehensible would be to mandate that bills be written in plain and accessible language, as Gibson (2010) has recommended. Another would be to simplify the types of special rules that can be issued. The Rules Committee should propose only closed, open, and modified special rules (which would open or close certain sections of the bill to amendment). The simplification would not significantly affect the majority's gatekeeping and agenda powers but would make floor proceedings and votes more transparent. It would also generate greater public confidence that Congress is not avoiding tough decisions or manipulating the regular legislative process.

Even when members discuss substantive issues, citizens have a hard time evaluating what is said. During debates, members are continually citing statistics, attributing ideas to different people, and generally making claims that are difficult to verify. Such remarks, of course, cannot be prospectively outlawed. But false claims and even unsubstantiated statements could be minimized by establishing a bipartisan and independent monitoring organization to evaluate floor remarks for their accuracy. Mucciaroni and Quirk (2006, 211) claim that "such an agency could authoritatively assess empirical issues that were central to a policy decision." Because congressional agencies such as the Congressional Budget Office have had problems maintaining political neutrality, Mucciaroni and Quirk suggest that this entity be external to Congress and recruit the popular media as outlets for its research. Examples of similar such operations include Fact Check at the Annenberg Public Policy Center at the University of Pennsylvania and Politifact, run by the *St. Petersburg Times*. According to Mucciaroni and Quirk (212), Fact Check "offers prompt, pointed assessments of prominent factual issues in political debate, almost in real time."

Transparency would also be enhanced if the public really watched what went on on the floor. C-SPAN's gavel-to-gavel coverage of House and Senate floor proceedings is all well and good, but only a minuscule proportion of the American population has the time or inclination to watch it closely. Instead, as Mayhew (2006, 234) has pointed out, we need "some organization or set of organizations ready to excerpt and package especially important or interesting congressional debates in watcher-friendly hour-long or half-hour-long presentations."

Finally, scholars and practitioners have suggested that the repackaging of legislative vehicles would boost the principle of deliberation. Two reforms are often discussed. Both come with significant costs. The contemporary Congress's penchant for omnibus legislation—"the unification of diverse measures within a single large bill" (Krutz 2001, 210)—means that many items are passed without much consideration. Proceedings on omnibus bills are inevitably about their central components, and distant provisions are frequently neglected. Mucciaroni and Quirk (2006, 209) go as far as to say that omnibus bills are so large that "they defy deliberation" and suggest that Congress separate the provisions within them from one another and compel each to be treated as stand-alone legislation. It seems to me, however, prohibitively difficult to identify in any objective way the various discrete components of any piece of legislation. Furthermore, omnibus legislation brings a discipline to policy making that a more fractured approach does not. Debating a huge budget reconciliation bill allows members to think simultaneously and thoroughly about all the parts of a large chunk of the nation's business. Legislators understand better that action in one particular issue area can have repercussions for another. If legislating were fragmented by placing items into numerous self-contained packages, members would lose this panoramic view of public policy.

The second proposal is the establishment of a biennial cycle for appropriations and defense reauthorization (Art 1989; Mucciaroni and Quirk 2006, 207; Smith 1989, 247; G. B. H. Solomon and Wolfensberger 1994, 363; Taylor 2000, 577–78). Appropriations and the defense reauthorization currently are "must-pass" pieces of legislation that need approval every year. Proponents of reform, like the more than 30 senators who co-sponsored Senator Johnny Isakson's (R-GA) biennial budget bill in 2011, argue that cutting back on these annual necessities of congressional business would release floor time for the consideration of other matters. But again, significant costs would result. Members of Congress are likely to engage in midstream adjustments and feel even greater need to pass supplemental appropriations, thereby eating up any savings in floor time and undermining the kind of medium-range planning benefits the biennial cycle is supposed to bring. In addition, congressional oversight of agency spending would be greatly diminished. As Representative Joe Moakley (D-MA) (2000) put it when he was ranking member of the Rules Committee, biennial budgets "would increase the power of executive branch bureaucrats, giving them a longer leash and two years worth of money to spend."

Final Thoughts

The reforms I have endorsed would make Congress better. They would strengthen the floor, invigorate floor rights, and improve floor proceedings. Unfortunately, however, they are unlikely to make a tremendous amount of difference unless they coincide with significant changes to two important characteristics of contemporary American politics and public life. The first of these is the elevated prominence of the two major parties. Congress is experiencing historically high levels of interparty polarization and intraparty homogenization. Some of the resultant partisanship is exacerbated by restrictive procedures that legislators can alter. But much is the product of deeper, stronger, and broader forces such as disparities in wealth and income (McCarty, Poole, and Rosenthal 2006) and the near-extinction of southern conservative white Democratic and northeastern and midwestern liberal Republican members (Berard 2001; Rae 1989, 1994). In the House, partisan polarization is augmented by redistricting and the tendency of state legislatures to create safe Democratic and Republican districts that are fertile ground for extreme liberal and conservative candidates (Carson et al. 2007). The partisanship is reinforced by the parties' tightening control over the distribution of government largesse (Balla et al. 2002; Martin 2003), the framing of issues for the legislative agenda and public debate (Cox and McCubbins 2005), and patronage—legislative staffers, campaign consultants, lobbyists, and many others in the Washington community are increasingly hired based on their partisan credentials (Koger and Victor 2009). The result is two strong parties with deep pockets, increasingly committed adherents, and divergent policy preferences.

Unless this situation changes, there is little incentive for the majority party to strengthen the floor and increase the rights members exercise on it. If individual members of the majority can mold legislative agendas in caucus meetings or standing committees, they will not want to push for rules changes that naturalize the body. In fact, we know that at least since the Civil War, strong and cohesive majority parties—like those we witness today—have pushed procedures in a restrictive direction. Even if the reforms I suggest could be imposed on Congress, moreover, it is unlikely that many of them would have much effect under current conditions. If floor rights were increased, the majority party leadership would likely respond by warning its members against exploiting those rights and by augmenting its control of the floor agenda. If floor proceedings were improved, the majority party leadership would just ignore debate and deliberation, particularly if they began to produce policy outcomes inconsistent with the party's preferences.

A further problem is persuading the majority's rank and file to look beyond their partisan interests on procedural issues. My research suggests that this can happen when the majority has experienced an influx of new members. It can also occur if the policy preferences of majority party members are quite heterogeneous. But other than those infrequent circumstances, it is unlikely under modern organizational arrangements that majority party members will want to support the naturalization of procedures.

A compelling case for a stronger and better floor must appeal to the majority's electoral and policy interests. Many surveys have revealed the low esteem in which Congress is held (Hibbing and Larimer 2008; Hibbing and Theiss-Morse 2002), and research has connected the general public's views of the institution with the electoral success of the majority party (Jones and McDermott 2009). Therefore, if majority party leaders could be persuaded that more natural procedures and better proceedings might enhance Congress's reputation and therefore their prospects of remaining in control, they might be interested in permitting reforms to bring about such changes. Given that the public seems more interested in policy outcomes than legislative processes (Hibbing 2002), however, this will be hard to accomplish.

Proponents of reform might also point to research that shows that bills passed by larger and bipartisan majorities become more durable laws (Maltzman and Shipan 2008). Bills generated by open and participatory processes—or natural procedures and quality floor proceedings—make a larger mark on American life. But because this kind of legislative process allows members of the minority more influence on outcomes, it will be very difficult for reformers to marshal a policy-based argument that will attract members of the majority party to their cause.

The nature of public debate is the second impediment to change. In Calhoun, Clay, and Webster's time, the public flocked to the congressional galleries and voraciously consumed the coverage of floor proceedings in the newspapers. Much public discussion of great national issues essentially happened on the floors of the House and Senate. There were, of course, exceptions, and members took their arguments on the road. The great 1858 Lincoln-Douglas debates in Illinois are a good example. So are Senator Charles Sumner's (R-MA) antislavery speeches, which were circulated in newspapers across the country.

Today, however, even more of the national political debate occurs outside the Capitol. One reason is that many of the most influential participants are not members of Congress. Candidates for political office engage in this debate—most importantly, presidential candidates, and the modern nominating process just seems to get longer and longer. The president and members of his administration are constantly called on to give their views about the nation's problems and their potential solutions. Debate also takes place in the media, think tanks, and academia. An army of journalists, pundits, analysts, bloggers, and public intellectuals discuss issues of national concern in newspapers and magazines; on the radio, television, and the Internet; in papers; and at conferences and symposia (Posner 2002; Sunstein 2007). Researchers have even discovered healthy doses of deliberative political discourse within the general public (Jacobs, Cook, and Delli Carpini

2009). There is no disputing the fact that the principals in the great national political discussion are not just members of Congress. In fact, lawmakers largely play bit parts. When tuning in to public life, citizens do not really listen to the federal legislature.

In addition, even when members of Congress participate in national debates on policy matters, today they do so off the floor rather than on it. Committees are still powerful on the Hill, and the reforms of the 1970s made their proceedings transparent. Party caucus meetings are a venue for substantive debate, although these gatherings are generally closed to reporters. Members' contributions seem also to occur with increasing frequency away from Capitol Hill. Legislators speak to think tanks and political groups in Washington and across the country. They write op-eds. They debate the president publicly and even directly. Early 2010 saw two unprecedented televised meetings between President Obama and congressional Republicans, the first at the House party's annual retreat and the second over health care. Members constantly appear on radio and television to give their views on issues and other political matters, and senators in particular populate the national Sunday morning television news shows and cable political talk programming. As journalist Caryn James (1998) put it during the Clinton impeachment proceedings, "Who needs Congress when there's *Crossfire?*"

There seems no obvious and plausible way to change this particular reality. If anything, it will be more difficult to alter than Congress's heightened partisanship. The situation is hardly catastrophic, however. Today's congressional floor proceedings may lack qualities such as debate, deliberation, reasoning, and concern for the general interest. But many Americans do not care. As Hibbing (2002) has argued, survey data reveal that the public is not particularly interested in a more transparent Congress willing to engage in public debate. Americans would not, it seems, pay too much attention to a rejuvenated floor on which members exercised strong floor rights and engaged in proceedings of the highest quality. Perhaps because the House and Senate floors have restricted access and diminishing influence, the public has turned to other institutions for meaningful discussions of the country's challenges. House and Senate floor proceedings should be better, but any gains might not appreciably impact American life.

Furthermore, although the House and Senate are moving in a restrictive direction, minority political interests, which obviously benefit from a powerful floor and strong floor rights, do have opportunities to influence policy outputs. With its separation of powers and federalist features, our system is still quite decentralized, and as I have shown, the Senate in particular maintains procedures that are quite natural in comparison to those of other legislative bodies. With their insatiable appetite for information, the pervasive, competitive, and influential electronic media are more than willing to provide a platform for members of the congressional minority parties, particularly those who can craft colorful sound bites or generate controversy. Congressional procedures ought to be less restrictive, but given the need for legislatures to be productive, today's House and Senate floors are reasonably powerful, and members still exercise some considerable rights on them.

Notes

1. Even in analyses of roll calls, members' individual votes are frequently deemed the product of pressures felt off the floor, such as those from all or some of their constituents (Bishin 2000; Clinton 2006), their party (Cox and Poole 2002; McCarty, Poole, and Rosenthal 2001; Snyder and Groseclose 2000), lobbying by and campaign contributions from interest groups (Fellowes and Wolf 2004; Hojnacki and Kimball 1998; Stratmann 2005), caucuses (Forgette 2004; Hammond 1997), the president (Bond and Fleisher 1990; Covington, Wrighton, and Kinney 1995; Sullivan 1990), personal ideology (Levitt 1996; Poole 2007; Poole and Romer 1993), and personal experiences (Burden 2007).

2. For Smith (1989, 4) this is the second of three meanings the floor has in the congressional vernacular. The first is the physical location in the Capitol. The third is a synonym for the parent chamber. I never use the floor in this third sense because I view it explicitly as a discrete part of the legislative process and a distinctive institution within each body.

The House has established the Committee of the Whole House, which debates private bills, and the much more important Committee of the Whole House on the State of the Union (usually just called the Committee of the Whole). It was established to expedite floor action. It has some different rules from the full House—for example, only 100 members (instead of 218) are needed for a quorum, the Speaker appoints a colleague, known as the chair, to preside, and the previous question and motion to recommit are not in order (Oleszek 2011, 180–82). Yet like the House in plenary session, it is really what I consider the floor. In Alexander's (1916, 256) words, the Committee of the Whole "is simply the House itself doing business under a special and less formal procedure, by means of which the entire membership is enabled to participate in the consideration of a bill, unhampered by roll-calls or the intervention of motions to adjourn, to refer, to postpone, for the previous question, and the like." When I talk about the floor in the House, therefore, I am also referring to the powers and proceedings of the Committee of the Whole.

3. Rule XIV dictates that all measures must be read on different legislative days before they can be assigned to committee. If a senator objects to further consideration of the bill after the second reading, it is placed on the calendar. From there, the majority leader can call it up for floor consideration (Oleszek 2011, 285–87).

CHAPTER 1

1. The Constitution says more about Congress's powers, including some that reveal intercameral differences. All revenue bills, for example, must originate in the House, while the Senate has the sole power to ratify treaties and confirm presidential appointments.

2. I could have used other terms to describe the poles of these dimensions. *Manufactured*, for example, is more obviously an opposite of *natural* than is *restrictive* but infers a body that has been subject to a relatively large number of procedural changes, whatever their magnitude and direction. *Decentralized* and *centralized* were plausible candidates, but they convey concrete meaning in existing congressional scholarship. For example, the postwar House was said to be decentralized prior to the reforms of the 1970s (Rieselbach 1994; Rohde 1991). Yet it also had strong and autonomous committees and a concomitantly weak floor. Moreover, when the body decided to increase the power of subcommittees, reign in standing committee chairs, and generally reform the committee system in the 1970s, it was said to have, in some ways at least, further decentralized power (Davidson 1992; Rieselbach 1994; Rohde 1991). This decentralization had little to do with the role of the floor in the legislative process or the strength of members' floor rights.

3. I also like the term *natural* because the Constitution says very little about how the two chambers should organize themselves. The members of the 1st Congress really were working with a blank slate. To be sure, the procedures and practices they created were shaped by the experiences of the British Parliament, Congress of the Confederation, and state legislatures (Alexander 1916; Bickford and Bowling 1989; Swift 1996; Wirls and Wirls 2004). But the Continental Congress—the natural precursor to Congress—was almost "institutionless." Committees had no power, there was no previous question, and no member or group of members controlled the agenda (Jillson and Wilson 1994; Stewart 2001, 57–62).

4. The House and Senate have always grown, with the major exception of the Civil War, when the withdrawal of delegations from the Confederate states meant that the House shrank from 238 to 183 after 1861 and the Senate dropped from 66 to 50. The House also shrank from 242 to 223 because of the 1842 Apportionment Act. This legislation was pushed by Whigs who believed that the House had become too disorderly. Their prime example was the

House of the 27th Congress (1841–43), which had behaved, it was said, like a "bear garden" (Shields 1985). In the 88th Congress (1963–65) the House also shrank to 435 from 437, where it had grown to accommodate Alaska's and Hawaii's admission into the Union.

5. See Taylor (2008, 459–60) for details on data collection. In chapter 2, I use an indicator derived from Binder's (1997) measure of workload. Because she employs elements constant to both chambers of Congress, Binder's House and Senate versions of the variable are essentially pegged to one another. I utilize the measure because it encapsulates a broad understanding of workload and can be easily extended across the expanse of congressional history. It also shows the secular increase in workload that is generally believed to have occurred.

6. This drop is generally attributed to changes in House cosponsorship rules. Until the 91st Congress (1969–71), the House did not permit cosponsorship, and the number of cosponsors per bill was limited to 25 until the 96th Congress (1979–81), when the cap was abolished completely. As a result, the number of bills introduced decreased dramatically after the mid-1970s.

7. Other types of work may disproportionately fall on senators. With more populous constituencies, senators presumably feel greater pressure to attend to their representation function, although this pressure is offset by senators' larger staffs, longer terms, and, presumably, their same-state colleague. Moreover, the upper chamber is uniquely responsible for ratifying treaties and confirming presidential appointments. Still, the House and Senate have had about the same number of roll-call votes since the 1st Congress.

8. The exception is Wawro and Schickler's (2006) analysis of chamber size and the establishment of the cloture procedure in the Senate. Koger (2010, 80–95) looks at the growth of the House and Senate and its implications for floor obstruction.

9. Binder (1997) argues that a weak majority party is a necessary but not sufficient condition for the creation of minority party rights. A cross-party coalition must be seeking this kind of change at the same time.

10. Gronke (2000, 37–59) argues that states are not necessarily more heterogeneous than congressional districts, especially when we look at such things as their racial composition.

11. Some factors mitigate this basic observation, including the Senate primary, which forces candidates towards the party median and presumably away from the general election median (Heckelman 2004), the decision by Senate parties to pick more extreme candidates for seats they have won previously (Fowler 2005), and the fact that legislators may feel less constrained by the median voter in heterogeneous districts (Gerber and Lewis 2004; Gronke 2000).

12. The House is therefore more prone to what scholars call "conditional party government" (Aldrich 1995; Aldrich, Berger, and Rohde 2002; Aldrich and Rohde 2001; Rohde 1991). In this situation, member preferences are homogenous within parties and polarized between them.

13. I will use measures of House and Senate majority party strength de-

rived from Binder's (1997) work in chapter 2. The mean House score for all Congresses from the 1st (1789–91) to 107th (2001–3) is slightly higher in the House but is not distinguishable from the Senate's at the p < .05 level in a difference-of-means test.

14. Under the general ticket, members were elected at large in separate contests or a single statewide vote with as many candidates elected as there were seats available.

15. However, when term length is correlated with an ordinal measure of debate termination in the 54 national legislative bodies presented in table 1.1, the product is small and not statistically significant. This is also the case for the relationship between constituency size and an ordinal measure of debate termination for the 99 state legislative bodies presented in the same table.

CHAPTER 2

1. Changes affecting the Rules Committee are important only after 1883 because since then, the committee has reported special rules that govern floor treatment of individual bills. Prior to that point the Rules Committee dealt with changes to the House's standing rules. As a result, I do not include the 1841 change that allowed the committee to report at all times or the 1880 change that promoted Rules to standing committee status.

The congressional reorganization measures of 1946 and 1970 seem, on the surface, to be matters involving power relations among standing committees. But both had important ramifications for the floor. I code the 1946 act as a change that both naturalized and restricted rules. It strengthened the floor in that it greatly decreased the number of committees over which the floor had to watch. It weakened the floor in that it gave committees important informational resources such as large staffs.

The 1970 act had marginal effects on floor procedure. It permitted recorded teller votes during the amending process and allowed the House to record floor votes electronically. The former change led to a surge in amendments during the 1970s and 1980s that were clearly part of the general openness of floor proceedings at the time (Smith 1989). The legislation's major effect, however, was to strengthen the floor by opening up committee proceedings and undermining chairs' ability to control their panels.

Some rules changes did not make my analysis because they were not mentioned enough. The creation of the first calendars in 1820 is a good example. Even if establishment of calendars had been deemed important enough, however, I am not sure how I would have coded it. The action merely simplified the business of going to the floor and separated bills into public and private and House and Senate categories.

I add the rules changes made at the beginning of the 104th Congress in the first days of the new Republican majority. The sources that were written after

1995 (Binder 1997; Oleszek 2011; Schickler 2001) discuss them in varying amounts of detail.

2. The rules change I code as either natural or restrictive is the five-minute rule for floor amendments passed in 1847. Guaranteeing at least five minutes to discuss an amendment in the Committee of the Whole suggests that floor rights were strengthened, especially since one result of a rule allowing for discharge of the Committee of the Whole passed six years earlier was that amendments were sometimes voted on without debate. But limiting members to five minutes of debate on an amendment—when they could have spoken for an hour under the extant rule—implies that the new rule weakened floor rights. The rule change is coded 1 in logit models of both natural and restrictive procedural alteration. Coding the 30th Congress 0 has no substantive effect on the statistical analyses I present.

3. Many of these alterations to the chamber's rules have already been scrutinized. For example, Binder (1997, 43–67) discusses the adoption of the previous question motion in great depth. Schickler (2001, 27–84, 189–248) examines such changes as Reed's Rules, the 1909–10 revolt against the centralized procedural arrangements under Speaker Joe Cannon (R-IL), and the weakening of committees in the 1970s.

Some rules changes have not been subject to much discussion, however. The changes in the 1st (1789–91), 3rd (1793–95), and 8th (1803–5) Congresses that establish the Speaker's primacy in the House do not make Binder's (1997) cut. But they get a great deal of play in many of the historical sources I use and are important to the story of how and why the House and Senate developed differently. Binder may not have considered them critical to majority or minority rights because, as I describe in chapter 3, the elevation of the Speaker's influence in the early years did not particularly affect interparty power relations.

4. The House, of course, grew infinitely when it was born. I give the 1st Congress a value of .44, since that is how much bigger the new House was than the Congress of the Confederation in 1788. A number of individuals and conventions in the 1st Congress were holdovers from the Congress of the Confederation. Coding the observation as 0 or 1.00 does not substantively change the results.

5. I thank Sarah Binder for providing the raw data for my workload variable.

6. Binder uses the size of the House as part of her workload measure. This is very different from and therefore is not endogenous to the way I conceptualize and operationalize chamber size. I examine the change in the size of the membership from one Congress to the next, arguing that the expansion or contraction in the number of legislators is critical, not the absolute number.

7. A measure that is the absolute value of workload created from either a continuous series or two series that are divided between the 53rd (1893–95)

and 54th (1895–97) Congresses generally performs worse than my change in workload measure.

8. A Rice cohesion score is calculated from all votes in a Congress as the absolute value of the average percentage of party members voting yes subtracted from those voting no.

9. Poole and Rosenthal's (1997; see also McCarty, Poole, and Rosenthal 1997) DW-NOMINATE scores use nonunanimous roll calls to place legislators on a unidimensional scale with scores ranging from −1 (the liberal pole) to +1 (the conservative pole). For the first dimension scores, classification is about 80 percent. The first dimension generally divides members by party.

Scores are generally comparable across Congresses after the Civil War. Prior to that time, flux in the party system makes temporal comparisons harder but does so largely because there are multiple dimensions and no stable coalitions. In of itself, this phenomenon suggests the kind of disconnect between member preferences on policy and procedures I discuss as prevalent at the time in chapter 3.

10. Schickler (2000) uses the change in this measure from one Congress to the next. Such a measure does not have coefficients that are statistically significant in my analysis.

11. I thank Eric Schickler for providing me with these data. I updated them through the 107th Congress and calculated the values for the 1st through 40th Congresses. The value for the 1st Congress is the raw value for that Congress. Put in terms of an equation, the calculation is as follows:

Ideological power balance = absolute(MEDIANfloor − MEDIANminority) − absolute(MEDIANfloor − MEDIANmajority).

Change in ideological power balance = Ideological power balance(t) − Ideological power balance(t − 1).

12. Simple descriptive statistics for the four principal variables over the 107 Congresses are as follows: Change in size, mean = .024, standard deviation = .087, minimum = −.23, maximum = .52; change in workload, mean = .014, standard deviation = .341, minimum = −1.20, maximum = .95; majority party strength, mean = .175, standard deviation = .129, minimum = −.015, maximum = .491; change in ideological power balance, mean = .005, standard deviation = .171, minimum = −.610, maximum = .320.

13. House Republicans campaigned in 1888 at least partially on the issue that power needed to be centralized and the rights of the minority reduced because the chamber was constantly gridlocked (Binder 1997, 126; Schickler 2001, 39). Indeed, Reed wrote regularly on this in such public forums as the *Saturday Evening Post* and *North American Review*. Here, a House minority party was advocating the restriction of procedures as part of an argument that it could govern more responsibly than the majority.

In some preliminary work on congressional organization, Rohde, Stiglitz, and Weingast (2008) forward a different argument. Looking particularly at the House, they contend that with ideal points likely distant from status quos, members of a new majority are willing to delegate agenda power to leaders to get bills passed into law. In my conceptualization of procedures, this is tantamount to restriction.

14. These two variables—changes in party control and the percentage of members who are freshmen—do not differ greatly across the chambers. Moreover, there is little theoretical reason to believe that switches in party control and large or small influxes of new members will have different effects in different chambers.

15. Wawro and Schickler (2006, 188–90) suggest the opposite. They argue that large numbers of freshmen are indicative of electoral instability and a willingness by members to increase their discount rate for the future and accept greater restriction to bring about legislative efficiency.

16. Cox and McCubbins (2005, 78–81) highlight rules changes related to "the Reed Rules, the Holman Rule (that allowed the Appropriations Committee to insert language into general appropriations bills), Calendar Wednesday, the discharge procedure, the twenty-one day rule, or the Rules Committee's powers."

17. Binder (2006) finds both to be significant to models in her analysis of procedural change as well.

18. In the model of Cox and McCubbins's rules that naturalize, a Congress is more likely to adopt procedural change when the majority party is relatively strong.

19. There is no substantive difference to the first and second specifications if the five-minute rule of the 30th Congress is coded 0.

20. Haynes (1938, 1:341) also claims, "In contrast with notable revisions of the House rules, the few Senate revisions have been significant of no urgent spirit of revolt or reform; they have been authorized when the accumulation of changes through a long series of years made a new codification desirable." This statement suggests that individual rules changes in the Senate are brought about not by the kinds of antecedents I am examining here but by a basic need to clean house after precedents have piled up.

21. This proposition is not uncontroversial (see, for example, Bruhl 2010). In 1959, majority leader Lyndon Johnson (D-TX) engineered an iteration of the continuing body argument in exchange for his support for a change to Rule XXII that permitted the invocation of cloture when two-thirds of members present voted for it rather than two-thirds of all members (Binder 1997, 194). Today the idea is in Rule V, Section 2: "The rules of the Senate shall continue from one Congress to the next Congress unless they are changed as provided in these rules."

22. Today, two-thirds of senators present and voting are required to invoke cloture on a rules change.

23. Wawro and Schickler (2006) do not analyze the successful attempts in their book but were kind enough to provide me with these data.

24. For example, Wawro and Schickler (2006, 185) do not include the five-minute limit on debate in secret sessions relating to the Civil War that was established in 1862 because it applied only to the session in which it was adopted.

25. Because these are efforts to restrict floor rights, I do not use an indicator of a change in party control.

26. Wawro and Schickler (2006), in turn, calculate their data from the work of Beth (1994) and Burdette (1940).

27. I report only a zero-inflated specification for attempts tried. An attempts successful version performed extremely poorly.

28. By historical standards, the majority party strength variable is not particularly high. It is .168 where the average for all Congresses from the 1st to 107th is .175. This is because the minority is quite large and cohesive—the minority-only score in the 65th Congress (1917–19) is .336, compared to a mean of .303 in all other Congresses from the 1st to 107th.

29. Schiller and Stewart (2008) show that the vast majority of Senate elections in the 1871–1913 period were decided by party-line votes in state legislatures.

30. Binder argues that opponents to reform repeatedly obtained explicit recognition within the revised rules that the Senate remained a continuing body. This process occurred in both 1959 and 1975. Binder (1997, 197–98) argues that the 1979 and 1986 changes had "mixed" effects because reformers did not get all that they wanted. In all four cases, however, the bar for cloture was clearly lowered.

31. For more on the history of changes to Rule XXII, see Gold and Gupta 2004.

32. Another way of bypassing recalcitrant committees, suspending the rules, requires a two-thirds vote, while the remaining approaches—using task forces to do the work of standing committees and having the Rules Committee utilize its power of extraction—are controlled by the majority leadership.

33. For discussions and analyses of the discharge petition, see especially Beth 1994; Burden 2003; Miller and Overby 2010, as well as Binder 1997, 135–55; Schickler 2001, 126–28.

34. Little work has been done on what the discharge petition says about congressional life. One exception is Miller and Overby 2010, which demonstrates that members will, as a result of party pressure, frequently refuse to sign petitions even if they prefer the bill to the status quo.

35. Here I essentially replicate Burden's (2003) technique. As he points out, the small number of cases makes it unnecessary to utilize such count models (8).

36. J. A. Robinson (1963, 44) reports that between 1939 and 1960, the House adopted 87 closed rules and 1,128 open rules. But that does not mean rules did not constrain before that time. J. M. Roberts (2010) reports that between 1893 and 1937, the House adopted 154 restrictive and 377 open rules.

37. For more on the controversy over restrictive rules at this time, see Binder 1997, 165–66; Schickler 2001, 235–38.

38. New majorities were proposing a reduced reliance on restrictive rules at the beginning of both the 110th Congress (2007–9) and the 112th Congress (2011–13).

39. It was Vice President John Garner (D-TX) who established the practice in 1937.

40. By many accounts, the practice continues at this high rate. Over the past several years, Minority leader Mitch McConnell has complained frequently about Majority leader Harry Reid's (D-NV) use of it (McConnell 2011).

41. The first instance of a UCA is reported to have been the effort to bring a bill providing for joint U.S.-British occupancy of Oregon to a vote in 1846 (*Congressional Quarterly* 1982, 219). Because we are unsure of exactly when UCAs came about and what their initial purposes were, I do not attempt to model what brought the practice into being.

42. These junior members pursued their interests successfully in other ways as well. To ensure that President Woodrow Wilson's progressive legislative program would be welcomed in the Senate, the Democratic Steering Committee was sometimes compelled to ignore seniority when making standing committee assignments.

43. Conditions here contrast with those surrounding the creation of Rule XXII just three years later. By 1916, direct election had been fully instituted and the number of senators who had been appointed was waning. What is more, turnover had decreased markedly—35.4 percent of senators were in their first terms in the 62nd Congress (1911–13), and 26 percent were freshmen in the 63rd Congress (1913–15), whereas only 10.4 percent were newcomers in the 64th Congress (1915–17) and 18.8 percent had that status in the 65th Congress (1917–19). The Democratic majority in 1917 was solidly progressive and maturing. It was ready to govern and force through its legislative agenda and was no longer in the mood to naturalize procedures.

CHAPTER 3

1. The story behind the 8th Congress's adoption of the rule formalizing the Speaker's ability to name committee chairs is interesting. A rule making the first appointed member of a committee its chair was passed on November 23, 1804, but only after it was amended to provide the committee's majority the right to name their chair if they so desired (*Annals of Congress*, 8th Cong., 2nd sess., 697–701).

In the next Congress, a concerted effort, led by Representative James Sloan (Rep-NJ), sought to strip the Speaker of the ability to name any members of committees. Sloan was particularly upset by the conduct of the chair of the Committee on Ways and Means, John Randolph (Rep-VA), who was accused of keeping the House in the dark about the spending needs of the government, delaying the processing of urgently needed appropriations requested by the Jefferson administration, and leaving Washington on personal business when the committee should have been conducting the nation's. Although Sloan's initial attempt to alter the rule was rebuffed, he did force the renewal of the provision allowing committees to choose their own chairs if they wished. As a temporary revision to the rules, this measure died in the 11th Congress (1809–11), and exclusive control of chair appointments reverted back to the Speaker.

2. The model fails to predict the 1822 rules change allowing House standing committees to report bills at their own discretion. Still, this alteration was part of a package of changes that included the establishment of a two-thirds vote to suspend the rules, a reform that naturalized procedures.

3. J. R. Rogers (1998, 2005) also argues that relatively large numbers of committees and support staff help bodies acquire information. These cannot be used to explain the House as an initiator of legislation in the early Congresses because there existed little to no intercameral differences in such matters at the time.

4. The Committee on Commerce and Manufactures was split in the 16th Congress (1819–21), so I show data only to the 15th Congress (1817–19).

5. Den Hartog and Goodman (2007) have shown, however, that majority party members with higher levels of party loyalty on important votes were more likely to get appointed to Ways and Means than their less loyal colleagues.

6. In the 1st Congress, Senate rules allowed the president to recognize members if more than one rose simultaneously.

7. On rare occasions, germaneness requirements have subsequently been tightened or relaxed, most importantly with regard to revenue bills in 1911 and 1924.

8. The actual wording was, "No new motion or proposition shall be admitted under color of amendment as a substitute for a question or proposition under debate until it is postponed or disagreed to."

9. It is unlikely that the regulation was adopted as a simple carryover from the Continental Congress, however. Whereas only 33 of the 65 (50.8 percent) initial members of the House in the 1st Congress had sat in the Continental Congress, 18 of the 24 (75 percent) of the original members of the Senate had attended the body.

10. The House had such a motion in its original rules, but it was used not to cut off debate but to delay undesired decisions (Alexander 1916, 180–83; Binder 1997, 49–50; Cooper 1962, 4).

The early Senate also did not use the previous question as we know it today. The provision was invoked only ten times before it was expunged by the body in 1806, and it did not have a consistent use. Indeed, Binder and Smith (1997, 35–37) reveal that opponents of bills generally used the procedure to postpone action.

11. Senate president Thomas Jefferson ruled the previous question motion out of order during a debate in the 6th Congress (1799–1801) (L. Rogers 1926, 165). Given that the normal removal of the previous question from the Senate

rule book has been deemed a housekeeping measure, we might argue that Jefferson's ruling represents the de facto death of the procedure in the Senate. As Binder's (1997, 64) data reveal, she regards the 6th Congress as a time when the Senate majority was relatively strong.

12. According to Representative Timothy Pitkin (Fed-CT), on December 2, 1803, the House voted 101–18 to reverse the chair's decision that the previous question ended debate (*Annals of Congress*, 12th Cong., 1st sess., 577).

13. The probabilities of a rules change restricting procedures produced by this model are 33.7 percent in the 8th Congress, 22.3 percent in the 10th Congress, and 7.9 percent in the 11th Congress.

14. Stewart (2007, 145) has argued that Porter was not the "fire-breathing" war hawk most historians have made him out to be.

15. Perkins (1961, 267) makes the case that the elections of 1810–11 were not clearly about the war, either. Not until after the spring of 1811 did the issue become so important.

16. The procedure was originally used to suspend the House's rules on the order of business so that it could deal with a measure. The first use of the motion to suspend the rules to proceed with a measure and adopt it came in 1868 (Bach 1990).

17. The model of procedural change assumes that members derive procedural preferences from fundamental interests in addition to policy. Electoral concerns are chief among these issues. But electoral interests are generally furthered through policy outcomes. Moreover, since members wish to be reelected and have their parties attain or keep majority status, I assume that electoral interests, when they do vary across members, almost always divide along party lines.

18. The gains-from-trade (Weingast and Marshall 1988) and informational (Krehbiel 1991) models conceptualize procedural design in a nonpartisan way. But they do not tell us much about how procedures are expected to change.

19. These days, the only exception is the Committee on Standards of Official Conduct.

20. Perhaps the most recent example of such a near thing came at the beginning of the 105th Congress in 1997. Because of a slim majority and controversy surrounding the previous speaker, Newt Gingrich (R-GA), it was a little unclear who the new presiding officer might be. Although nine Republicans did not vote for him, Gingrich managed to hang on.

21. I discuss the unusual Senate of the 47th Congress in additional detail in chapter 5.

22. Jenkins, Schickler, and Carson (2004) have used constituency-based measures such as the presidential vote and per capita value of the manufacturing sector to show that House parties were not, especially when compared to the mid-1890s, particularly polarized and homogenous during the Civil War and Reconstruction.

23. As Jenkins and Nokken (2000) show, however, the coalition that elected Banks was made up largely of opposition members—the individuals who were soon to become Republicans. This group held a plurality of seats in the 34th Congress (1855–57).

24. Not until 1823 were 62 percent of all bills in the House referred to standing committees (Gamm and Shepsle 1989, 47). The Senate used as many as 114 select committees as late as the 14th Congress (1815–17).

25. Gamm and Shepsle (1989) and G. L. Robinson (1954, 20–21) have argued that Federalist philosophy also was not particularly compatible with standing committees. Agenda setting, Federalists believed, should be undertaken by executive departments.

26. Canon and Stewart (2002) test a series of hypotheses about the motivations for House committee assignments in a model of the 1st (1789–91) to 22nd (1831–33) Congresses. None of their independent variables—measuring such phenomena as profession, education, legislative experience, state, and distance from party median preference—has a statistically significant coefficient.

27. Some observers believe that the "property right norm" did not really develop until as late as the 1890s (Katz and Sala 1996).

28. In the same year, the House established the rule that prevented the appropriation of funds unless they had been previously authorized by law. The rule had little real effect but it was an expression of the importance of authorizing committees in the critical enterprise that is the funding of government (McConachie 1898, 178–79).

29. In 1882, the Republicans had inched toward empowering the Rules Committee and providing the majority control of the floor agenda by determining that resolutions reported from Rules could not be filibustered (Alexander 1916, 201–2).

30. The disappearing quorum ban was repealed in the 52nd (1891–93) Congress but reestablished in the 53rd (1893–95).

31. Smith (2007, 140–41) has argued that although Cox and McCubbins (2005, 65–73) believe that Reed's Rules are the basis for the majority party's considerable negative agenda powers in the House, the procedures in fact provide the foundation for its grip on the positive agenda.

32. In the preceding 50th Congress (1887–89), the Republican scores had a standard deviation of .121. In the 51st the score was .111. Before the Civil War, standard deviations were very rarely this low.

33. Wawro and Schickler (2006, 61–88) have taken issue with this assertion, arguing that Senate rules are quite mutable.

CHAPTER 4

1. As Freeman (2001) reveals, many of these incidents were the product of a kind of honor code that permeated American public life in the country's early years.

2. Wirls's (2007) analysis of four important debates in the 19th century reveals no demonstrable intercameral differences in the quality of floor proceedings, however.

3. Porter (1987) asked 26 historians to rank their 10 greatest senators. Although floor performance was not one of the criteria, only 7 of the top 19 served any time after World War II: J. William Fulbright (D-AR), Hubert H. Humphrey (D-MN), Lyndon B. Johnson (D-TX), Richard Russell (D-GA), Robert Taft (R-OH), Arthur Vandenberg (R-MI), and Robert Wagner (D-NY).

4. Floor managers literally manage the debate on a bill. The manager for the majority side is often the chair of the committee that reported the bill, and his or her counterpart is frequently the ranking minority member on that committee. One of their main responsibilities is to manage the time given to their side under the special rule or unanimous consent agreement.

5. Pappas's song began,

Twinkle, twinkle Kenneth Starr,
Now we see how brave you are.
Up above the Pentagon sting,
Like a fair judge in the ring
(*Congressional Record*, July 21, 1998, H5967).

6. Some observers have argued that live television coverage elevated the quality of floor proceedings. Senator Robert Byrd noted that his colleagues were making "better speeches" and that the television cameras improved debate "from a substantive point of view" (S. V. Roberts 1986). Norman Ornstein (Dart 1994, 264) argued in the mid-1990s that C-SPAN had "improved the quality of deliberations." In their extensive book about C-SPAN, Frantzich and Sullivan (1996, 263) claim that the videotaped record of floor proceedings "encourages members to think through their comments more carefully."

7. Mayhew (2000), for example, has written extensively about members' actions outside of Congress.

8. I do not include statements submitted for the record by senators after votes on removal had been taken. Sigelman, Deering, and Loomis (2001) analyze these statements in an article on senatorial language. I exclude them from my work because most were not spoken on the floor but were submitted in writing.

I also talk a little about a similar case that I do not code, the Senate censure of Andrew Jackson in 1834.

I do not analyze the House's first debate on an article to impeach Johnson, which took place in late 1867. The article was rejected handily.

9. In the case of Iraq in 1991, I do not include proceedings on House Concurrent Resolution 32. This resolution encompassed a congressional assertion that the legislative branch maintained the right to declare war and was not directly about the Gulf conflict.

10. Jenkins, Peck, and Weaver (2010) argue that race was an important part of the congressional agenda in the 50 years between 1890 and 1940. They point to the legislative activity on anti-lynching to make their case.

11. These bills are: the Tariff Act (1824), Tariff of Abominations (1828), Adams Compromise (1832), Clay Compromise (1833), Tariff Act (1842), Walker Tariff (1846), Tariff Act (1857), Morrill Tariff (1861), Tariff Act (1875), Morrison Bill (1884), Mills Bill (1888), McKinley Tariff (1890), Gorman Tariff (1894), Dingley Tariff (1897), Payne-Aldrich Tariff (1909), Underwood Tariff (1913), Fordney-McCumber Tariff (1922), Smoot-Hawley Tariff (1930), Reciprocal Trade Agreements Act (1934), Reciprocal Trade Agreements Act Extension (1937), Reciprocal Trade Agreements Extension (1945), Reciprocal Trade Agreements Extension (1955), Trade Expansion Act (1962), Mills Bill (1970), Trade Reform Act (1974), Trade Remedies Reform Act (1984), Disapproval of Fast-Track (1991), North American Free Trade Agreement (1993), Uruguay Round Agreement (1994), Permanent Normal Trade Relations with China (2000), and Trade Promotion Authority (TPA) (2002). The McIntyre Amendment of 1974 that Hiscox analyzes is discussed in the Senate during the debate on the Trade Reform Act, so I do not treat it separately. There are House debates only on the 1884, 1970, and 1984 legislation. The 2002 legislation passed the House and Senate in quite different forms. The legislative vehicle for the House's debate on TPA was HR 3005. The Senate never debated HR 3005 but instead incorporated an amendment on TPA into the Andean Trade Bill, HR 3009. I therefore code the debate on HR 3005 in the House and HR 3009 in the Senate.

12. A number of scholars think about deliberation a little differently (Granstaff 1999; Mucciaroni and Quirk 2006; Quirk 2005). They see it as providing factual accuracy and making claims that have logical consistency. My measures of deliberation do not tap this approach, largely because measuring factual accuracy and logical consistency in a systematic way across congressional history is prohibitively difficult.

13. Hibbing and Theiss-Morse (1995, 2002) show that members of the public do not think particularly highly of legislative debate and deliberation. This does not mean, however, that in a normative sense, these qualities contribute to poor proceedings.

14. Gutmann and Thompson (1996, 124) argue that "publicity" is generally important for salubrious government activity—especially representation—but they also recognize that it can sometimes have the opposite effect. Greater transparency, they argue, allows "cheap talk" to drive out "quality talk." Along similar lines, Mayer and Canon (1999, 148–51) argue that closed committee meetings allow for frank discussion and meaningful debate.

Journalist David Brooks (2007) similarly argues that many members of Congress are naturally both SIPB (self-important pathetic blowhards) when the cameras are on them or their words are being recorded and RIP (reasonable in private) when they are together out of the media glare. Brooks feels that they should have greater opportunities to be the latter.

15. The *House Journal* and *Senate Journal* present recorded votes, the history of bills, procedural matters, and presidential messages since 1789. They include no verbatim or summary remarks of debates. The *Annals of Congress* provide another record of floor proceedings. First published by Joseph Gales and William Seaton in 1834, however, the *Annals* were summaries of debates and actions in the first eighteen congresses—that is, through 1824. As a result, they did not provide a contemporaneous record.

The *Register of Debates in Congress* was the first contemporaneous attempt to report accurately the leading debates and incidents in Congress. It covers the period from 1824 to 1837. It is not a verbatim account—coverage is very patchy, speeches sometimes are reported in their entirety, sometimes chunks of debate are omitted—and is often written in the third person.

The *Congressional Globe* began as a newspaper in 1833. The *Globe* initially provided what its early subtitle called only "sketches of the debates and proceedings" of Congress. By 1851, however, the *Globe* was using corps of reporters trained in the latest stenographic techniques and began publishing close to a verbatim record. The *Globe* was replaced in 1873 by the *Congressional Record*.

More unofficial records also exist. The most famous of these is William Maclay's (1890) journal of the Senate during the First Congress.

16. Nonvoting delegates are excluded from the analysis.

17. One problem with the *Congressional Globe*'s reporting is that members of Congress insisted on revising their spoken remarks before providing them to the publication. These remarks were then placed in the appendix. It is sometimes impossible, therefore, to differentiate spoken from revised remarks. When this is the case, I treat everything as if it were spoken on the floor

Similar problems exist with the *Congressional Record*. For example, although the modern publication has designated space for "extensions to remarks," words not spoken on the floor are often seamlessly interwoven with those that are. Again, when I cannot tell them apart, these words are all considered as if they were uttered on the floor.

18. The language is remarkably consistent across Congresses and publications. I am assuming, however, that the *Congressional Globe* and *Congressional Record* were consistent in creating their indexes.

19. Both publications reference remarks in multiple ways. For example, A member's discussion of a trade bill and its effects on the environment might be indexed under both "trade" and "environment." The use of double or greater referencing is indubitably haphazard and impossible to gauge systematically.

20. The *Congressional Globe* had a three-column-per-page format. The *Congressional Record* had a two-column-per-page format until 1941, when it switched to a three-column format.

21. During the early Congresses, a reporter might note that "several" or a

"group of" members engaged in a discussion or asked a question of a colleague. These instances are counted as one colloquy.

22. Many words and phrases are used to convey the public good. I generally took a liberal view in this respect and coded as mentions of commonweal phrases such as *common good, national interest, public necessity, collective interest, societal need*, and so forth. Ultimately, of course, whether a member cloaked an argument in the public good was a judgment call.

23. Several American and European scholars have constructed a discourse quality index (DQI) to measure the nature of debate in European legislative bodies (Steiner et al. 2004). This instrument attempts to capture characteristics such as participation, civility, interaction, reasoning, and commonweal.

I do not think that the DQI lends itself well to this study of congressional proceedings for two reasons. First, using the DQI is extremely time-consuming and labor-intensive. Steiner et al. (2004) examine 52 debates in four countries—a massive undertaking. In many ways, a study of floor proceedings designed to span congressional history is considerably more ambitious. Second, I have measures similar to those in the DQI (Steiner et al. 2004, 56–61). My measure of commonweal, for example, seems identical to that in the DQI. Moreover, my indicators can take advantage of the fact that they are crafted for a single chamber, hence the use of colloquies and yields as proxies of interaction. They are often, that is, simpler than those in the DQI. Simplicity is a virtue here in that it makes the measures less prone to error across time and chambers.

CHAPTER 5

1. The Senate's formal record of days in session can be found at www.senate.gov/reference/resources/pdf/congresses2.pdf.

2. For more on the battle over Senate secrecy, see Wirls and Wirls 2004, 166–70.

3. For more on the newspapers analyzed and her methodology, see Swift 1996, 60–61, 189–94.

4. The Internet has dramatically altered member-constituent communication (Johnson 2004), but at this point it is difficult to see what influence it will have on the transparency of floor proceedings beyond live video streams of them. Some observers have argued that the Internet will allow a "virtual" Congress in which members hold proceedings from remote locations, a development that would clearly undermine the principle of interaction (Johnson 2004, 175–80). Thinking of this sort accelerated after the 9/11 attacks set into motion all types of contingency plans for national emergencies.

5. As Barbara Sinclair and Donald Wolfensberger argued in testimony to the House's Subcommittee on Rules and Organization in the late 1990s, heightened partisanship—itself not necessarily deleterious—is often confused with incivility (Subcommittee on Rules and Organization of the House 1999).

6. By *comity*, Uslaner (1993, 8) is basically referring to courtesy.

7. Candidates' personal attributes had previously affected election outcomes, but as Carson, Engstrom, and Roberts (2007) show, one such critical factor, political experience, had at best an indirect effect because parties were much better equipped to recruit quality candidates than they are today.

8. It is hard to pinpoint when exactly this practice began. It was certainly in place by the mid-19th century, however.

9. Requests for veterans' pensions and disability benefits were particularly prevalent both before and just after the Civil War (Finocchiaro and Jenkins 2006).

10. Sanders (1997) has shown that the less educated tend not to enjoy deliberative settings.

11. The Senate expunged the resolution against Jackson in January 1837. No president has been formally censured, but other episodes similar to the Jackson one have occurred. In 1800, the House debated and passed a motion rebuking President John Adams for asking a federal judge to grant a British request to extradite Jonathan Robbins, a sailor impressed into service and accused of murder and mutiny. In 1842, the House approved a resolution reported by a committee headed by John Quincy Adams that condemned President John Tyler for two vetoes he had issued to Whig-proposed tax bills. In June 1860, the House adopted a resolution stating that President James Buchanan's actions were worthy of "reproof" in a matter concerning navy contracts and kickbacks to campaign contributors. In 1909, a lame-duck Theodore Roosevelt was chastised when the House passed a resolution condemning remarks he had made during an interbranch spat over the proper usage of the Secret Service. Roosevelt had flippantly remarked that the House had introduced an amendment to control Secret Service actions because its members "did not themselves wish to be investigated" and that the amendment "has been of benefit only, and could be of benefit only, to the criminal class" (Brands 1997, 633).

It is hard to know what to make of all of these cases because they are very different and have occurred in different chambers. They are also of varying degrees of importance. As a result, I do not think detailed analysis of them would be fruitful here.

12. The score for Senate remarks during the Clinton trial omits the large number of contributions majority leader Trent Lott (R-MS) made while advising members on parliamentary procedures.

13. *Congressional Record*, December 18, 1998, H11777.

14. For more analysis of the content of the Johnson and Clinton impeachment proceedings, see Sigelman, Deering, and Loomis 2001.

15. In February 1917, German foreign minister Arthur Zimmerman sent Mexico a note inviting it to join the German side and attack the United States to seize back Arizona, New Mexico, and Texas. The note also stated that Germany would begin to attack all American ships headed for Britain. The Ger-

mans had previously promised not to sink vessels belonging to neutral countries.

16. Both the war/authorization of force and the trade data reveal fewer colloquies in the House than the Senate. Some of this finding may be a function of House rules that state that members should address the chair.

17. Over time, it becomes easier to determine what remarks are spoken on the floor and what were submitted for the record or subsequently extended. In the late 19th century, it is sometimes a little trickier to distinguish between spoken and written contributions, so quantity figures for proceedings in those years might be slightly inflated.

18. In the years before a verbatim record of debate is available, stenographers regularly failed to distinguish between members who had the same last name, thereby potentially undermining the data from before 1850. I distribute remarks where a member cannot be identified because he shares a last name with a colleague evenly across all members with the same last name.

Stenographers in this era also frequently noted "conversations" that took place on the floor and listed their participants. The recorders did not note how many times a member spoke. Consequently, I count a mention of a member's name in such conversation as one remark.

19. Special orders are not recognized by formal House rules but have evolved as a common practice under unanimous consent. Members of both parties are recognized to speak after legislative business for periods ranging from five minutes to one hour. One-minute speeches take place at the beginning of the day after the approval of the previous day's journal but before legislative business. The chair recognizes members who signal their intent to participate by sitting in the front row of benches. Members of the majority and minority speak alternately.

20. Harris (2005) has a supply-rather than demand-side explanation for one-minutes. He says party leaders tightly control distribution of speaking slots and use them to reward loyalists.

CONCLUSION

1. The Senate uses its discharge procedure only very rarely because it is seen as undercutting committees and because there are other ways around committee obstruction. It was last employed successfully in 1964 (Oleszek 2011, 287–88). If debate on the motion to discharge is not completed in morning hour—when it must be introduced—it is subject to a filibuster.

2. The data are from Taylor n.d.

3. Nokken and Sala (2002) have shown the House's Tuesday-Thursday Club emerged in the early 20th century as a response to congressional careerism and electoral pressures for members to engage in more "home style"—the Australian ballot is particularly important in this regard—as well as new technologies that permitted members to travel back to their districts more easily.

4. Mann, Reynolds, and Holmes (2008) show that for the first year of the 110th Congress, 2007, the legislature was in session greater than 20 days and 300 hours more than the first year of the 109th, 2005.

5. For more on the proposals to increase the length of time members spend at the Capitol, see Beth 2001b. The "three weeks on, one week off" policy was recommended in the Joint Committee on the Organization of Congress's important December 1993 report (Joint Committee, 1993a).

6. As Wolfensberger (2003) and Ornstein (2010a) have shown, the motion to recommit was not always guaranteed. Indeed, the Democratic majority prior to 1995 issued special rules that explicitly prevented the motion from being made. The current rule protecting the right was established at the beginning of the 104th Congress, in 1995.

7. In the 110th Congress, Republicans tended to use the word *promptly* instead of *forthwith* in their motion to recommit motions. Believing this was an effort to send bills back to committee and kill them rather than offer meaningful alternatives, the Democratic majority prohibited the use of *promptly* motions at the beginning of the 111th Congress, in 2009 (Oleszek 2011, 208–9).

8. Ornstein (2010a) accused Republicans of employing the motion to recommit under the current limited rules for precisely these political reasons during the 100th and 111th Congresses. As minority leader, John Boehner (R-OH) put it in 2007, "Sometimes we offer motions to recommit to improve legislation—sometimes it's to force Democrats in marginal districts to make tough choices" (Layton 2007).

9. Congressional Research Service, Earmarks in Appropriations Acts: FY1994, FY1996, FY1998, FY2000, FY2002, FY2004, FY2005. Memorandum, January 26, 2006.

10. Crespin, Finocchiaro, and Wanless (2009) show, however, that earmarks are as likely to be contained in small bills as in big ones.

11. The rule change was enacted as the Honest Leadership and Open Government Act of 2007—House Resolution 6 and Senate Bill 1 in the Senate.

12. This was also in House Resolution 6. The practical effect of this change is negligible at best, however. Conference committees continue to be run by the majority party, and little increased transparency has resulted (Hulse 2007b).

13. This was Senate Resolution 10, which also included a provision to prohibit a filibuster on the motion to proceed.

14. The health care debate is in the *Congressional Record*, March 16, 1994, H1419–36; the welfare debate is in the *Congressional Record*, May 4, 1994, H3042–54; and the trade debate is in the *Congressional Record*, July 20, 1994, H5937–49.

15. The debate can be found in the *Congressional Record*, November 3, 1993, H8784–91.

16. The debate can be found in the *Congressional Record*, September 22, 2003, S11739–46.

17. The debate can be found in the *Congressional Record*, November 12, 2003, S14528–785. The three judges were Carolyn Kuhl, Priscilla Owen, and Janice Rogers Brown.

18. Binder and Smith (1997, 210–12) support this proposal. As they report, in 1957, Senator Paul Douglas (D-IL) suggested a 15-day advance notice requirement for cloture within a proposed 51-vote rule.

19. Of course, the Senate could rid itself of the deleterious effects of the filibuster by doing away with the practice altogether. Merkley suggested in 2009 that the Senate adopt a rule prohibiting filibusters. To avoid obviously advantaging one party or the other, he argued that the change should take effect sometime in the future—six years is the time frequently mentioned (Klein 2009).

Bibliography

Adams, Greg D. 1996. "Legislative Effects of Single-Member vs. Multi-Member Districts." *American Journal of Political Science* 40:129–44.

Ahuja, Sunil. 1994. "Electoral Status and Representation in the United States Senate: Does Temporal Proximity to Election Matter?" *American Politics Quarterly* 22:104–18.

Ahuja, Sunil. 2008. *Congress Behaving Badly: The Rise of Partisanship and Incivility and the Death of Public Trust.* Westport, CT: Praeger.

Ainsworth, Scott H., and Marcus Flathman. 1995. "Unanimous Consent Agreements as Leadership Tools." *Legislative Studies Quarterly* 20:177–95.

Aldrich, John H. 1995. *Why Parties? The Origin and Transformation of Political Parties in America.* Chicago: University of Chicago Press.

Aldrich, John H., Mark M. Berger, and David W. Rohde. 2002. "The Historical Variability of Conditional Party Government, 1877–1994." In *Party, Process, and Political Change in Congress: New Perspectives on the History of Congress,* ed. David W. Brady and Mathew D. McCubbins. Stanford, CA: Stanford University Press.

Aldrich, John H., and Ruth W. Grant. 1993. "The Antifederalists, the First Congress, and the First Parties." *Journal of Politics* 55:295–326.

Aldrich, John H., and David W. Rohde. 1997–98. "Theories of Party in the Legislature and the Transition to Republican Rule in the House." *Political Science Quarterly* 112:541–67.

Aldrich, John H., and David W. Rohde. 2000. "The Republican Revolution and the House Appropriations Committee." *Journal of Politics* 62:1–33.

Aldrich, John H., and David W. Rohde. 2001. "The Logic of Conditional Party Government: Revisiting the Electoral Connection." In *Congress Reconsidered,* ed. Lawrence C. Dodd and Bruce I. Oppenheimer. 7th ed. Washington, DC: Congressional Quarterly Press.

Alexander, De Alva Stanwood. 1916. *History and Procedure of the House of Representatives.* Boston: Houghton Mifflin.

Art, Robert J. 1989. "The Pentagon: The Case for Biennial Budgeting." *Political Science Quarterly* 104:193–214.

Atlas, Cary, Robert Hendershott, and Marty Zupan. 1997. "Optimal Effort Allocation by U.S. Senators: The Role of Constituency Size." *Public Choice* 92:221–29.

Babington, Charles. 2004. "Pelosi Seeks House Minority Bill of Rights." *Washington Post*, June 24, A23.

Bach, Stanley. 1986. "Representatives and Committees on the Floor: Amendments to Appropriations Bills in the House of Representatives, 1963–82." *Congress and the Presidency* 13:40–58.

Bach, Stanley. 1990. "Suspension of the Rules, the Order of Business, and the Development of Congressional Procedure." *Legislative Studies Quarterly* 15:49–63.

Bach, Stanley, and Steven S. Smith. 1988. *Managing Uncertainty in the House of Representatives: Adaptation and Innovation in Special Rules*. Washington, DC: Brookings Institution.

Baker, Peter. 2000. *The Breach: Inside the Impeachment and Trial of William Jefferson Clinton*. New York: Scribner.

Baker, Peter, and David M. Herszenhorn. 2009. "An Earmarked Bill, and Limits for the Next One." *New York Times*, March 12, A18.

Baker, Ross. 2001. *House and Senate*. 3rd ed. New York: Norton.

Balla, Steven J., Eric D. Lawrence, Forrest Maltzman, and Lee Sigelman. 2002. "Partisanship, Blame Avoidance, and the Distribution of Legislative Pork." *American Journal of Political Science* 46:515–25.

Barnes, Julian E., Naftali Bendavid, and Adam Entous. 2010. "GOP Halts Repeal of 'Don't Ask, Don't Tell.'" *Wall Street Journal*, September 22, A3.

Baron, David P., and John A. Ferejohn. 1989. "Bargaining in Legislatures." *American Political Science Review* 89:1181–1206.

Battista, James S. Coleman. 2003. "An Ambition-Theoretic Approach to Legislative Organizational Choice." *Legislative Studies Quarterly* 28:333–55.

Bensel, Richard F. 2000. *The Political Economy of American Industrialization, 1877–1900*. New York: Cambridge University Press.

Bensel, Richard F. 2004. *The American Ballot Box in the Mid-19th Century*. New York: Cambridge University Press.

Benton, Thomas Hart. 1856. *Thirty Years' View*. New York: Appleton.

Berard, Stanley P. 2001. *Southern Democrats in the U.S. House of Representatives*. Norman: University of Oklahoma Press.

Bernhard, William, and Brian R. Sala. 2006. "The Remaking of an American Senate: The 17th Amendment and Ideological Responsiveness." *Journal of Politics* 68:345–57.

Bernstein, Robert A. 1991. "Strategic Shifts: Safeguarding the Public Interest? U.S. Senators 1971–1986." *Legislative Studies Quarterly* 16:263–80.

Bessette, Joseph M. 1982. "Is Congress a Deliberative Body?" In *The United States Congress*, ed. Dennis Hale. Chestnut Hill, MA: Boston College Press.

Bessette, Joseph M. 1994. *The Mild Voice of Reason: Deliberative Democracy and American National Government.* Chicago: University of Chicago Press.

Beth, Richard S. 1994. "Control of the House Floor Agenda: Implications from the Use of the Discharge Rule, 1931–1994." Paper presented at the annual meeting of the American Political Science Association.

Beth, Richard S. 2001a. *The Discharge Rule in the House: Recent Use in Historical Context.* Congressional Research Service report 97–856. Washington, DC: Government Printing Office.

Beth, Richard S. 2001b. *House Schedule: Recent Practices and Proposed Options.* Congressional Research Service report 30825. Washington, DC: Government Printing Office.

Bickford, Charlene Bangs, and Kenneth R. Bowling. 1989. *Birth of the Nation: The First Federal Congress, 1789–1791.* Madison, WI: Madison House.

Biglaiser, Glen, David J. Jackson, and Jeffrey S. Peake. 2004. "Back on Track: Support for Presidential Trade Authority in the House of Representatives." *American Politics Research* 32:679–97.

Binder, Sarah A. 1995. "Partisanship and Procedural Choice: Institutional Change in the Early Congress, 1789–1823." *Journal of Politics* 57:1093–1117.

Binder, Sarah A. 1996. "The Partisan Basis of Procedural Choice: Allocating Parliamentary Rights in the House, 1789–1990." *American Political Science Review* 90:8–20.

Binder, Sarah A. 1997. *Minority Rights, Majority Rule: Partisanship and the Development of Congress.* New York: Cambridge University Press.

Binder, Sarah A. 2003. *Stalemate: Causes and Consequences of Legislative Gridlock.* Washington, DC: Brookings Institution Press.

Binder, Sarah A. 2005. "Elections, Parties, and Governance." In *The Legislative Branch*, ed. Paul J. Quirk and Sarah A. Binder. New York: Oxford University Press.

Binder, Sarah A. 2006. "Parties and Institutional Choice Revisited." *Legislative Studies Quarterly* 31:513–32.

Binder, Sarah A., and Steven S. Smith. 1995. "Acquired Procedural Tendencies and Congressional Reform." In *Remarking Congress*, ed. James A. Thurber and Roger H. Davidson. Washington, DC: Congressional Quarterly Press.

Binder, Sarah A., and Steven S. Smith. 1997. *Politics or Principle? Filibustering in the United States Senate.* Washington, DC: Brookings Institution.

Birkhead, Nathaniel, John Hulsey, Christopher Kam, William Bianco, Itai Sened, and Regina Smyth. 2010. "A Multi-Dimensional Analysis of Rules Changes and Party Influence in the U.S. House." Paper presented at the annual meeting of the Midwest Political Science Association.

Bishin, Benjamin G. 2000. "Constituency Influence in Congress: Do Subconstituencies Matter?" *Legislative Studies Quarterly* 25:389–415.

Blanchard, Robert O. 1974. "The Congressional Correspondents and Their World." In *Congress and the News Media*, ed. Robert O. Blanchard. New York: Hastings House.

Bolling, Richard W. 1968. *Power in the House: A History of the Leadership of the House of Representatives.* New York: Dutton.

Bond, Jon R., and Richard Fleisher. 1990. *The President in the Legislative Arena.* Chicago: University of Chicago Press.

Brands, H. W. 1997. *T.R.: The Last Romantic.* New York: Basic Books.

Brooks, David. 2007. "Private Virtue, Public Vice." *New York Times*, February 8, A21.

Brown, George Rothwell. 1922. *The Leadership of Congress.* Indianapolis: Bobbs-Merrill.

Bruhl, Aaron-Andrew P. 2010. "Burying the 'Continuing Body' Theory of the Senate." *Iowa Law Review* 95:1401–65.

Buchanan, James M., and Gordon Tullock. 1962. *The Calculus of Consent: Logical Foundations of Constitutional Democracy.* Ann Arbor: University of Michigan Press.

Bullock, Charles S. 1972. "House Careerists: Changing Patterns of Longevity and Attrition." *American Political Science Review* 66:1295–1300.

Burden, Barry C. 2003. "The Discharge Rule and Minority Rights in the U.S. House of Representatives." Paper presented at the annual meeting of the American Political Science Association.

Burden, Barry C. 2007. *The Personal Roots of Representation.* Princeton: Princeton University Press.

Burdette, Franklin L. 1940. *Filibustering in the Senate.* Princeton: Princeton University Press.

Burnett, Edmund C. 1926. *Letters of Members of the Continental Congress.* Vol. 3, January 1–December 31, 1778. Washington, DC: Carnegie Institution.

Burnham, Walter Dean. 1967. "Party Systems and the Political Process." In *The American Party Systems: Stages of Political Development*, ed. William Nisbet Chambers and Walter Dean Burnham. New York: Oxford University Press.

Byrd, Robert C. 1991. *The Senate, 1789–1989: Addresses on the History of the United States Senate.* Vol. 2. Washington, DC: U.S. Government Printing Office.

Byrd, Robert C. 1994. *The Senate 1789–1989: Classic Speeches, 1830–1993.* Washington, DC: U.S. Government Printing Office.

Canon, David T., Garrison Nelson, and Charles Stewart III. 2002. *Committees in the U.S. Congress.* Washington, DC: Congressional Quarterly Press.

Canon, David T., and Charles Stewart III. 2001. "The Evolution of the Committee System in Congress." In *Congress Reconsidered*, ed. Lawrence C. Dodd and Bruce I. Oppenheimer. 7th ed. Washington, DC: Congressional Quarterly Press.

Canon, David T., and Charles Stewart III. 2002. "Committee Hierarchy and Assignments in the U.S. Congress: Testing Theories of Legislative Organization, 1789–1946." Paper presented at the annual meeting of the Midwest Political Science Association.

Carrubba, Clifford J., and Craig Volden. 2000. "Coalitional Politics and Logrolling in Legislative Institutions." *American Journal of Political Science* 44:261–77.

Carrubba, Clifford J., and Craig Volden. 2001. "Explaining Institutional Change in the European Union: What Determines the Voting Rule in the Council of Ministers?" *European Union Politics* 2:5–30.

Carson, Jaime L., Michael Crespin, Charles Finocchiaro, and David W. Rohde. 2007. "Redistricting and Party Polarization in the U.S. House of Representatives." *American Politics Research* 35:878–904.

Carson, Jamie L, Eric J. Engstrom, and Jason M. Roberts. 2007. "Candidate Quality, the Personal Vote, and the Incumbency Advantage in Congress." *American Political Science Review* 101:289–301.

Clinton, Joshua D. 2006. "Representation in Congress: Constituents and Roll Calls in the 106th House." *Journal of Politics* 68:397–409.

Clinton, Joshua D., Simon Jackman, and Douglas Rivers. 2004. "The Statistical Analysis of Roll-Call Voting: A Unified Approach." *American Political Science Review* 98:355–70.

Clinton, Joshua D., and John Lapinski. 2008. "Laws and Roll-Calls in the U.S. Congress, 1889–1994." *Legislative Studies Quarterly* 33:511–42.

Congressional Quarterly. 1982. *Origins and Development of Congress.* Washington, DC: Congressional Quarterly.

Congressional Quarterly. 1999. *Congressional Quarterly's Guide to Congress.* 5th ed. Washington, DC: Congressional Quarterly Press.

Congressional Research Service. 2006. "Earmarks in Appropriations Acts FY 1994, FY 1996, FY 1998, FY 2000, FY 2002, FY 2004, FY 2005." Memorandum, January 26. Washington, DC: Government Printing Office.

Conley, Richard S. 1999. "Derailing Presidential Fast-Track Authority: The Impact of Constituency Pressure and Political Ideology on Trade Policy in Congress." *Political Research Quarterly,* 54:785–99.

Connor, George E., and Bruce I. Oppenheimer. 1993. "Deliberation: An Untimed Value in a Timed Game." In *Congress Reconsidered,* ed. Lawrence C. Dodd and Bruce I. Oppenheimer. 5th ed. Washington, DC: Congressional Quarterly Press.

Cook, Timothy E. 1988. "Press Secretaries and Media Strategies in the House of Representatives: Deciding Whom to Pursue." *American Journal of Political Science* 32:1047–69.

Cook, Timothy E. 1989. *Making Laws and Making News: Media Strategies in the U.S. House of Representatives.* Washington, DC: Brookings Institution.

Cooper, Joseph. 1962. *The Previous Question: Its Standing as a Precedent for Cloture in the United States Senate.* Senate Document 87-104. Washington, DC: U.S. Government Printing Office.

Cooper, Joseph. 1970. *The Origins of the Standing Committees and the Development of the Modern House.* Houston, TX: Rice University Press.

Cooper, Joseph. 1988. *Congress and Its Committees.* New York: Garland.

Cooper, Joseph, and Elizabeth Rybicki. 2002. "Analyzing Institutional Change: Bill Introduction in the Early Senate." In *U.S. Senate Exceptionalism*, ed. Bruce Oppenheimer. Columbus: Ohio State University Press.

Cooper, Joseph, and Cheryl D. Young. 1989. "Bill Introduction in the 19th Century: A Study of Institutional Change." *Legislative Studies Quarterly* 14:67–105.

Covington, Cary R., J. Mark Wrighton, and Rhonda Kinney. 1995. "A Presidency-Augmented Model of Presidential Success on House Roll-Call Votes." *American Journal of Political Science* 39:1001–24.

Cox, Gary W. 2000. "On the Effects of Legislative Rules." *Legislative Studies Quarterly* 25:169–92.

Cox, Gary W. 2005. "The Organisation of Democratic Legislatures." In *The Oxford Handbook of Political Economy*, ed. Barry R. Weingast and Donald A. Wittman. New York: Oxford University Press.

Cox, Gary W., Chris Den Hartog, and Mathew D. McCubbins. 2007. "The Motion to Recommit in the U.S. House of Representatives." In *Party, Process, and Political Change in Congress: Further New Perspectives on the History of Congress*, vol. 2, ed. David W. Brady and Mathew D. McCubbins. Stanford, CA: Stanford University Press.

Cox, Gary W., and Mathew D. McCubbins. 1993. *Legislative Leviathan: Party Government in the House.* Berkeley: University of California Press.

Cox, Gary W., and Mathew D. McCubbins. 2002. "Agenda Power in the U.S. House of Representatives." In *Party, Process, and Political Change in Congress: New Perspectives on the History of Congress*, ed. David W. Brady and Mathew D. McCubbins. Stanford, CA: Stanford University Press.

Cox, Gary W., and Mathew D. McCubbins. 2005. *Setting the Agenda: Responsible Party Government in the U.S. House of Representatives.* New York: Cambridge University Press.

Cox, Gary W., and Mathew D. McCubbins. 2007. *Legislative Leviathan: Party Government in the House.* 2nd ed. New York: Cambridge University Press.

Cox, Gary W., and Keith T. Poole. 2002. "On Measuring Partisanship in Roll Call Voting: The U.S. House of Representatives, 1877–1999." *American Journal of Political Science* 46:477–89.

Crespin, Michael H., Charles Finocchiaro, and Emily Wanless. 2009. "Perception and Reality in Congressional Earmarks." *The Forum* 7:Article 1.

Crespin, Michael H., and Nathan Monroe. 2005. "Are Partisan Theories of Agenda Control in the Senate Plausible?" Paper presented at the annual meeting of the Midwest Political Science Association.

Crook, Sarah B., and John R. Hibbing. 1997. "A Not-So-Distant Mirror: The Seventeenth Amendment and Congressional Change." *American Political Science Review* 91:845–53.

Dart, Bob. 1994. "C-SPAN Celebrates 15th Anniversary of Showing Congress to America." Cox Wire Service, March 16.

Davidson, Roger H., ed. 1992. *The Postreform Congress.* New York: St Martin's.

Deering, Christopher, and Steven S. Smith. 1997. *Committees in Congress.* 3rd ed. Washington, DC: Congressional Quarterly Press.

Den Hartog, Chris. 2004. "Limited Party Government and the Majority Party Revolution in the 19th-Century House." Ph.D. diss., University of California, San Diego.

Den Hartog, Chris, and Craig Goodman. 2007. "Committee Composition in the Absence of a Strong Speaker." In *Party, Process, and Political Change in Congress: Further New Perspectives on the History of Congress,* vol. 2, ed. David W. Brady and Mathew D. McCubbins. Stanford, CA: Stanford University Press.

Den Hartog, Chris, and Nathan Monroe. 2008a. "Agenda Influence and Tabling Motions in the U.S. Senate." In *Why Not Parties? Party Effects in the U.S. Senate,* ed. Nathan W. Monroe, Jason M. Roberts, and David W. Rohde. Chicago: University of Chicago Press.

Den Hartog, Chris, and Nathan Monroe. 2008b. "UCAs and the Majority Party's Bargaining Advantage over Scheduling in the U.S. Senate." Paper presented at the annual meeting of the American Political Science Association.

Den Hartog, Chris, and Nathan Monroe. 2011. *Agenda Setting in the U.S. Senate: Costly Consideration and Majority Party Advantage.* New York: Cambridge University Press.

Dennis, Steven T., and Jessica Brady. 2010. "Spotlight Shines on Reform Debate." *Roll Call,* June 10, 3.

Dennis, Steven T., and Jackie Kucinich. 2010. "Hoyer and Cantor Just Can't Play Nice." *Roll Call,* June 9, 1.

Diermeier, Daniel. 1995. "Commitment, Deference, and Legislative Institutions." *American Political Science Review* 89:344–55.

Dion, Douglas. 1997. *Turning the Legislative Thumbscrew: Minority Rights and Procedural Change in Legislative Politics.* Ann Arbor: University of Michigan Press.

Dion, Douglas, and John D. Huber. 1996. "Procedural Choice and the House Committee on Rules." *Journal of Politics* 58:25–53.

Dixit, Avinash K. 2004. *Lawlessness and Economics: Alternative Modes of Governance.* Princeton: Princeton University Press.

Dodd, Lawrence C., and Scot Schraufnagel. 2007. "A Conflict-Theory of Policy Productivity in Congress: Party Polarization, Member Incivility, and Landmark Legislation, 1891–1993." Paper presented at the annual meeting of the American Political Science Association.

Durkheim, Emile. 1947. *The Division of Labor in Society.* Glencoe, IL: Free Press.

Eilperin, Juliet. 2006. *Fight Club Politics: How Partisanship Is Poisoning the House of Representatives.* Lanham, MD: Rowman and Littlefield.

Elving, Ronald. 1993. "Brighter Lights, Wider Windows: Presenting Congress in the 1990s." Paper presented at the Congress, the Press, and the Public conference, Washington, DC.

Enelow, James. 1981. "Saving Amendments, Killer Amendments, and an Expected Utility Theory of Sophisticated Voting." *Journal of Politics* 43:1062–89.

Erickson, Nancy. 2008. *Pro Tem: Presidents Pro Tempore of the United States Senate since 1789*. Washington, DC: U.S. Government Printing Office.

Evans, C. Lawrence, and Daniel Lipinski. 2005. "Obstruction and Leadership in the U.S. Senate." In *Congress Reconsidered*, ed. Lawrence C. Dodd and Bruce I. Oppenheimer. 8th ed. Washington, DC: Congressional Quarterly.

Evans, C. Lawrence, and Walter J. Oleszek. 1998. "If It Ain't Broke Bad, Don't Fix It a Lot." *PS: Political Science and Politics* 31:24–28.

Evans, C. Lawrence, and Walter J. Oleszek. 2000. "The Procedural Context of Senate Deliberation." In *Esteemed Colleagues: Civility and Deliberation in the U.S. Senate*, ed. Burdett A. Loomis. Washington, DC: Brookings Institution.

Evans, C. Lawrence, and Walter J. Oleszek. 2001. "Message Politics and Senate Procedures." In *The Contentious Senate: Partisanship, Ideology, and the Myth of Cool Judgment*, ed. Colton C. Campbell and Nicol C. Rae. Lanham, MD: Rowman and Littlefield.

Farrand, Max. 1966. *The Records of the Federal Convention of 1787*. New Haven: Yale University Press.

Fellowes, Matthew, and Patrick Wolf. 2004. "Funding Mechanisms and Policy Instruments: How Campaign Contributions Influence Congressional Votes." *Political Research Quarterly* 57:315–24.

Fenno, Richard F., Jr. 1973. *Congressmen in Committees*. Boston: Little, Brown.

Fenno, Richard F., Jr. 1982. *The United States Senate: A Bicameral Perspective*. Washington, DC: American Enterprise Institute.

Fink, Evelyn C. 2000. "Representation by Deliberation: Changes in the Rules of Deliberation in the U.S. House of Representatives, 1789–1844." *Journal of Politics* 62:1009–25.

Finocchiaro, Charles J., and Jeffery A. Jenkins. 2006. "The Politics of Military Service Pensions in the Antebellum U.S." Paper presented to the Midwest Political Science Association.

Finocchiaro, Charles J., and Jeffery A. Jenkins. 2008. "In Search of Killer Amendments in the Modern U.S. House." *Legislative Studies Quarterly* 33:263–94.

Fiorina, Morris P. 1977. *Congress: Keystone of the Washington Establishment*. New Haven: Yale University Press.

Fishkin, James S. 1995. *The Voice of the People: Public Opinion and Democracy*. New Haven: Yale University Press.

Fleisher, Richard, and Jon Bond. 1983. "Beyond Committee Control: Committee and Party Leader Influence on Floor Amendments in Congress." *American Politics Quarterly* 11:131–61.

Fleming, Thomas. 2003. *The Louisiana Purchase*. Hoboken, NJ: Wiley.

Follett, Mary Parker. 1896. *The Speaker of the House of Representatives*. New York: Longmans, Green.

Forgette, Richard G. 1997. "Reed's Rules and the Partisan Theory of Legislative Organization." *Polity* 29:375–96.

Forgette, Richard G. 2004. "Congressional Party Caucuses and Coordination: Assessing Caucus Activity and Party Effects." *Legislative Studies Quarterly* 29:407–30.

Forgette, Richard G., and James V. Saturno. 1994. "302(b) or Not 302(b): Congressional Floor Procedures and House Appropriators." *Legislative Studies Quarterly* 3:385–96.

Fowler, James H. 2005. "Dynamic Responsiveness in the US Senate." *American Journal of Political Science* 49:299–31.

Frantzich, Stephen E., and John Sullivan. 1996. *The C-Span Revolution.* Norman: University of Oklahoma Press.

Freeman, Joanne Barrie. 2001. *Affairs of Honor: National Politics in the New Republic.* New Haven: Yale University Press.

Freeman, Joanne Barrie. 2004. "Opening Congress." In *The American Congress,* ed. Julian E. Zelizer. New York: Houghton Mifflin.

Froman, Lewis. 1967. *The Congressional Process.* Boston: Little, Brown.

Fuller, Herbert Bruce. 1909. *The Speakers of the House.* Boston: Little, Brown.

Gabardi, Wayne. 2001. "Contemporary Models of Democracy." *Polity* 33:547–68.

Gailmard, Sean, and Jeffery A. Jenkins. 2007. "Negative Agenda Control in the Senate and House of Representatives: Fingerprints of Majority Party Power." *Journal of Politics* 64:689–700.

Gailmard, Sean, and Jeffery A. Jenkins. 2009. "Agency Problems, the 17th Amendment, and Representation in the Senate." *American Journal of Political Science* 53:324–42.

Galloway, George B. 1976. *History of the House of Representatives.* 2nd ed. New York: Crowell.

Gamm, Gerald, and Kenneth Shepsle. 1989. "Emergence of Legislative Institutions: Standing Committees in the House and Senate, 1810–1825." *Legislative Studies Quarterly* 14:39–66.

Gamm, Gerald, and Steven S. Smith. 2000. "Last among Equals: The Senate's Presiding Officer." In *Esteemed Colleagues: Civility and Deliberation in the U.S. Senate,* ed. Burdett A. Loomis. Washington, DC: Brookings Institution.

Gamm, Gerald, and Steven S. Smith. 2002. "Policy Leadership and the Development of the Modern Senate." In *Party, Process, and Political Change in Congress: New Perspectives on the History of Congress,* ed. David W. Brady and Mathew D. McCubbins. Stanford, CA: Stanford University Press.

Garay, Ronald. 1984. *Congressional Television: A Legislative History.* Westport, CT: Greenwood.

Gerber, Elisabeth R., and Jeffrey B. Lewis. 2004. "Beyond the Median: Voter Preferences, District Heterogeneity, and Representation." *Journal of Political Economy* 112:1364–83.

Gibson, Joseph. 2010. *A Better Congress: Change the Rules, Change the Results— A Modest Proposal.* Alexandria, VA: Two Seas.

Gilligan, Thomas W., and Keith Krehbiel. 1987. "Collective Decision Making and Standing Committees: An Informational Rationale for Restrictive Amendment Procedures." *Economics and Organization* 3:287–335.

Gilligan, Thomas W., and Keith Krehbiel. 1990. "Organization of Informative Committees by a Rational Legislature." *American Journal of Political Science* 34:531–64.

Gold, Martin B., and Dimple Gupta. 2004. "The Constitutional Option to Change Senate Rules and Procedures: A Majoritarian Means to Overcome the Filibuster." *Harvard Journal of Law and Public Policy* 28:206–66.

Goodwin, George, Jr. 1970. *The Little Legislatures.* Amherst: University of Massachusetts Press.

Granstaff, Bill. 1999. *Losing Our Democratic Spirit: Congressional Deliberation and the Dictatorship of Propaganda.* Westport, CT: Praeger.

Gronke, Paul. 2000. *Settings, Campaigns, Institutions, and the Vote: A Unified Approach to House and Senate Elections.* Ann Arbor: University of Michigan Press.

Gutmann, Amy, and Dennis Thompson. 1996. *Democracy and Disagreement.* Cambridge: Belknap Press of Harvard University Press.

Habermas, Jürgen. 1989. *The Structural Transformation of the Public Sphere.* Cambridge: MIT Press.

Hall, Richard L., and Bernard Grofman. 1990. "The Committee Assignment Process and the Conditional Nature of Committee Bias." *American Political Science Review* 84:1149–66.

Hamilton, Alexander, James Madison, and John Jay. 1961. *The Federalist Papers.* Ed. Clinton Rossiter. New York: Mentor.

Hammond, Susan Webb. 1997. *Congressional Caucuses in National Policymaking.* Baltimore: Johns Hopkins University Press.

Harlow, Ralph V. 1917. *The History of Legislative Methods in the Period before 1825.* New Haven: Yale University Press.

Harris, Douglas B. 1998. "The Rise of the Public Speakership." *Political Science Quarterly* 113:193–212.

Harris, Douglas B. 2005. "Orchestrating Party Talk: A Party-Based View of One-Minute Speeches in the House of Representatives." *Legislative Studies Quarterly* 30:127–41.

Hasbrouck, Paul. 1927. *Party Government in the House of Representatives.* New York: Macmillan.

Haynes, George H. 1938. *The Senate of the United States: Its History and Practice.* Boston: Houghton Mifflin.

Heckelman, Jac C. 2004. "A Spatial Model of U.S. Senate Elections." *Public Choice* 118:87–103.

Herrera, Richard, and Michael Yawn. 1999. "The Emergence of the Personal Vote." *Journal of Politics* 61:136–50.

Hess, Stephen. 1991. *Live from Capitol Hill! Studies of Congress and the Media*. Washington, DC: Brookings Institution.

Hibbing, John R. 2002. "How to Make Congress Popular." *Legislative Studies Quarterly* 27:219–44.

Hibbing, John R., and Christopher W. Larimer. 2008. "The American Public's View of Congress." *The Forum* 6:Article 6.

Hibbing, John R., and Elizabeth Theiss-Morse. 1995. *Congress as Public Enemy: Public Attitudes towards American Political Institutions*. New York: Cambridge University Press.

Hibbing, John R., and Elizabeth Theiss-Morse. 2002. *Stealth Democracy: Americans' Beliefs about How Government Should Work*. New York: Cambridge University Press.

Hickey, Donald. 1989. *The War of 1812: A Forgotten Conflict*. Champaign: University of Illinois Press.

Hill, Kim Quaile, and Patricia A. Hurley. 2002. "Symbolic Speeches in the U.S. Senate and Their Representational Implications." *Journal of Politics* 64:219–31.

Hinds, Asher C. 1907. *Hinds' Precedents of the House of Representatives*. Washington, DC: U.S. Government Printing Office.

Hiscox, Michael J. 2002. *International Trade and Political Conflict: Commerce, Coalitions, and Mobility*. Princeton: Princeton University Press.

Hojnacki, Marie, and David C. Kimball. 1998. "Organized Interests and the Decision of Whom to Lobby in Congress." *American Political Science Review* 92:775–90.

Hook, Janet. 2010. "New Push to Ban Earmarks in Senate." *Wall Street Journal*, November 9, A5.

Hulse, Carl. 2007a. "Congress Continues Its Pursuit of Earmarks." *New York Times*, December 20, A30.

Hulse, Carl. 2007b. "In Conference: Process Undone by Partisanship." *New York Times*, September 26, A1.

Hulse, Carl. 2010a. "Senate Ends an Impasse over Extending Jobless Benefits." *New York Times*, March 3, 13.

Hulse, Carl. 2010b. "With Tea Party in Mind, Republicans Have Change of Heart about Earmarks." *New York Times*, November 16, A17.

Hurley, Patricia A., and Rick K. Wilson. 1989. "Partisan Voting Patterns in the U.S. Senate, 1877–1986." *Legislative Studies Quarterly* 14:225–50.

Jacobs, Lawrence R., Fay Lomax Cook, and Michael X. Delli Carpini. 2009. *Talking Together: Public Deliberation and Political Participation in America*. Chicago: University of Chicago Press.

James, Caryn. 1998. "It Was All Too Familiar, Like a 'Nightline' Rerun." *New York Times*, October 6, A21.

Jamieson, Kathleen Hall. 1997. *Civility in the House of Representatives*. Philadelphia: Annenberg Public Policy Center, University of Pennsylvania.

Jamieson, Kathleen Hall, and Erika Falk. 1998. *Civility in the House of Representatives: An Update*. Philadelphia: Annenberg Public Policy Center, University of Pennsylvania.

Jansen, Bart. 2009. "Capitol Hill's Conferences: Can They Be Revived?" *Congressional Quarterly Weekly Report*, January 5, 18–19.

Jefferson's Manual. 2005. 109th Congress., House Document 108-241.

Jenkins, Jeffery A. 1998. "Property Rights and the Emergence of Standing Committee Dominance in the 19th-Century House." *Legislative Studies Quarterly* 23:493–519.

Jenkins, Jeffery A., and Michael C. Munger. 2003. "Investigating the Incidence of Killer Amendments in Congress." *Journal of Politics* 65:498–517.

Jenkins, Jeffery A., and Timothy P. Nokken. 2000. "The Institutional Emergence of the Republican Party: A Spatial Voting Analysis of the House Speakership Election of 1855–56." *Legislative Studies Quarterly* 25:101–30.

Jenkins, Jeffery A., Justin Peck, and Vesla M. Weaver. 2010. "Between Reconstructions: Congressional Action on Civil Rights, 1891–1940." *Studies in American Political Development* 24:57–89.

Jenkins, Jeffery A., Eric Schickler, and Jamie L. Carson. 2004. "Constituency Cleavages and Congressional Parties: Measuring Homogeneity and Polarization across Time." *Social Science History* 28:537–73.

Jenkins, Jeffery A., and Charles H. Stewart III. 1998. "Committee Assignments as Side Payments: The Interplay of Leadership and Committee Development in the Era of Good Feelings." Paper presented at the annual meeting of the Midwest Political Science Association.

Jenkins, Jeffery A., and Charles H. Stewart III. 2002. "Order from Chaos: The Transformation of the Committee System in the House, 1816–22." In *Party, Process, and Political Change in Congress: New Perspectives on the History of Congress*, ed. David W. Brady and Mathew D. McCubbins. Stanford, CA: Stanford University Press.

Jenkins, Jeffery A., and Charles H. Stewart III. 2003. "Out in the Open: The Emergence of *Viva Voce* Voting in House Speakership Elections." *Legislative Studies Quarterly* 28:481–508.

Jillson, Calvin, and Rick K. Wilson. 1994. *Congressional Dynamics: Structure, Coordination, and Choice in the First American Congress, 1774–1789*. Stanford, CA: Stanford University Press.

Johnson, Dennis. 2004. *Congress Online: Bridging the Gap between Citizens and Their Representatives*. New York: Routledge.

Joint Committee on the Organization of Congress. 1993a. *Final Report on the Organization of Congress*. Washington, DC: U.S. Government Printing Office.

Joint Committee on the Organization of Congress. 1993b. *Floor Deliberations and Scheduling*. Hearing, May 20.

Jones, David R., and Monika L. McDermott. 2009. *Americans, Congress, and Democratic Responsiveness: Public Evaluations of Congress and Electoral Consequences*. Ann Arbor: University of Michigan Press.

Josephy, Alvin M., Jr. 1975. *History of the Congress of the United States.* New York: McGraw-Hill.

Josephy, Alvin M., Jr. 1979. *On the Hill: A History of the American Congress.* New York: Simon and Schuster.

Kahane, Leo H. 1996. "Senate Voting Patterns on the 1991 Extension of the Fast-Track Trade Procedures: Prelude to NAFTA." *Public Choice* 87:35–53.

Kassebaum, Nancy Landon. 1988. "The Senate Is Not in Order." *Washington Post*, January 27, A19.

Katz, Jonathan N., and Brian R. Sala. 1996. "Careerism, Committee Assignments, and the Electoral Connection." *American Political Science Review* 90:21–33.

Kernell, Samuel. 1977. "Toward Understanding 19th Century Congressional Careers: Ambition, Competition, and Rotation." *American Journal of Political Science* 21:669–93.

Kerr, Clara H. 1895. *The Origin and Development of the United States Senate.* Ithaca, NY: Andrus and Church.

Key, V. O., Jr. 1955. "A Theory of Critical Elections." *Journal of Politics* 17:3–18.

Kiewiet, D. Roderick, and Mathew D. McCubbins. 1991. *The Logic of Delegation: Congressional Parties and the Appropriations Process.* Chicago: University of Chicago Press.

King, David C. 1997. *Turf Wars: How Congressional Committees Claim Jurisdiction.* Chicago: University of Chicago Press.

Klein, Ezra. 2009. "After Health Care, We Need Senate Reform." *Washington Post*, December 27, B1.

Koger, Gregory. 2006. "Cloture Reform and Party Government in the Senate, 1918–1925." *Journal of Politics* 68:708–19.

Koger, Gregory. 2010. *Filibustering: A Political History of Obstruction in the House and Senate.* Chicago: University of Chicago Press.

Koger, Gregory, and Jennifer Victor. 2009. "Polarized Agents: Campaign Contributions by Lobbyists." *PS: Politics and Political Science* 42:485–88.

Kravitz, Walter. 1974. "Evolution of the Senate's Committee System." *Annals of the American Academy of Political and Social Science* 411:27–38.

Krehbiel, Keith. 1991. *Information and Legislative Organization.* Ann Arbor: University of Michigan Press.

Krehbiel, Keith. 1997. "Restrictive Rules Reconsidered." *American Journal of Political Science* 41:919–44.

Krehbiel, Keith. 1998. *Pivotal Politics: A Theory of U.S. Lawmaking.* Chicago: University of Chicago Press.

Krehbiel, Keith, Kenneth A. Shepsle, and Barry R. Weingast. 1987. "Why Are Congressional Committees Powerful?" *American Political Science Review* 81:929–45.

Krutz, Glen S. 2001. *Hitching a Ride: Omnibus Legislating in the U.S. Congress.* Columbus: Ohio State University Press.

Kuklinski, James H. 1978. "Representativeness and Elections: A Policy Analysis." *American Political Science Review* 72:165–77.

Lancaster, Lance W. 1928. "The Initiative of the United States Senate in Legislation, 1789–1809." *Southwestern Political and Social Science Quarterly* 9:67–75.

Lapinski, John S. 2004. "Direct Election and the Emergence of the Modern Senate." Unpublished manuscript.

Lascher, Edward L., Jr. 1996. "Assessing Legislative Deliberation: A Preface to Empirical Analysis." *Legislative Studies Quarterly* 21:501–19.

Lawson, Gary, and Guy Seidman. 2005. "The First 'Incorporation' Debate." In *The Louisiana Purchase and American Expansion*, ed. Sanford Levinson and Bartholomew H. Sparrow. Lanham, MD: Rowman and Littlefield.

Layton, Lyndsey. 2007. "House GOP Uses Procedural Tactic to Frustrate Democratic Majority." *Washington Post*, May 19, A1.

Lee, Frances E., and Bruce I. Oppenheimer. 1999. *Sizing up the Senate: The Unequal Consequences of Equal Representation*. Chicago: University of Chicago Press.

Lehnan, Robert G. 1967. "Behavior on the Senate Floor: An Analysis of Debate in the U.S. Senate." *Midwest Journal of Political Science* 11:505–21.

Levitt, Steven. 1996. "How Do Senators Vote? Disentangling the Role of Voter Preferences, Party Affiliation, and Senator Ideology." *American Economic Review*. 86:425–41.

Lichtblau, Eric. 2010a. "Leaders in House Block Earmarks to Corporations." *New York Times*, March 11, A1.

Lichtblau, Eric. 2010b. "Rivals Reach Consensus on New Earmark Rules." *New York Times*, September 29, A19.

Lichter, S. Robert, and Daniel R. Amundson. 1994. "Less News Is Worse News: Television News Coverage of Congress, 1972–92." In *Congress, the Press, and the Public*, ed. Thomas E. Mann and Norman J. Ornstein. Washington, DC: American Enterprise Institute and Brookings Institution.

Lijphart, Arend. 1999. *Patterns of Democracy: Government Forms and Performance in Thirty-Six Countries*. New Haven: Yale University Press.

Londregan, John, and James M. Snyder. 1994. "Comparing Committee and Floor Preferences." *Legislative Studies Quarterly* 19:233–66.

Longley, Lawrence D., and Walter J. Oleszek. 1989. *Bicameral Politics: Conference Committees in Congress*. New Haven: Yale University Press.

Lord, Clifford L. 1943. *The Atlas of Congressional Roll Calls for the Continental Congresses, 1777–1781*. Cooperstown: New York State Historical Association.

Lowi, Theodore J. 1964. "American Business, Public Policy, Case Studies, and Political Theory." *World Politics* 16:677–715.

Luce, Robert. 1922. *Legislative Procedure: Parliamentary Practices and the Course of Business in the Framing of Statutes*. Boston: Houghton Mifflin.

Maclay, William. 1890. *Journal of William Maclay, United States Senator from Pennsylvania, 1789–1791*. Ed. Edgar Maclay. New York: Appleton.

Main, Jackson Turner. 1967. *The Upper House in Revolutionary America, 1763–1788.* Madison: University of Wisconsin Press.

Malbin, Michael J. 1987. "Congress during the Convention and Ratification." In *The Framing and Ratification of the Constitution,* ed. Leonard W. Levy and Dennis J. Mahoney. New York: Macmillan.

Malecha, Gary Lee, and Daniel J. Reagan. 2004. "News Coverage of the Postreform House Majority Party Leadership: An Expanding or a Shrinking Public Image?" *Congress and the Presidency* 31:53–76.

Maltzman, Forrest. 1997. *Competing Principals: Committees, Parties, and the Organization of Congress.* Ann Arbor: University of Michigan Press.

Maltzman, Forrest, and Charles R. Shipan. 2008. "Continuity, Change, and the Evolution of the Law." *American Journal of Political Science* 52:252–67.

Maltzman, Forrest, and Lee Sigelman. 1996. "The Politics of Talk: Unconstrained Floor Time in the U.S. House of Representatives." *Journal of Politics* 58:819–30.

Mann, Thomas E., and Norman J. Ornstein. 1992. *Renewing Congress: A First Report.* Washington, DC: Brookings Institution and American Enterprise Institute.

Mann, Thomas E., and Norman J. Ornstein. 2006. *The Broken Branch: How Congress Is Failing America and How to Get It Back on Track.* New York: Oxford University Press.

Mann, Thomas E., Molly Reynolds, and Nigel Holmes. 2008. "Could Congress Be Waking Up?" *New York Times,* January 19, A19.

Marbut, F. B. 1971. *News from the Capitol: The Story of Washington Reporting.* Carbondale: Southern Illinois University Press.

Margulies, Herbert F. 1996. *Reconciliation and Revival: James R. Mann and the House Republicans in the Wilson Era.* Westport, CT: Greenwood.

Marshall, Bryan W. 2002. "Explaining the Role of Restrictive Rules in the Postreform House." *Legislative Studies Quarterly* 27:61–85.

Martin, Paul S. 2003. "Voting's Rewards: Voter Turnout, Attentive Publics, and Congressional Allocation of Federal Money." *American Journal of Political Science* 47:110–27.

Martorano, Nancy. 2006. "Balancing Power: Committee System Autonomy and Legislative Organization." *Legislative Studies Quarterly* 31:205–34.

Matthews, Donald R. 1960. *U.S. Senators and Their World.* New York: Vintage.

Mayer, Kenneth R., and David T. Canon. 1999. *The Dysfunctional Congress? The Individual Roots of an Institutional Dilemma.* Boulder, CO: Westview.

Mayhew, David R. 1974. *Congress: The Electoral Connection.* New Haven: Yale University Press.

Mayhew, David R. 2000. *America's Congress: Actions in the Public Sphere, James Madison through Newt Gingrich.* New Haven: Yale University Press.

Mayhew, David R. 2005. *Divided We Govern: Party Control, Lawmaking, and Investigations, 1946–2002.* 2nd ed. New Haven: Yale University Press.

Mayhew, David R. 2006. "Congress as Problem Solver." In *Promoting the Gen-*

eral Welfare: New Perspectives on Government Performance, ed. Alan S. Gerber and Eric M. Patashnik. Washington, DC: Brookings Institution.

McCarty, Nolan, Keith T. Poole, and Howard Rosenthal. 1997. *Income Redistribution and the Realignment of American Politics*. Washington, DC: AEI Press.

McCarty, Nolan, Keith T. Poole, and Howard Rosenthal. 2001. "The Hunt for Party Discipline in Congress." *American Political Science Review* 95:673–88.

McCarty, Nolan, Keith T. Poole, and Howard Rosenthal. 2006. *Polarized America: The Dance of Ideology and Unequal Riches*. Cambridge: MIT Press.

McConachie, Lauros. 1898. *Congressional Committees*. New York: Cromwell.

McConnell, Mitch. 2011. "Don't 'Fix' the Filibuster." *Washington Post*, January 15, A15.

McKelvey, Richard D. 1976. "Intransitives in Multidimensional Voting Models and Some Implications for Agenda Control." *Journal of Economic Theory* 12:471–82.

McKelvey, Richard D. 1986. "Covering Dominance and Institution Free Properties of Social Choice." *American Journal of Political Science* 30:283–314.

Meinke, Scott R. 2007. "Slavery, Partisanship, and Procedure in the U.S. House: The Gag Rule, 1836–45." *Legislative Studies Quarterly* 32:33–57.

Michel, Robert H. 1987. "The Minority Leader Replies." *Washington Post*, December 29, A14.

Michels, Robert. 1949. *Political Parties: A Sociological Study of the Oligarchical Tendencies of Modern Democracy*. Glencoe, IL: Free Press.

Miller, Susan M., and L. Marvin Overby. 2010. "Parties, Preferences, and Petitions: Discharge Behavior in the Modern House." *Legislative Studies Quarterly* 35:187–210.

Mixon, Frank, Jr., David Hobson, and Kamal Upadhyaya. 2001. "Gavel-to-Gavel Congressional Television Coverage as Political Advertising: The Impact of C-SPAN on Legislative Sessions." *Economic Inquiry* 39:351–64.

Mixon, Frank, Jr., David Hobson, and Kamal Upadhyaya. 2003. "Institutional Arrangement as Free Advertising Opportunities in Congress: The Impact of C-SPAN2 on Senate Filibustering." *Public Choice* 115:139–62.

Moakley, John Joseph. 2000. *Biennial Budgeting: A Tool for Improving Government Fiscal Management and Oversight*. U.S. Congress. House Committee on Rules, 106th Congress, 2nd sess. Washington, DC: U.S. Government Printing Office.

Monroe, Nathan W., and Gregory Robinson. 2008. "Do Restrictive Rules Produce Non-Median Outcomes? A Theory with Evidence From the 101st–108th Congresses." *Journal of Politics* 70:217–31.

Montgomery, Lori, and Paul Kane. 2010. "House May Try to Pass Senate Health Care Bill without Voting on It." *Washington Post*, March 16, A1.

Moore, Joseph West. 1895. *The American Congress: A History of National Legislation and Political Events*. New York: Harper.

Morris, Jonathan S. 2001. "Reexamining the Politics of Talk: Partisan Rhetoric in the 104th House." *Legislative Studies Quarterly* 26:101–21.

Mucciaroni, Gary, and Paul J. Quirk. 2006. *Deliberative Choices: Debating Public Policy in Congress.* Chicago: University of Chicago Press.

The Nation. 1910. "The Value of Debate." February 17, 154–55.

Niven, David. 1996. "Shaping the Congressional Debate on the Gulf War." *Congress and the Presidency* 23:33–56.

Nokken, Timothy P., and Brian R. Sala. 2002. "Institutional Evolution and the Rise of the Tuesday–Thursday Club in the House of Representatives." In *Party, Process, and Political Change in Congress: New Perspectives on the History of Congress*, ed. David W. Brady and Mathew D. McCubbins. Stanford, CA: Stanford University Press.

O'Halloran, Sharyn. 1994. *Politics, Process, and American Trade Policy.* Ann Arbor: University of Michigan Press.

Oleszek, Walter J. 2011. *Congressional Procedures and the Policy Process.* 8th ed. Washington, DC: Congressional Quarterly Press.

Olson, Alison G. 1992. "18th-Century Colonial Legislatures and Their Constituents." *Journal of American History* 79:543–67.

Onuf, Peter S. 2005. "'The Strongest Government on Earth': Jefferson's Republicanism, the Expansion of the Union, and the New Nation's Destiny." In *The Louisiana Purchase and American Expansion*, ed. Sanford Levinson and Bartholomew H. Sparrow. Lanham, MD: Rowman and Littlefield.

Ornstein, Norman J. 2000. "Civility, Deliberation, and Impeachment." In *Esteemed Colleagues: Civility and Deliberation in the U.S. Senate*, ed. Burdett A. Loomis. Washington, DC: Brookings Institution.

Ornstein, Norman J. 2006. "Part-Time Congress." *Washington Post*, March 7, A17.

Ornstein, Norman J. 2010a. "The Motion to Recommit, Hijacked by Politics." *Roll Call*, May 19, 31.

Ornstein, Norman J. 2010b. "Time to Reassess Filibuster to Keep Senate Functioning." *Roll Call*, January 20, 6.

Ornstein, Norman J., Thomas E. Mann, and Michael J. Malbin. 2002. *Vital Statistics on Congress, 2001–2.* Washington, DC: American Enterprise Institute Press.

Owens, John, and J. Mark Wrighton. 2008. "Partisan Polarization, Procedural Control, and Partisan Emulation in the U.S. House: An Examination of Rules Restrictiveness over Time." Paper presented to the History of Congress Conference.

Packer, George. 2010. "The Empty Chamber." *New Yorker*, August 9, 38–51.

Parker, Edward G. 1857. *The Golden Age of American Oratory.* Boston: Whittemore, Niles, and Hall.

Pearson, Kathryn L., and Eric Schickler. 2009. "Discharge Petitions, Agenda Control, and the Congressional Committee System, 1929–1976." *Journal of Politics* 71:1238–56.

Perkins, Bradford. 1961. *Prologue to War: England and the United States, 1805–1812.* Berkeley: University of California Press.

Peters, Ronald. 1997. *The American Speakership: The Office in Historical Perspective.* 2nd ed. Baltimore: Johns Hopkins University Press.

Peterson, Merrill D. 1987. *The Great Triumvirate: Webster, Clay, and Calhoun.* New York: Oxford University Press.

Polsby, Nelson W. 1968. "Institutionalization of the United States House of Representatives." *American Political Science Review* 62:144–68.

Poole, Keith T. 2007. "Changing Minds? Not in Congress!" *Public Choice* 131:435–51.

Poole, Keith T., and Thomas Romer. 1993. "Ideology, 'Shirking' and Representation." *Public Choice* 77:185–96.

Poole, Keith T., and Howard Rosenthal. 1997. *Congress: A Political Economic History of Roll-Call Voting.* New York: Oxford University Press.

Porter, David L. 1987. "America's Ten Greatest Senators." In *The Rating Game in American Politics: An Interdisciplinary Approach*, ed. William D. Pederson and Ann M. McLaurin. New York: Irvington.

Posner, Richard A. 2002. *Public Intellectuals: A Study of Decline.* Cambridge: Harvard University Press.

Price, H. Douglas. 1977. "Careers and Committees in the American Congress: The Problem of Structural Change." In *The History of Parliamentary Behavior*, ed. William O. Aydelotte. Princeton: Princeton University Press.

Quinn, Kevin M., Burt L. Monroe, Michael Colaresi, Michael H. Crespin, and Dragomir R. Radev. 2010. "How to Analyze Political Attention with Minimal Assumptions and Costs." *American Journal of Political Science* 54:209–28.

Quirk, Paul J. 2005. "Deliberation and Decision Making." In *The Legislative Branch*, ed. Paul J. Quirk and Sarah A. Binder. New York: Oxford University Press.

Rae, Nicol C. 1989. *The Decline and Fall of the Liberal Republicans.* New York: Oxford University Press.

Rae, Nicol C. 1994. *Southern Democrats.* New York: Oxford University Press.

Rawls, John. 1997. "The Idea of Public Reason Revisited." *University of Chicago Law Review* 94:765–807.

Rehfeld, Andrew. 2005. *The Concept of Constituency: Political Representation, Democratic Legitimacy, and Institutional Design.* New York: Cambridge University Press.

Remini, Robert V. 2006. *The House: The History of the House of Representatives.* New York: Smithsonian.

Richardson, Lilliard, Brian E. Russell, and Christopher A. Cooper. 2004. "Legislative Representation in a Single-Member versus Multiple-Member District System: The Arizona State Legislature." *Political Research Quarterly* 57:337–44.

Riddick, Floyd M. 1949. *The U.S. Congress: Organization and Procedure.* Manassas, VA: National Capitol.

Rieselbach, Leroy N. 1994. *Congressional Reform: The Changing Modern Congress.* Washington, DC: Congressional Quarterly Press.

Riker, William H. 1980. "Implications for the Disequilibrium of Majority Rule for the Study of Institutions." *American Political Science Review* 74:432–46.

Risjord, Norman. 1965. *The Old Republicans: Southern Conservatives in the Age of Jefferson.* New York: Columbia University Press.

Roberts, Jason M. 2010. "The Development of Special Orders and Special Rules in the U.S. House, 1881–1937." *Legislative Studies Quarterly* 35: 307–26.

Roberts, Jason M., and Steven S. Smith. 2007. "The Evolution of Agenda-Setting Institutions in Congress: Path Dependency in the House and Senate Institutional Development." In *Party, Process, and Political Change in Congress: Further New Perspectives on the History of Congress,* vol. 2, ed. David W. Brady and Mathew D. McCubbins. Stanford, CA: Stanford University Press.

Roberts, Steven V. 1986. "TV May Quicken the Senate's Pulse." *New York Times,* June 8, E5.

Robinson, George L. 1954. "The Development of the Senate Committee System." Ph.D. diss., New York University.

Robinson, James A. 1963. *The House Rules Committee.* Indianapolis: Bobbs-Merrill.

Robinson, Michael J. 1981. "Three Faces of Congressional Media." In *The New Congress,* ed. Thomas Mann and Norman J. Ornstein. Washington, DC: American Enterprise Institute.

Robinson, William A. 1930. *Thomas B. Reed: Parliamentarian.* New York: Dodd, Mead.

Rocca, Michael S. 2007. "Nonlegislative Debate in the House of Representatives." *American Politics Research* 35:489–505.

Rogers, James R. 1998. "Bicameral Sequence: Theory and State Legislative Evidence." *American Journal of Political Science* 42:1025–60.

Rogers, James R. 2001. "An Informational Rationale for Congruent Bicameralism." *Journal of Theoretical Politics* 12:129–57.

Rogers, James R. 2005. "Empirical Determinants of Bicameral Sequence in State Legislatures." *Legislative Studies Quarterly,* 30:29–42.

Rogers, Lindsay. 1926. *The American Senate.* New York: Knopf.

Rohde, David W. 1991. *Parties and Leaders in the Postreform House.* Chicago: University of Chicago Press.

Rohde, David W., Edward H. Stiglitz, and Barry R. Weingast. 2008. "Parties, Committees, and Pivots: A Reassessment of the Literature on Congressional Organization." Paper presented at the annual meeting of the American Political Science Association.

Rusk, Jerrold. 1970. "The Effect of the Australian Ballot Reform on Split Ticket Voting: 1876–1908." *American Political Science Review* 64:1220–38.

Rybicki, Elizabeth. 2003. "Resolving Bicameral Differences in the U.S. Congress, 1789–2002." Paper presented at the annual meeting of the American Political Science Association.

Rybicki, Elizabeth. 2007. "Bicameral Resolution in Congress, 1863–2002." In *Party, Process, and Political Change in Congress: Further New Perspectives on the History of Congress*, vol. 2, ed. David W. Brady and Mathew D. McCubbins. Stanford, CA: Stanford University Press.

Rybicki, Elizabeth, Ryan Vander Wielen, and Steven S. Smith. 2003. "Congressional Conference Committee Bias, 1963–2002." Paper presented at the annual meeting of the American Political Science Association.

Sanders, Lynn M. 1997. "Against Deliberation." *Political Theory* 25:347–76.

Schickler, Eric. 2000. "Institutional Change in the House of Representatives, 1867–1998: A Test of Partisan and Ideological Power Balance Models." *American Political Science Review* 94:267–88.

Schickler, Eric. 2001. *Disjointed Pluralism: Institutional Innovation and the Development of the U.S. Congress.* Princeton: Princeton University Press.

Schickler, Eric, Eric McGhee, and John M. Sides. 2003. "Remaking the House and Senate: Personal Power, Ideology, and the 1970s Reforms." *Legislative Studies Quarterly* 28:297–333.

Schiller, Wendy. 2000. *Partners and Rivals: Representation in U.S. Senate Delegations.* Princeton: Princeton University Press.

Schiller, Wendy, and Charles Stewart III. 2004. "Senate Elections before 1914." Paper presented at the annual meeting of the American Political Science Association.

Schiller, Wendy, and Charles Stewart III. 2008. "The Effect of Party Loyalty on the Election of U.S. Senators, 1871–1913." Paper presented at the annual meeting of the American Political Science Association.

Schneider, Judy. 2003a. *One-Minute Speeches: Current House Practices.* Congressional Research Service Report RL30135. Washington, DC: Government Printing Office.

Schneider, Judy. 2003b. *Special Order Speeches: Current House Practices.* Congressional Research Service Report RL30136. Washington, DC: Government Printing Office.

Senate Rules Committee. 1993. Hearing 103-26, March 18.

Shapiro, Catherine R., David W. Brady, Richard A. Brody, and John A. Ferejohn. 1990. "Linking Constituency Opinion and Senate Voting Scores: A Hybrid Explanation." *Legislative Studies Quarterly* 15:599–621.

Shepsle, Kenneth A., and Barry R. Weingast. 1987. "The Institutional Foundations of Committee Power." *American Political Science Review* 81:85–104.

Shields, Johanna Nicol. 1985. "Whigs Reform the 'Bear Garden': Representation and the Apportionment Act of 1842." *Journal of the Early Republic* 5:355–82.

Sigelman, Lee, Christopher J. Deering, and Burdett A. Loomis. 2001. "'Wading Knee Deep in Words, Words, Words': Senatorial Rhetoric in the Johnson and Clinton Impeachment Trials." *Congress and the Presidency* 28:119–39.

Sinclair, Barbara. 1989. *The Transformation of the U.S. Senate.* Baltimore: Johns Hopkins University Press.

Sinclair, Barbara. 2000. "Change the Rules: Arcane Senate Procedures Lead to Gridlock." *Roll Call*, January 24, A46.

Singer, Paul. 2010. "Coburn Bill Targets Earmarks." *Roll Call*, May 11, 3.

Skladony, Thomas W. 1985. "The House Goes to Work: Select and Standing Committees in the U.S. House of Representatives." *Congress and the Presidency* 12:165–88.

Smith, Steven S. 1985. "New Patterns of Decisionmaking in Congress." In *The New Direction in American Politics*, ed. John E. Chubb and Paul E. Peterson. Washington, DC: Brookings Institution.

Smith, Steven S. 1989. *Call to Order: Floor Politics in the House and Senate.* Washington, DC: Brookings Institution.

Smith, Steven S. 2007. *Party Influence in Congress.* New York: Cambridge University Press.

Smith, Steven S. 2010. "The Procedural Senate, 1960–2010." Unpublished paper.

Smith, Steven S., and Marcus Flathman. 1989. "Managing the Senate Floor: Complex Unanimous Consent Agreements since the 1950s." *Legislative Studies Quarterly* 14:349–92.

Snyder, James M., Jr., and Tim Groseclose. 2000. "Estimating Party Influence in Congressional Roll Call Voting." *American Journal of Political Science* 44:193–211.

Solomon, Burt. 2000. "Gone Are the Giants." *National Journal*, May 27, 1668–73.

Solomon, Gerald B. H., and Donald R. Wolfensberger. 1994. "The Decline of Deliberative Democracy in the House and Proposals for Reform." *Harvard Journal of Legislation* 31:321–70.

Stealey, Orlando O. 1906. *Twenty Years in the Press Gallery.* New York: Publishers.

Steiner, Jürg, André Bächtiger, Markus Spörndli, and Marco R. Steenbergen. 2004. *Deliberative Politics in Action: Analyzing Parliamentary Discourse.* New York: Cambridge University Press.

Stevenson, Charles A. 2010. "In Senate, 'Motion to Proceed' Should Be Non-Debatable." *Roll Call*, April 19, 4.

Stewart, Charles, III. 1989. *Budget Reform Politics: The Design of the Appropriations Process in the House, 1865–1921.* New York: Cambridge University Press.

Stewart, Charles, III. 1999. "The Inefficient Secret: Organizing for Business in the U.S. House of Representatives, 1789–1861." Paper presented at the annual meeting of the American Political Science Association.

Stewart, Charles, III. 2000. "Speakership Elections and Control of the U.S.

House, 1839–59." Paper presented at the annual meeting of the American Political Science Association.

Stewart, Charles, III. 2001. *Analyzing Congress*. New York: Norton.

Stewart, Charles, III. 2007. "Architect or Tactician? Henry Clay and the Institutional Development of the U.S. House of Representatives." In *Party, Process, and Political Change in Congress: Further New Perspectives on the History of Congress*, vol. 2, ed. David W. Brady and Mathew D. McCubbins. Stanford, CA: Stanford University Press.

Stewart, Charles, III, and Wendy J. Schiller. 2004. "Party Control and Legislator Loyalty in Senate Elections before the Adoption of the Seventeenth Amendment." Paper presented at the annual meeting of the American Political Science Association.

Strahan, Randall W. 2002. "Leadership and Institutional Change in the 19th Century House." In *Party, Process, and Political Change in Congress: New Perspectives on the History of Congress*, ed. David W. Brady and Mathew D. McCubbins. Stanford, CA: Stanford University Press.

Strahan, Randall W. 2007. *Leading Representatives: The Agency of Leaders in the Politics of the U.S. House*. Baltimore: Johns Hopkins University Press.

Strahan, Randall W., Matthew Gunning, and Richard L. Vining Jr. 2006. "From Moderator to Leader: Floor Participation by U.S. House Speakers, 1789–1841." *Social Science History* 30:51–74.

Strahan, Randall W., Vincent Moscardelli, Moshe Haspel, and Richard Wike. 2000. "The Clay Speakership Revisited." *Polity* 32:561–93.

Stratmann, Thomas. 2005. "Some Talk: Money in Politics. A (Partial) Review of the Literature." *Public Choice* 124:135–56.

Subcommittee on Rules and Organization of the House. 1999. "Proposals Emanating from the Second Bipartisan Congressional Retreat." H. Hearing 106-64.

Sullivan, Terry. 1990. "Bargaining with the President: A Simple Game and New Evidence." *American Political Science Review* 84:1167–96.

Sundquist, James L. 1983. *Dynamics of the Party System: Alignment and Realignment of Political Parties in the United States*. Washington, DC: Brookings Institution.

Sunstein, Cass. 2007. *Republic.com 2.0*. Princeton: Princeton University Press.

Swift, Elaine D. 1996. *The Making of the American Senate: Reconstitutive Changes in Congress, 1787–1841*. Ann Arbor: University of Michigan Press.

Taibbi, Matt. 2006. "The Worst Congress Ever: How Our National Legislature Has Become a Stable of Thieves and Perverts—in Five Easy Steps." *Rolling Stone*, November 2, 46–84.

Taylor, Andrew J. 2000. "The Congressional Budget Process in an Era of Surpluses." *PS: Political Science and Politics* 33:575–80.

Taylor, Andrew J. 2006. "Size, Power, and Electoral Systems: Exogenous Determinants of Legislative Procedural Choice." *Legislative Studies Quarterly* 31:323–45.

Taylor, Andrew J. N.d. "Professionalism and Legislative Procedures in the American States." Unpublished manuscript.

Taylor, Andrew J., and John T. Rourke. 1995. "Historical Analogies in the Congressional Foreign Policy Process." *Journal of Politics* 57:460–68.

Theriault, Sean M. 2004. "The Case of the Vanishing Moderates: Party Polarization in the Modern Congress Procedures and their Impact on Party Polarization." Paper presented at the annual meeting of the Midwest Political Science Association.

Theriault, Sean M. 2006. "Party Politics during the Louisiana Purchase." *Social Science History* 30:293–323.

Theriault, Sean M. 2008. *Party Polarization in Congress.* New York: Cambridge University Press.

Tocqueville, Alexis de. 2004. *Democracy in America.* Trans. Arthur Goldhammer. New York: Library of America.

U.S. House of Representatives. Rules Committee. 1997. "Proposals Emanating from the First Bipartisan Congressional Retreat." Hearing, April 17.

Uslaner, Eric M. 1993. *The Decline of Comity in Congress.* Ann Arbor: University of Michigan Press.

Uslaner, Eric M. 1998. "Let the Chits Fall Where They May? Executive and Constituency Influences on Congressional Voting on NAFTA." *Legislative Studies Quarterly* 23:347–71.

Uslaner, Eric M. 2000. "Is the Senate More Civil Than the House?" In *Esteemed Colleagues: Civility and Deliberation in the U.S. Senate*, ed. Burdett A. Loomis. Washington, DC: Brookings Institution.

Victor, Kirk. 2004. "The Lack of True Debate in the Senate." *National Journal*, January 10, 94–95.

Waldron, Jeremy. 2009. "Representative Lawmaking." *Boston University Law Review* 89:335–55.

Ware, Alan. 2002. *The American Direct Primary.* New York: Cambridge University Press.

Wawro, Gregory J., and Eric Schickler. 2006. *Filibuster: Obstruction and Lawmaking in the U.S. Senate.* Princeton: Princeton University Press.

Weber, Max. 1947. *The Theory of Social and Economic Organization.* New York: Oxford University Press.

Weingast, Barry. 1989. "Floor Behavior in the United States Congress: Committee Power under the Open Rule." *American Political Science Review* 83:795–815.

Weingast, Barry W., and William J. Marshall. 1988. "The Industrial Organization of Congress; or, Why Legislatures, Like Firms, Are Not Organized as Markets." *Journal of Political Economy* 96:132–63.

Wilkerson, John D. 1999. "'Killer Amendments' in Congress." *American Political Science Review* 93:535–52.

Wilson, Woodrow. 1981. *Congressional Government: A Study in American Politics.* Baltimore: Johns Hopkins University Press.

Wirls, Daniel. 2007. "The 'Golden Age' Senate and Floor Debate in the Ante-bellum Congress." *Legislative Studies Quarterly* 32:193–222.

Wirls, Daniel, and Stephen Wirls. 2004. *The Invention of the United States Sen-ate*. Baltimore: Johns Hopkins University Press.

Wolfensberger, Donald. 2003. "The Motion to Recommit in the House: The Creation, Evisceration, and Restoration of a Minority Right." Paper pre-sented to the History of Congress Conference.

Wolfensberger, Donald. 2010a. "Fiscally Unaccountable Debt-Limit Maneu-ver Puts House on Autopilot." *Roll Call*, February 9, 6.

Wolfensberger, Donald. 2010b. "Supplemental Bill Defies Emergency Label." *Roll Call*, July 20, 27.

Young, James Sterling. 1966. *The Washington Community, 1800–1828*. New York: Columbia University Press.

Zelizer, Julian E. 2004. *On Capitol Hill: The Struggle to Reform Congress and Its Consequences*. New York: Cambridge University Press.

Index